# IN THE SHADOW OF PAPILLON

**FRANK KANE** with **JOHN TILSLEY**

MAINSTREAM
PUBLISHING
EDINBURGH AND LONDON

363.45

First published in Great Britain in 2006 by
MAINSTREAM PUBLISHING COMPANY
(EDINBURGH) LTD
7 Albany Street
Edinburgh EH1 3UG

ISBN 1 85496 184 6

A catalogue record for this book is available
from the British Library

Typeset in Bembo and News Gothic

Printed in Great Britain by
William Clowes Ltd, Beccles, Suffolk

# CONTENTS

# AUTHOR'S NOTE

Drug smuggling is a way of life for some people, but you have to be a certain type of person to get away with it. You have to be without fear and have no conscience. As you read this, there are people all over the world, travelling in planes, trains, cars, boats and many other means of transport, some even crossing frontiers on foot, risking their freedom for that pot of gold at the end of the rainbow.

I never aspired to be one of those people, and neither did my girlfriend. I was just an ordinary guy whose business had collapsed. Under pressure from impatient creditors, I foolishly allowed myself in desperation to be enticed by old supposed friends into an apparently easy way to make enough money to keep the hounds at bay and have enough money left over to start a new life. Maybe we didn't look the part; maybe it was time for me to follow a karmic pattern of suffering from past lifetimes. 'Sam' wasn't supposed to have been involved; she shouldn't have been with me, but she'd insisted. Maybe we were both overdue a lesson in life. Whatever the reason, things went drastically wrong and we paid the price for our foolishness.

Although parts of my account may seem incredible, unbelievable in some cases, the story you are about to read is without exaggeration. Some names have been changed and others omitted completely for obvious reasons, and to protect the privacy of some individuals I have altered sensitive information. The experience had such an impact on me that I have no difficulty whatsoever in remembering each vivid detail – every minute of every torturous day has been imprinted in my mind for ever.

For those of you who may be tempted to smuggle drugs, let this story be a warning: it doesn't always go according to plan.

*Frank Kane*

# FOUR AND A HALF YEARS IN

In a dangerous mood and very drunk, José, the prison boss, staggered over to where Mancho lay propped on one elbow. He dragged the surprised informer off the bed by his shirt and ordered him to kneel down in front of him. We all sat transfixed and silent, nobody daring to move or utter a sound. José held the muzzle of the .38 automatic close to the man's forehead. Mancho started to sob, then pleaded, 'Please don't kill me!' Those were to be the last words that passed his lips.

'Cocksucking *sapo*! You know what happens to people with long tongues,' replied José coldly. While the gun at his head drew Mancho's attention, Carlo Pino, one of José's lieutenants and a cold-blooded killer of repute, moved in behind the kneeling man and with a practised motion slipped the loop of a home-made garrotte over Mancho's head and pulled it taut around his throat, tightening the wire while at the same time placing his knees between the shoulder blades. It was as though Mancho had accepted the fact he was about to die. Like a lamb to the slaughter, he didn't even put up a struggle. At one point, both men toppled backwards, Mancho landing across Carlo Pino's legs, but Carlo kept his grip tight for almost two minutes during which time Mancho's legs and feet twitched uncontrollably. With bulging eyes, his sphincter muscle loosened and his bowels emptied, a dark wet patch appearing around his crotch as his bladder discharged. Although I was a couple of yards away from the scene, the smell hit me immediately. I fought to suppress the vomit rising in my throat.

After more than four and a half years in Latino hellholes, I'd almost become immune to the unending cycle of violence and murder. What had happened to me? It didn't seem that long ago I was wining and dining clients in fancy restaurants; now I was witnessing yet another act of cold-blooded murder with little compassion.

José watched Mancho's life force drain from his body with a huge smile, then knelt down, removed a suture kit from his pocket, broke the seal and proceeded to sew up the snitch's mouth. It was an established ritual for that kind of execution.

'He won't be talking to anyone else,' he laughed. His whisky-glazed eyes looked around the room. 'Are you all watching?' he shouted. 'This is what happens to people who talk.'

Still nobody uttered a sound. Eighteen prisoners had been forced to watch the horrific execution and not one dared say a word for fear of a repeat performance.

While all that was going on, another lieutenant, known as Chivo Loco or Crazy Goat, was busy ripping up a sheet he'd snatched from the nearest bed. The owner was another English guy, and he wasn't about to argue. José and Chivo quickly fashioned a makeshift noose and hung Mancho's now lifeless body from one of the concrete window slats. There it would stay until the following morning when it would be discovered that, once more, there was one short at six o'clock headcount. From past experience, I knew every single one of us would pay for that act of retribution.

# 1

# FIRST ENCOUNTER

I remember the voices in my head as clearly as if it were yesterday. 'Don't do it, Frank,' one said. No, it'll be OK, the other silently replied. I was in two minds. Should we leave it behind on the coach? What if it all goes tits up? Stop worrying, it'll be fine. Dump it, Frank. It's not much money to lose. Just get on with the job. It's a risk you don't have to take. It'll be OK. Stay cool.

The coach eased out from the plush Flamingo Beach Hotel for the 30-minute ride to the international airport near Porlamar. It was eleven o'clock in the morning, 10 December 1996. As we swung through the *barrios* of Pampatar, a town on La Isla de Margarita, a small island in the south Caribbean, kids were playing and families going about their everyday business on street corners and dusty slopes. Old rusting American automobiles dotted the kerbsides and landscape. Most had wings, doors or bonnets missing. Here it didn't seem to matter. They were drivable whatever the condition. Huge parts of the island's population live in poverty and squalor, while others are wealthy and live in luxury. A perfect breeding ground for crime and corruption, and only four hours by ferry from its mother country Venezuela.

The voices came again as I watched people and colour all around me. We weren't tourists any more. On a normal holiday, we

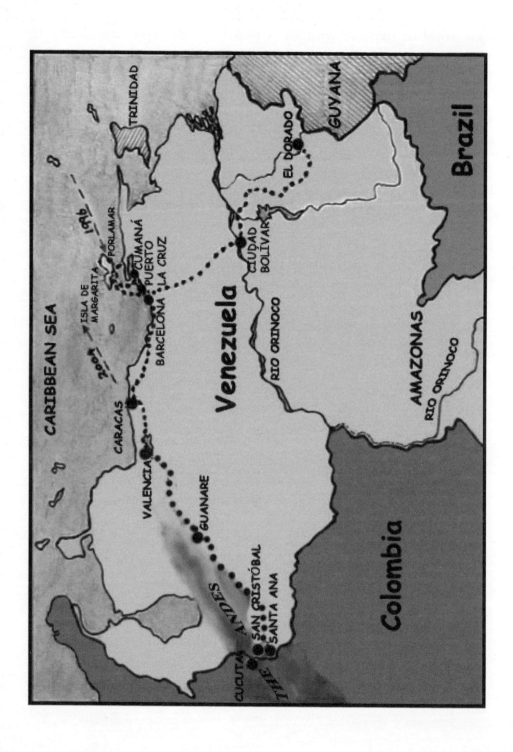

would be taking in what we were leaving behind, but not today. Our conversation was strained, it was too late now for any more deliberation. The coach turned a corner and the airport loomed up ahead. There was no turning back; we had to go through with it.

As the coach pulled up across from the entrance, 'Sam' and I turned and looked at each other. I smiled reassuringly. She smiled back, but in that instant I noticed something was different about her. I could see the hint of doubt in her eyes, the usual sparkle had gone. We'd been together for 18 months and I thought I knew her inside out; I'd never seen that look before. Had she been thinking the same thoughts as me? It didn't inspire me with much confidence.

Waiting for the cases to be offloaded from the luggage compartments, I hailed a porter. He was one of a huge crowd always available for the '*gringo* flights', as I later learned they were called. The going rate for tourists was 1,000 bolivares. Small wonder the guy's smile reached from ear to ear as he shuffled over, pushing his two-wheeled trolley. A meagre amount for a tourist on holiday but quite a princely sum for him, especially when the average salary for anyone lucky enough to have a job was around 30,000 bolivares a month: roughly £40 sterling.

We walked across the concrete area towards the one and only airport building, which was shimmering in the blistering heat. The sun beat down on our heads; it was a far cry from the coolness of the air-conditioned coach. My head began to throb and I started to sweat profusely, small rivulets running from my hairline, drenching my shirt collar. The heat didn't seem to trouble Sam. She could lie in the sun all day, every day, which she'd proven over our two-week stay. The heat didn't seem to faze our grinning porter either, who stuck to us like a faithful dog. An emaciated character, he was no more than five feet tall, black as coal and dressed in poor-quality shirt and pants, which stopped a good four inches above his ankle line. There were no socks to protect his feet against the tattered Nike trainers he wore.

We entered the airport building and felt the air conditioning's instant chill. Ten yards ahead was the first obstacle to cross. Several stern-looking soldiers of odd shapes and sizes manned passport control. These were men of the Guardia Nacional, each one dressed in ill-fitting US Army-pattern fatigues, red berets and black boots. All sported the mandatory machine gun. There wasn't a smile on any of their faces.

Two lines of tourists moved forwards slowly as every face was examined and matched against the passport handed to them. After what felt like hours but in fact was only a minute or two, it was our turn. I handed over our passports to a particularly ugly brute whose jacket appeared to be several sizes too small. The nametag over his left breast pocket read 'Guirez'. The procedure seemed to take for ever, repeatedly checking the photos and scrutinising our faces. Finally he paused, leafed through the pages one more time and focused on Sam, his glinting eyes lingering longer than I cared – he was blatantly undressing her in his mind. It wasn't surprising really because she was a real stunner. Twenty-one years old, long blonde hair, bleached almost white by two weeks of Caribbean sun, her almond-shaped, piercing green eyes, and slim and suntanned figure: who could blame him?

She returned his shameless stare with a smile. The guy was mesmerised. Eventually, he handed our passports back to me. He didn't give me another glance, he was still staring at Sam. He waved us through and our porter met us, smiling and visibly eager to claim his reward. So far, so good, I thought, walking towards the ticket counter.

'That monster really fancied the arse off you, Sam,' I said.

She pulled a face, as if she'd eaten something past its sell-by date. 'Yuk,' she replied.

The mood lightened and we laughed. They hadn't even searched our suitcases and travel bag. I looked at the porter – he was still beaming, and little wonder. For pushing our cases no more than 50 yards, he was about to earn the equivalent of a day's pay. Those thoughts briefly distracted my attention from the job at hand and as a result, I failed to stop at the next obstacle, a booth set in the wall where airport tax had to be paid before passengers could leave the country. I'd never come across airport taxes before. I remembered being told about them and had made a mental note. I even had the correct amount – 26,000 bolivares – folded in my rear pocket. There was no excuse, I had made a serious error, and it wasn't until we'd reached the queue of holidaymakers waiting to collect their boarding passes that I realised what I'd done. The booth was no more than 20 yards back; I had to think quickly. Would it look more suspicious if I left Sam in the queue with the cases and paid the taxes myself? Or should we walk back together? I looked around, the porter had disappeared in search of fresh custom. I decided on the first option and went back on my own. There was nobody waiting at the booth and it wouldn't take too long.

I was only gone a couple of minutes, but it was long enough for that little voice in my head to reappear and tell me, 'You shouldn't have done it, Frank.' Walking back towards Sam, I could see a worried frown on her face; it dawned on me that even though we'd been separated for only a minute or two our collective strength, the link that held us close, had somehow been broken. My immediate thoughts centred on how I appeared myself. Did I too look guilty? Sliding by her side, I soon realised what was troubling her.

'There's a little guy over there who's been watching me,' she whispered, pointing with her eyes. 'He had his eye on you, too, as you walked back.'

'Don't worry about it,' I said. 'He probably fancies you, the same as the guy who checked our passports.'

'No, seriously, he's still there . . . Shit, now there's two of them.'

I couldn't stop myself. I turned to look and, sure enough, she was right. There were two men dressed exactly the same, wearing black pants, sky-blue shirts and shiny black shoes. Each holstered a side arm and was so similar in looks they could have passed as twins. They had short, black, curly hair, dark skin, moustaches and thin weasel faces. For a moment, I thought I was seeing double but was soon proven wrong when one of them raised his arm and pointed directly at me. There was no doubt about it. They were on to us.

Fuck!!

It's difficult to explain exactly how I felt at that moment. The background noise of the busy airport concourse narrowed into a deep hum. My mind raced, yet everything around me seemed to slow right down like the frames of a flickering film, my vision changing from peripheral to tunnel and edged in fogginess.

The same weasel-faced character raised his right hand and pointed at me again. My heart began to race. We went through the whole routine: I pointed to myself with the best innocent face I could muster under the circumstances; he nodded solemnly and beckoned me with his crooked index finger; I pointed to myself again, and lowered my eyebrows in a quizzical frown. I tried to swallow, but the finger kept beckoning. With hunched shoulders, I showed the palms of my hands in the classic gesture, 'Who me?'

At that point, barring a miracle, I realised we were in deep shit. On the outside, everything was still in slow motion, while inside my head the best that little voice could come up with was, 'I told you so, Frankie. You've fucked up big-time.' My stomach turned. Sweat began to saturate my clothing. I knew my face looked as guilty as hell. My heart literally bounced out of my chest and everything went hazy. As I walked towards them, my feet became leaden, as if anchored to the floor by heavy weights. In my mind's eye, I could see my sluggish movements from outside of my body, an experience I will never forget.

Looking back, I knew it was my good spirit leaving me behind. 'I told you so,' it was saying. 'You should have listened.' I had a gut-wrenching feeling that this was the beginning of a terrible nightmare.

After what appeared to be an eternity, I made my way over to the two officials, who turned out to be airport police. Each took one of my arms and very gently guided me to a door to one side of the airport tax booth. Once through the door, things started to get a little rougher: a gun was swiftly slipped from its holster and placed firmly against my cheekbone. The man holding the gun pushed me roughly against the wall and held me forcefully with his free hand. His breath reeked of garlic. His hold tightened, though I couldn't understand the need, the gun alone being enough to frighten the life out of me.

The other one started to pat me down. This happened in the corridor, a few strides inside the door we had come through. It smelled strongly of cigar smoke on entering. The walls were painted a dull brown and yellow. When the police officer reached the small of my back and touched gold, his face lit up with a huge grin. His twin beamed too. They made gestures for me to unbutton the baggy denim shirt I'd purchased especially for the job. I did so very slowly but couldn't drag it out longer than the six buttons. The shirt opened and they started to jabber in quick-fire Spanish. At that time, my knowledge of the Spanish language was limited to *por favor*, *gracias* and a few odd words. Now, as they saw taped across my stomach the waistcoat I'd made in the hotel room several days earlier, they became more excitable.

'*Dólares*,' one of them whispered at me, looking shiftily around.

At the bottom of the corridor to the right, maybe 15 yards away, I saw through the open door of an office a white-shirted man sitting behind a desk littered with files. He busied away on an old-fashioned typewriter, apparently oblivious to what was going on. He had probably witnessed the procedure many times.

'*Dólares*,' he said again.

The puzzled look on my face lit a bulb in his head because he spoke slowly, with extenuated gestures and hand movements. '*Si me das muchas dólares y es suficiente, puedes irse como nada paso.*'

Was he asking me for dollars? I was struggling to fully understand what had been said, but his body language told the story. I couldn't believe what was happening. If I were to give him a sufficient amount of dollars, I would walk out of there as if nothing had happened? I had no dollars on me at all. I had a few pounds in my jeans back pocket, so reached back slowly, very much aware of the pistol now being waved in my face. I came out with a bundle of £20 notes, somewhere between four hundred and five hundred quid.

'No dollars,' I said shakily. 'Pounds sterling – English.'

'*No! Dólares!*'

I tried to make them understand using the same manner of gestures they had that the English pound was worth much more than the dollar. It was all to no avail, the black-market currency in Venezuela was the good old American dollar, and those guys knew no better. Only people 'in the know' would appreciate the value of the pound, which was very unfortunate for me because they weren't having any of it. I may as well have waved a fistful of coloured paper at them. I put the money back in my pocket, and I could tell by the look on their faces that they were angry with me. Their patience was up and the gun holstered. They grabbed my arms and roughly manhandled me down the corridor towards the open doorway.

At first, it was a bit of a struggle for them because I wasn't too sure I wanted to go. But my six-foot-one-inch, fourteen-stone frame put up only token resistance. They were only small men but quite insistent. I knew after a few shuffled steps it would be pointless to fight it.

At the bottom of the corridor, we entered the room with the open door. The man behind the desk got up immediately and walked to another doorway to my right into a much larger room, in which I could see several Guardia Nacional soldiers milling around. A few seconds later, an officer with an array of coloured ribbons on his chest came into the office. He looked me up and down with a sour expression and stopped short to take in the waistcoat. His left hand moved down, unclipped his holster and pulled out a nasty-looking pistol.

'Sit!' he shouted, pointing somewhere behind me with the gun.

I looked around for a chair and saw there was one against the wall. In that instant, I actually thought about making a dash through the open doorway. But what would I do about Sam? Crazy idea. I couldn't leave her. Where would I go to anyway? I would have the corridor to negotiate, giving *Señor* Ribbons or one of the policemen plenty of time to put a bullet or two in my back. No, I had to sit down and think clearly. This guy could know the value of my currency, and this mess could still be sorted out.

As I sat, I noticed the colourful chest had the nametag 'Sanchez' stitched upon it. He turned and spoke sharply to the two airport policemen, and it was clear to see who was the boss.

'*Y la mujer?*' he asked.

I understood that to mean 'and the woman', and that meant Sam.

'*Si, señor,*' replied the two airport officers in unison and without further instruction took off in search of Sam, who no doubt was in a panic over the length of my disappearance. I somehow hoped she'd been quick-witted enough to go to the toilets and dump the waistcoat she was wearing. I snapped out of my thoughts and wondered if 'Sanchez' was 'in the know'. I would try him out.

'Pounds sterling?' I said to him hopefully.

Nothing. No reply.

Sanchez pushed a pile of folders to the centre of the table, perched himself on the corner and swung his leg back and forth. He looked at me coldly. I saw no compassion in him, but I thought I'd try him one more time.

'Pounds sterling,' I said again.

'*Silencio!*' he barked.

My heart pounded once again, temples throbbing in time with my quickening pulse. My mind raced. I'd lost the numbness of before: I was back in the real world and realised beyond any doubt we were up to our necks in deep, deep shit.

Sanchez was a short, barrel-chested guy, broad shouldered and impeccably dressed in what I took to be a high-ranking officer's uniform. He wore black leather shoes as opposed to the boots I'd seen soldiers wearing. His red beret was cocked on the side of his head but perfectly arranged. Placing the pistol in its holster, he lit a cigarette. His eyes never left me for a second. His left hand came to rest on his thigh closest to the holstered gun, his right lifted the cigarette to his mouth. He took long, deep drags, then exhaled a cloud of smoke upwards into the air. His hair was cut very short, which accentuated his well-fed face. Thick bushy eyebrows topped his dark, swarthy skin and bulbous nose. His eyes were black and malevolent, the mouth under a well-trimmed moustache was cupid-shaped yet mean, with the corners turned down. A couple of chins finished the look.

His stare was hate-filled. I stared back for a few moments, until his eyes veered to the doorway and the corridor beyond. It was obvious

Sam was going through the same pat-down as me. It hadn't taken them very long because just then she walked through the door, her head lowered, a bewildered expression on her face as she turned and looked down at me. It was a stupid thing to say, but I started to ask if she was all right. Sanchez cut me short.

'*Silencio!*' he yelled. 'No talk! OK.'

The airport police were right behind her, carrying our luggage: two cases and a holdall. With all those extra people and baggage, the already small office was suddenly overcrowded. One policeman said something rapidly to Sanchez, who looked at me and said in broken English, 'Open case.' Mine was a grey Samsonite with a combination lock; Sam's a black, canvas suitcase zipped all the way around. The holdall was our hand luggage, containing the usual holiday paraphernalia.

I inserted the right code and opened the catch, whereupon Sanchez drew his pistol. Using the barrel as a pointer, he said, 'Dis way,' and waved us into the next room. Once through the doorway, we were ushered to the right and brought to a halt in front of a large desk. Sat there was none other than 'Guirez', the passport official. He motioned with his hand for us to remove whatever we had under our clothes, his greedy eyes taking in Sam's breasts when she lifted her flowery top in order to remove her waistcoat. His breathing became somewhat laboured and it looked as if his ill-fitting uniform was about to burst at the seams.

I felt a stab of anger and wanted to hit him, but it would have been madness; there were at least a dozen soldiers of the Guardia Nacional around us, two of them pointing machine guns at me. I wondered if this was some horrific dream I was having and any moment I would wake up in the hotel room.

An exchange of words took place between Guirez and the two soldiers, who left the room briefly and returned with our luggage, dumping it on the floor behind and to the side of us. They opened the suitcases and started to take everything out, item by item. Clothing was shaken and everything meticulously checked. We'd taken off our waistcoats by this time and placed them on the table in front of

Guirez. Again using gestures, he told us to empty our pockets. We were wearing baggy, lightweight jeans and had used our pockets for all sorts. Out came a set of keys from one of Sam's pockets – the key ring had a photo of me inside it. Then a wallet-type purse, where she kept her little treasures: photos of her family, little notes from me, and other personal things. I could tell she was reluctant to put them down.

Then along came Sanchez. He spoke a little English, albeit badly with an American twang. Walking across the room, he said, 'Trafficking cocaine is very bad offence.' He came so close I had to look down on him as he spoke. 'You go to jail for very long time,' he added coldly.

Stunned by his words, I felt numb. Sam and I looked at each other for a second, the seriousness of the situation beginning to sink in. I emptied my pockets – out came my money, keys, two passports and other papers.

Guirez examined the four packs he'd taken from the waistcoat pockets, cut into one with a knife, wet his finger and stuck it in the package, ready to test it with his tongue. As our passports landed on the desk, he stopped what he was doing and swooped on them; it was the second time that day he'd had our passports in his grubby little hands. He didn't bother looking at them this time. Opening a drawer on the right-hand side of his desk, he dropped them inside, closed it and looked up with a satisfied smile.

After recovering a little from the shock of what Sanchez had said, I became more aware of things happening around us: conversations in the background, the clack-clack of an old-fashioned typewriter, a telephone ringing, even the sound of a plane taxiing on the runway. I looked at my watch. We should have been on that plane. Shit, I thought to myself, we've been caught. Look for an opportunity to get out of this mess!

'*Por allí!*' said Guirez, pointing over toward the wall on our right. The wall had a clear space about six feet wide and was painted off-white. When we turned, he said loudly, '*No, no, no, asi!*' He picked up one of the waistcoats – each had two kilos of cocaine placed on the top – and struck a pose, holding the garment at arm's length.

21

He passed the waistcoat to me, picked up the other and gave it to Sam.

We turned and moved over to the wall. As we did so, the person who'd earlier been sitting behind the desk in the first office walked over with a camera, an old-fashioned contraption with a flash-bulb attachment. He appeared to be a civilian worker: short-sleeved white shirt, black pants and shoes. He wasn't dark-skinned as such, rather he had a jaundiced face with slicked-back dark hair – a nondescript character really. He obviously seconded as photographer and took up his position.

Poof! For a few seconds I couldn't see a thing. My sight returned just in time to see he'd changed the bulb and was ready to blind us again. Poof! This happened four times in all. When it was over, we were told to return the waistcoats. It took a minute for the bright spots dancing in front of my eyes to disappear. As my sight returned, I saw the two soldiers with machine guns were still pointing their weapons at us. They were young men, 19 or 20 at the most, though I could tell by the look in their eyes they wouldn't give us any sympathy if we tried anything. They'd shoot us for sure.

Events began to speed up. Transport had been arranged. We were handcuffed together and faced towards the way we'd entered. I turned and looked back at our belongings still lying on the table, nothing signed for and no receipts of any kind; however, that was the least of our worries. The cuff was so tight it bit into my skin. Sam was a bit luckier, as her wrists were so slim that even on the last notch the cuff wouldn't close tight.

Four soldiers jostled us unceremoniously through the door and down the corridor. The two in front held our clothes with a tight grip, while the other two young machine-gunners stayed behind, prodding us with the barrels from time to time. I prayed the safety catches were on. We passed the door through which the police had brought us and down to the bottom end of the corridor where, just around the corner, a doorway led outside. There sat an old, American army jeep-type vehicle with the back door open.

We were pushed inside, the door slammed shut and locked. It

stank of urine. The heat was so intense it stuck to our skin. The vehicle had been converted for this particular kind of service, the tiny windows made up of a tight diamond-shaped mesh. Rusting metal seats ran either side with the spare wheel in the middle of the floor. The interior was absolutely filthy. Before too long, I was mopping the sweat with the tail of my shirt. Outside, there was enough room for two soldiers to sit one either side. One more soldier stood on the back step, holding on to a bar that ran from floor to roof. I could see them through the grille in the door.

The journey wasn't long, maybe ten minutes or so, but it was so bumpy it felt like the driver was purposely aiming at every pothole he could find. I didn't have a clue where we were heading and, to be honest, I wasn't in the mood for sightseeing. Now we were alone, Sam and I began to make conversation. It wasn't easy, the words forming lumps in my throat. Sam sat with a stunned expression on her face, her eyes wide open.

'Oh God, love, I'm so sorry,' I said to her.

'It's all right, it's not your fault,' she said. It was as if she knew a huge cloud of guilt had enveloped me.

I tried to sound convincing. 'Maybe we can get out of this somehow. I've heard that you can buy yourself out of situations like this. Don't give up just yet.'

'I won't,' she replied. 'Maybe someone here will help us, eh?'

I nodded. 'Yeah, maybe,' I said, praying inwardly.

# 2

# THE INTERROGATORS

The jeep bumped and bounced through narrow streets, then turned a sharp right that almost threw us from our seats. The soldiers at the rear laughed amongst each other loudly, probably amused at our discomfort. The vehicle stopped abruptly, causing me to crush Sam into the bulkhead momentarily.

'These fuckers are really having a ball with us, aren't they?' I said angrily.

'Calm down, Frank, you've got to keep your head,' she replied.

She was right, of course. I was getting angry, mad at myself for doing something so stupid in the first place, despite all the warnings in my head.

What Sam had said made sense: I needed to keep my head. I'd once learned a saying used by friends in martial arts circles – if you allow your opponent to get you angry, then he has already won. This would be the time to put those wise words into practice.

We'd stopped short of a large set of metal gates, a shaded sentry box stood against the wire fence, manned by three soldiers of the Guardia Nacional. One got to his feet lazily and ambled over to the jeep's passenger window. A few words were hastily exchanged and he walked away clutching a piece of paper that he waved at the other two soldiers, motioning them to open the gates.

Sam joined me to look out of the window, and as the jeep lurched off we banged our heads together. We rubbed the pain with our free hands. Under normal circumstances, we would have laughed it off, but the mood was darkening by degrees. The driver sped through the gates and swept the jeep in a wide arc, jammed on his brakes, backed up a dozen yards or so and jerked to a halt. The two soldiers in front jumped out and made their way to the rear; the door to our sweatbox was unlocked and snatched open. Bright sunlight flooded in, while one of the soldiers motioned us out. They were more relaxed with their machine guns now, probably safe in the knowledge we posed no threat in the heavily manned Guardia Comando post.

As we emerged, I could see some ten yards in front double doors fitted with opaque glass and painted bright blue. One of the doors swung open and a soldier stepped out, holding the door with one hand and beckoning with the other. Neither of us needed a degree to know where we had to go, but before we had the chance to step forward the five soldier escorts began to manhandle us.

There were a few seconds of scorching heat from the early afternoon sun as we made our way over to the waiting soldier, but once inside the door, the chill of air conditioning hit me like an icy blast. In the large office, three men stood to one side of a table that held an archaic computer and printer. Other desks were scattered around, littered with papers, ashtrays and files. One held a bank of telephones. On the far wall, two glass-panelled doors led into other rooms. The men, smartly dressed in khaki suits, shirts and ties, carried side arms. They were huddled together discussing our fate, from time to time glancing in our direction.

The soldier who had led us in stood with his back to the door, a machine gun strapped over his shoulder in the ready position, forefinger resting on the trigger guard, his face deadpan. It didn't look as if we were going anywhere for a while.

It was some minutes before one of the trio broke away and made his way over. He looked down at our handcuffs. 'Don't worry, we'll soon have them off,' he said in excellent English. Again, there was that strong American twang. '*Busca la llave!*' he barked at the soldier guarding the door.

'*Si, señor,*' replied the soldier. He opened the door and smartly took his leave. The man who gave the orders had no markings on his uniform except for a row of coloured ribbon. He was almost as tall as I was, around my age too, early 40s. His hair was very thin, almost balding, and he was pale-skinned. His thick, grey eyebrows overshadowed dark, piercing eyes and his beaked nose hooked over thin, cruel lips. After he'd spoken, he smiled. It sent a shiver down my spine. He was playing the good guy, but my instincts told me he wasn't to be trusted. I had no money to bargain with, it had been left at the airport – not that five hundred quid would possibly have bought those men anyway.

The soldier returned with the key to our handcuffs and passed them to our interrogator, then repositioned himself by the door as before.

'Good,' said the English-speaking officer, taking off our handcuffs. When he saw the mark around my wrist, he tutted and slowly shook his head. 'They get a little excited,' he smiled. Who was he kidding? This guy had evil written all over him.

The remaining two officers split as if on cue. One placed two wooden chairs in front and to the side of the computer table. The other sat down and prepared himself at the keyboard.

'Sit down, both of you,' the English speaker ordered.

As we sat, I had the feeling it was going to be a long day. I wasn't about to tell them anything about my connections back in England or on the island; it was more than my life was worth. Sam didn't know anything anyway, so it would be down to me. We gave our full names, addresses in England, ages, dates of birth and parents' names, and were asked for our identity numbers, which threw us completely. We didn't have identity cards or numbers.

'Passport number then,' said the officer.

'Can't remember,' I replied.

'Me neither,' said Sam.

'What? You can't remember?' he said incredulously.

In Venezuela, it seemed everyone possessed an identity card and number.

'No *cédula*? What kind of country do you come from?'

'A free one,' I replied, almost too quickly. I'd reacted with a smart-arsed reply and as soon as it left my lips I realised I couldn't take it back. It was too late now anyway; I noticed something in his eyes had changed in that instant. He recovered quickly; the thin, watery smile never wavered.

'Now,' he said firmly, 'where did you buy the drugs?'

'Off a guy on the beach,' I replied, and again it was almost too quickly. It was the first thing that popped into my head. For some unfathomable reason, I hadn't reckoned on this part.

'No, no, no, you know that's not the truth. Where did you buy the drugs?'

'I told you, I bought them off a guy on the beach!'

'Are you asking me to believe you bought four kilos of cocaine from a man you met on the beach?' he said, looking across at Sam, as if for encouragement.

She shrugged her shoulders. 'I don't know anything,' she said flatly.

She was telling the truth. Sam had stayed in the hotel complex for the whole two weeks of our holiday and had never been present during the transactions. I knew the 'man on the beach' story was a bit feeble, but I needed time to think of something to make it ring true.

The officer turned in his chair. 'Go and sit outside for a while, I want to talk to you separately,' he said to Sam. After instruction, the soldier guarding the door took Sam outside. He never came back, so I assumed he'd been told to watch over her.

The officer slipped his smile and set his face. 'OK, let's not fool around any more. Who did you buy the drugs from?'

'I told you already—' Smack! The flat of a hand struck the right side of my face. It came unexpectedly from behind me, knocking my head sideways. My face smarted. Turning, I saw a fist coming towards me. My reactions were a bit slow and he caught me a glancing blow on the cheekbone.

'*No, no, no. Asi, no,*' said Mr Nice Guy to the man who'd hit me.

'Sorry about that,' he said to me. 'He sometimes loses his temper. I've told him, I said to him, "Pedro, one day you're really gonna hurt someone." That's what I said to him.'

I wasn't impressed; nevertheless, they had my full attention.

'Just tell the truth and everything will go painlessly,' the officer said in a fatherly manner.

'Look! I've told you already—'

'OK, so what did he look like, this guy on the beach?'

'He was Venezuelan and he spoke very good English. A Negro type.'

'And what was his name, this *negro*?'

I ransacked my mind for a suitable Spanish name. 'Miguel,' I told him after a few seconds.

'I think you're making all this up,' said my interrogator.

'No, I'm not, I'm—' Smack! Again, another good crack to the side of the head, this time from the interrogator himself.

Leaning forward, and inches from my face, he screamed, '*Tell me the truth!*'

'I'm telling the truth, I met the guy on the hotel beach one day and got to know him. He seemed OK, so—'

Everything went dark as a black plastic bag was placed over my head. The stench of something repulsive filled my nostrils. I tried to breathe, but the fumes burned my nose. I felt a sharp pain around my throat. I couldn't breathe, my head was swimming. I tried desperately to unhook the hands behind my head holding the plastic bag tight around my neck. The fumes inside the bag took all the oxygen. I felt myself going, then I blacked out.

When I came round, I was still in the office, everything dancing and swirling about dizzily through the blur of my watery eyes. I gasped for air, coughing and wheezing. As my head began to clear, I heard the tail end of a conversation going on behind me. The only words that rang any bells were '*no*' and '*cónsulado*'. I turned around slowly, just in time to see a door slam. The door was set in the opposite wall, and I wondered if maybe it was their chief's office. I never did find out, though I wasn't mistreated for the rest of the time I spent with those three gentlemen.

I gave the English speaker my story, which I made up and embellished along the way. While doing so, he translated it to the man at the keyboard. All the time, I glared at the third man, who'd perched himself on the table edge. He looked back at me with just the faint glimmer of a smile in his eyes. When everything was typed out and printed, the computer man placed the pages on the desktop and passed me a pen to sign them.

'You've got to be kidding,' I said in response after trying to read and understand what I was supposed to have said. 'I don't understand a word of this. It could say anything!'

He smiled and said, 'You have to sign it, my friend, because the process does not start until you sign the statement. If you don't sign, you will be here for ever.'

After some thought, I still refused. Better to be sure and wait until I was certain that what was written on the statement was what I'd actually said. I had no idea how I would go about this, but I was sure something or someone would turn up.

They had finished with me now and seemed unaffected by my refusal to sign. 'OK,' said the interrogator, 'we'll talk to your woman now. Maybe *she'll* be more helpful.'

His intonation made me see red. I snapped at him with new-found bravado. 'Don't you hurt that girl, she doesn't know anything – don't even fucking touch her!'

'And who is it that's going to stop me, *gringo*!' He spat the last word at me. Gringo echoed in my head. For some reason, the way he delivered it made my skin crawl.

My tormentor walked briskly to the door. 'Come with me,' he said sharply. He opened the door wide and shouted an order to the soldier across the courtyard guarding Sam. Through the opened doorway, I could see her sitting on a concrete bench. She got to her feet and walked towards us, the soldier following closely. Making eye contact as we passed each other, I had a chance to say to her quietly,

'Don't sign any papers, OK?' She knew me well enough to know my expression was serious.

Once outside, the heat pounded at me like a hammer. My head throbbed, my cheek ached but most of all I dared not think what was happening to Sam. The day was unfolding to be a page in my life I would remember for ever. The soldier made a point of prodding me with the barrel of his gun and pointed to the concrete seats 20 yards away on the other side of the courtyard. I made my way over unsteadily, taking deep breaths as I went, the smell of ammonia still hanging in my nostrils.

There was no shade where I sat. I looked at my watch: it was four o'clock. The soldier placed himself ten feet away in the shade of a large tree. Looking at me unblinking, he ejected the magazine from his machine gun, glanced down briefly to check the round count, and snapped it back. He looked at me again. He was only a kid. An evil smirk crossed his boyish face; he had made his point, he was macho. I wondered if he'd done the same thing with Sam. I could only speculate as to what was happening to her right then.

Slowly, I recovered my senses and began to take in the scene around me. I was sitting on the edge of an oval courtyard in a large compound filled with concrete buildings – their windows, doors and soffits all painted a vivid blue. Vehicles were parked all around, including the jeep we'd arrived in. The main gate and entrance were to my right, trees and bushes were dotted here and there; it was a busy place, soldiers going back and forth in all directions. One stopped to chat with my guard. Dressed in camouflage trousers, green T-shirt and sandals, he wasn't armed and was obviously off duty. As he walked away, he pointed at me and crooked his finger twice, as if pulling a trigger. 'Pow, pow,' he laughed. He walked on down the path and disappeared behind a block building. At that moment, I questioned what went on in their heads.

I sat there for an hour, feeling like a freak in a sideshow. Everyone that passed stared at me and made some comment to my guard, who just laughed. By 5 p.m., the sun had dipped and long shadows were forming across the courtyard. The terrific heat eased and a gentle breeze began to blow. The door across the yard opened and Sam came out, followed by the interrogator. She walked over and sat next to me. I studied her face and was relieved she wasn't marked.

'I'm OK,' she said. 'I just kept telling them I didn't know anything. I didn't sign anything, though. Why did you say that to me?'

'Because we don't understand anything they've put down. Besides, it's best we don't admit to anything just yet. There might be a way out.'

She lifted her eyes to me. 'I hope so, this is a bloody nightmare.'

'Yeah,' I said, agreeing with her. 'I'm puzzled as to why they pulled us. I get the feeling it wasn't pot luck; they knew.'

'What makes you say that?'

'Just little things. Those two airport police were pretty sure of themselves when they got me in the corridor. I'm sure they don't just pull tourists out of the queue and put a gun to their heads.'

'They did sort of zoom in on us, didn't they?'

'That officer, Sanchez, he told the two policemen to go and get the woman. I'm almost certain they hadn't mentioned you to him. It all seems a bit strange, that's all.'

We remained sitting on the bench. A couple more guards were sent to watch over us. We tried to work out if we'd been double-crossed, and why? By 6.30 p.m. it was going dark, and we sat in the glare of halogen floodlights until just after seven. Several more soldiers appeared and we were beckoned towards the jeep we had arrived in. We were handcuffed together, my discomfort amusing the soldier who had tightened the cuff as hard as he possibly could. Once inside the jeep, we sped off through the gate.

'I'm scared. Where do you think they're taking us this time?' asked Sam.

'I don't know, love,' I said, 'but I'm pretty sure it's not going to be nice, wherever it is.' Sam gripped my hand tightly. I realised I'd said the wrong thing.

It was a 15-minute ride in relative darkness. Sam and I made little conversation during the journey, both nurturing our own thoughts. I didn't know exactly what Sam was thinking, but I imagined it would be similar to what was going through my mind. I cursed myself for being so stupid. A crazy mixture of questions buzzed inside my head, each one fighting for attention. What went wrong? What's going to happen to us? Why, oh why hadn't I listened to my inner thoughts on the coach? What did Sam think of me now? That voice had told me over and over, why hadn't I listened? These things went round and round in my head until I felt dizzy. The swerves and bumps caused by our driver's erratic moves didn't help either.

Eventually, we pulled up alongside a brightly lit building. Its entrance was easily 20 feet wide and the whole front section, from floor to ceiling, a construction of iron bars. Two wide concrete steps led up to the entrance in which a gate was set. Inside, we could see three men sitting around a table. One of them got up with great effort, picked up a set of keys and made his way to unlock the gate, swinging it inwards as he opened it.

The back door to the jeep was opened and we were ordered out. '*Vamos!*' said one soldier sharply. Walking towards the open gate, I looked up at the twinkling stars in the clear night sky. I noticed the same constellations I'd seen on those lazy, balmy nights I'd enjoyed with Sam during our stay at the complex and wondered if I would ever enjoy the beauty of it all again.

Two soldiers accompanied us through the gate, which was slammed and locked behind us. Our handcuffs were removed and we were ushered over to a table. The three men on duty were all dressed the same: blue, short-sleeved, open-necked shirts with dark-blue epaulettes, which bore silver numbers on them. Dark-blue pants and black shoes completed their attire. All carried side arms. Their shirt pockets were emblazoned with an official-looking emblem, which I didn't recognise at the time; I would soon find out they were local police and we were back in Pampatar at a station called El Cinco (Number Five).

After an exchange of paperwork, the soldiers took their leave. The policeman with the keys slammed the gate so hard we both jumped. The whole wall of bars rattled for a second or two. I turned around and it was only then, under the glow of several bare light bulbs, I noticed the garish blue paintwork on the bars. It was the same colour as I'd seen at the guardia post. Under the circumstances, it was strange that I found myself wondering whether the government had bought a job lot of this paint.

I was brought back to the present by the sound of keys landing heavily on the metal desktop. I turned and looked at Sam.

'What now?' I said to her.

She just shrugged, a look of hopelessness on her face. I could tell she had already resigned herself to the worst possible outcome.

The two policemen still sitting were dark-skinned, while the other had a lighter complexion. He had greased black hair, a clipped moustache, a mean mouth and coal-black eyes. He did all the talking. Neither of us could understand a word he said but got the general picture from his exaggerated gestures. The other two sat and watched with amused looks on their faces.

We were ordered to empty our pockets. I tried to explain to the officer that we had absolutely nothing, that our belongings had been taken from us at the airport, but he insisted, so we went through the motions. The smiles of the policemen faded and frowns took their place, all three obviously disappointed: there was no booty for them. One pointed at my watch. I'd kept it on my wrist so far and hadn't really thought about it, except to check the time here and there.

'Oh no, mate, you're not having that,' I muttered under my breath. It wasn't an expensive watch, but its sentimental value was priceless. 'No, no,' I said, shaking my finger from side to side to emphasise the point.

The speaker made it very clear, using a slicing motion with his finger across his throat, that if I were to go back there in the cells wearing the watch I would lose my life. I didn't trust the guy one bit, but I couldn't take the chance. I took the watch off and passed it over to him. He opened a drawer, pulled out an envelope and offered me a pen.

'*Nombre*,' he said, pointing at me, then the envelope. I took the pen and wrote my name, all the time thinking it was a sham, that this would be the last I saw of it.

The speaker exchanged a few words with one of the other policemen. I heard the word '*mujer*' and knew they were talking about Sam again. I'd heard that word several times since our arrest earlier in the day. Was it only eight hours ago? It felt like a lifetime already. The policeman picked up the keys and beckoned Sam towards a steel door in the wall. There was nothing I could do, I felt powerless. Was this the last time we would see each other? I didn't know what the hell was going on. She looked back at me with pleading, frightened eyes for which I could muster no words of comfort. I tried to say something but nothing came out. I watched with a heavy heart until she disappeared and the door closed behind her.

I turned towards the desk. A questioning look on my face prompted the policeman to say, '*Tranquilo.*' He made a calming gesture with his hands to emphasise the point and shrugged a plausible '*Mañana*' as an afterthought.

The policeman came back through the steel door and handed the keys to the man who'd spoken to me. '*Vamos,*' he said, rising from the chair and motioning me to follow him. We went through the same door and turned left into a corridor illuminated by two bare light bulbs hanging from the ceiling. The further we walked, the more an indescribable smell crept into my nostrils. At the end of the corridor was a solid metal door and when the policeman unlocked and opened it inwards, it revealed a barred gate. The stench hit me so hard I reeled back in disgust. Fucking hell, don't tell me I've got to go in there, I almost shouted.

The noise of babbling, shouting people bombarded my ears and echoed off the bare concrete walls. The policeman unlocked the gate and pulled me through by my shirtsleeve. I took a deep, nauseating breath and prepared myself mentally. By the sound of the rabid baying only yards away, I knew I'd be eaten alive if I showed any sign of weakness.

There were three cells in this part of the building: two were completely empty, the third crammed full of local thugs and miscreants. Jabbering faces pressed tight to the bars; it was like something from a scene depicting a lunatic asylum. Pulled by my sleeve towards the cell,

I was convinced they'd fucking kill me once inside. In no position to argue, along I went like a doomed man. Looking at the human flotsam, I reflected that the policeman had been right about the watch. They shook the bars like wild, caged animals, mouths agape, each with missing teeth. It was a frightening sight. The policeman shouted at them and they fell silent.

Why was he putting me in there with all those deranged people? I understood from my experience at the airport that if I'd had money to bribe with maybe things would have been different. He opened the gate and shoved me in. The crowd initially stepped back, more in fear of the policeman's authority than my humble self, but soon they encircled me. I clenched my fists, adrenalin kicking in. There was no place to go. I heard the clank of the cell door, then the iron gate. Finally, the metal door to the corridor slammed shut.

They were at me like a pack of wolves. Not hitting but touching, poking, searching my pockets. Without a thought, I lashed out with everything I could muster: head-butts, punches, kicks. I completely lost control for what felt like an age but could have only been a few seconds. They cautiously backed away. I was amazed; it had been a long time since I'd reacted in such a way and without hesitation. My heart pounded like a jackhammer. I stood firmly, fists raised, my face twisted and distorted with anger and fear.

'Hey, man, do you speak English?' The voice caught me completely off guard, its reverberation so bizarre in the situation I shook my head to let it free. Again, the voice called across, 'Over here.' I turned and looked in the direction the voice had come from, and through the crowd, I saw the owner, a tough-looking bearded guy, a deep scar running from his forehead into the left eyebrow. He spoke English like a mainland European.

He pushed his way roughly through the crowd. 'You did right, man. You have to beat these monkeys, it's the only way to earn their respect! Ha, ha!'

My eyes quickly gathered in the mob once more, fearful this was some kind of apparition. Their eyes darted shiftily but none made contact with mine. They were a filthy, bedraggled bunch; only a few of them wore a top, and those that didn't revealed heavy scar tissue on arms and chests. Some wore shorts, some tattered jeans; in either case, they were filthy. Not one of them owned a pair of shoes or footwear of any kind. I could only relate to them as savages. The place stank of excrement and urine. I'd never imagined such squalor in my life before.

'Does the smell ever go away?' I asked my new friend.

'No, but you'll get used to it,' he laughed.

'I don't fuckin' think so,' I replied.

He took my arm and guided me through the crowd. They parted as he raised his hand and shoved one or two violently aside. We reached the far right-hand corner of the cell, where the stench was horrendous. Pointing down to a bucket just outside the bars, he said, 'That's where you take a piss.' It was three-quarters full already.

'What happens when it's full?'

'Then it goes on the floor like always,' he replied. 'Over there is where you're supposed to shit.' He pointed through the bars to a cubicle two yards away. From where I stood, I could see what passed for a toilet pan, full and overflowing with excrement. A cloud of flies buzzed around, the floor was littered with plastic bags and newspaper.

'You've got to be joking with me,' I said.

'Well,' he said nonchalantly, 'you can always shit in a plastic bag or some newspaper and throw it over there with the rest of it.'

I heaved and almost threw up.

'I am called Eric, and welcome to the Hilton,' he said with an outstretched hand.

I took his grip and we shook. 'My name's Frank.'

Eric obviously carried a dark sense of humour. He led me over to where he'd been sitting against the one solid wall and made a space for me to sit. He'd claimed his space in this four-yards-square cell several nights previously after being arrested in a club for brawling. The police had found a small amount of marijuana in his pocket, and he'd been brought here. He'd left Holland some years ago to live in Venezuela, so he knew the ropes. His lawyer was talking with the judge, money would be exchanged, and he would go free in a day or so, he seemed sure of it. Then it *was* possible. My spirits were momentarily lifted, then deflated. Where the hell would I get my money from, or a lawyer I could trust? Eric explained that a huge number of lawyers in the country were crooked and corrupt, along with judges, guardia and almost any official with power. Anything could be bought if the 'price was right', which would be laughable if this was the TV show. But there I was, in dire straits, without two pennies to rub together. How would I get Sam and myself out of this mess?

'What about food?' I asked Eric. 'I haven't eaten anything since this morning and neither has my girlfriend.' I explained our story to him.

'So, you don't have money?' he said. 'Then you are fucked, my friend; they don't feed you here.'

'How do you eat?' I asked.

'Me, I have some food coming shortly from a café across the street. My lawyer pays the police and one of them will bring it to me. Don't worry, you can share mine tonight. But don't make a habit of it, all right?'

Sure enough, one of the black policemen delivered a parcel to Eric within the hour.

How on earth I managed to keep food down amid the stench and filth would be anyone's guess, but eat I did, ripping into a fried chicken with unwashed hands. The chicken came with maize-flour cakes deep fried in oil. The locals call them *arepas*. On their own they were tasteless but filling. Eric showed me how to break one open and make a chicken sandwich.

All the time we ate, the locals watched from under hooded eyes; they didn't miss a mouthful. The only guilt I felt was when I thought of Sam – she wouldn't have eaten either, and here I was stuffing my face. I explained my feelings to Eric.

'Don't worry about her,' he said, between mouthfuls, 'women prisoners are treated very differently. They get food sent in regularly and they'll share with her. Your woman will not starve.'

When we'd had our fill, Eric said to me mockingly, 'Would sir like a dessert perhaps?' He laughed loudly and passed what food was left to one of the locals. Immediately, a group joined him and squatted in a circle around the leftovers scattered on the floor. Like hungry dogs, they squabbled and fought each other for scraps. Skin and bones, they devoured everything. There wasn't a crumb left when they'd finished; they too were hungry.

A couple of hours after my arrival, everyone began to settle. Now and then, the odd local crept over to scrounge something. It must have been obvious to all and sundry that I was as destitute as they were but try they did, time after time. Eric didn't smoke and I was dying for a cigarette. I hadn't bought any that morning, as the flight was non-smoking. If there was a time when I needed tobacco, this was surely it.

It got so hot I took my shirt off and draped it over what I first took to be a black string line running diagonally across the cell at head height. It was black on account of the thousands of flies that had settled on it. They buzzed about furiously when I disturbed them, then settled on the shirt I'd taken so much trouble to have laundered and pressed for the flight home. As the night closed in, so did the mosquitoes. Before too long, I was swatting, slapping and scratching continuously. Luckily, I'd been vaccinated with every jab known to mankind before leaving England.

I tried to settle on the concrete floor using my boots as a pillow, but it was so uncomfortable I could only doze. My eyes opened at the slightest sound, and hearing the steel door and gate open, I raised my head slightly to look. A prisoner was let in, laughing and joking with the guard. The gate and door were locked again as the prisoner made his way past our cell and down to the far end. He entered the first cell, which was unlocked. In my somewhat heavy-eyed state, I wondered what part he played in the system to be granted a cell all on his own. It came to mind he must be a trustee or cleaner for the police.

I'd taken a headcount earlier: there were sixteen men in a cell four yards square. Every inch of floor space was covered with sleeping bodies; cockroaches crawled everywhere. I tried to settle again, and eventually dozed fitfully. Something woke me – a feeling, a sound, I couldn't tell. I opened my eyes and saw the trustee reaching into our cell, holding out a broom handle and trying to unhook my shirt from the line above me. I was up in a flash. Without even thinking, I grabbed the handle and snatched it from his grasp. My reaction surprised him greatly; he stood stock-still on the other side of the bars, his mouth wide open. I lifted the handle, took aim between the bars and brought it crashing down onto his head. Crack! The handle broke in two.

He howled for a second or two, shook his head, then waved his arms about like an angry gorilla. A string of obscenities followed, all in Spanish, and delivered with such venom the commotion woke everyone up.

'What's going on?' asked Eric sleepily.

'This fuckin' monkey was trying to steal my shirt,' I shouted. Eric, unwittingly or not, had introduced the word 'monkey' into my vocabulary.

'Watch that one,' he said, 'he's a piece of shit. Works for the police.'

'I'll break his fucking fingers if he tries thieving my shirt again,' I spat. I took down the shirt, put it on and turned to see the trustee had gone.

'That's the way, my friend,' said Eric, yawning. 'Let's get some sleep.'

Despite the heat, I kept my clothes on all night. The bare bulbs glowed above. Sleep was difficult, and I dropped off here and there, but was wide awake when the steel door and gate were opened. '*Buenos dias!*' the policeman shouted.

People stirred. Then the gate and steel door slammed shut again and prisoners collapsed back into slumber. Not the trustee, though; he was up and wandering, eyeing me coldly every time he passed our cell. He walked to where the bucket sat and picked it up, urine slopping out onto the floor. I gathered it must have been his job to empty it somewhere. I was right. He held the bottom of the bucket with his other hand, swung it back and threw the whole contents into our cell, soaking everyone with the night's piss.

The whole place erupted, people jumped up, screaming and cursing the trustee, who by now had retreated to the safety of his cell. Even Eric lost his cool.

'*Te voy a matar, bastardo!*' he screamed after the trustee. 'I'm gonna kill that bastard!' he shouted at me. 'He's pissed off about last night,' he said, 'but if we get a chance, my friend, we'll give it to him good, eh?'

'Too right,' I replied. I was livid. All my clothes were soaked with urine, and if that wasn't bad enough, flies were multiplying by the thousand.

Within the hour, we were let out to wash. The 'washing facilities' were situated at the far end past the trustee's cell. I followed the crowd and spotted the trustee lying on the floor smoking a cigarette. Without a thought, I pushed open the cell door and ran towards him. He'd only managed to get up on one elbow when my booted foot crashed into his face. I bore down on him and I hit him repeatedly until he was bloodied and unconscious. Getting to my feet and turning to go, I noticed everyone had stopped to watch.

I stood for a moment and took stock. What the hell was happening to me? I didn't want this, but if violence was all they respected, so be it. I had grown up in a tough area, and although I'd moved on and established a better lifestyle, I knew how to handle myself. Leaving the trustee lying there, I went out to clean up. The washing amenities were six twenty-five-litre tubs containing grimy water and several sawn-off plastic Coca-Cola bottles to use as scoops. There was no soap. I stripped, taking care to leave my clothes where I could see them. On close inspection, I could see clearly how marked the locals were, particularly their backs and buttocks.

I rinsed off quickly and grabbed half a tub from the pestering locals, who were actually drinking the stuff. I growled at them, raised my fist, and they backed off. I used the water to rinse my shirt and jeans. Wringing them out tightly, I shook them and put them on wet. I walked back to the cell carrying my socks and boots. The trustee was still sprawled out where I'd left him. There was no breakfast. Our cell was locked again.

'You did good with that cocksucker,' said Eric. 'You didn't need me.'

We made small talk, then I dozed for a while, so tired I could have slept for a week, but it was impossible. I woke to the sound of the steel door opening again.

'*Holandés!*' shouted the guard.

'That's me,' said Eric. 'Good luck, my friend. Don't be fooled by these monkeys; they'd cut your throat while you were asleep if they thought you had anything. But I can see you can look after yourself, you'll be all right.'

We shook hands, and he was up and gone in a matter of seconds. I never saw him again. I'd even missed the chance to ask for his lawyer's name.

I felt desolate and alone. The locals jabbered at me all day long, it didn't seem to matter that I didn't understand them. Maybe they thought I did. Over and over again, a couple re-enacted the pounding I'd given the trustee, who wasn't to be seen. I was surprised there was no retribution, either from him or the police. At least he'd kept his mouth shut. There was to be no food that day, or night. Clouds of flies buzzed around incessantly. My clothes dried on me, only slightly cleaner than before. I felt filthy, I hadn't shaved, and my mouth tasted like a cesspit, my skin was hot and sticky and I felt dispirited and demoralised.

I spent the rest of the day avoiding conversation and eye contact, and cursing myself for being a prick. I worried about Sam, and how she was faring. Later in the evening, as people settled down for the night, my thoughts focused on home for the first time. I could lose my clean, comfortable life, the precious time with my daughter from a previous marriage, my loving relationship with Sam; we were crazy about each other. I had planned to start another business. That dream seemed shattered.

Two years before the trip, I had been the managing director of a thriving company. Bad debts, bankruptcies and cut-throat competition contributed to liquidation a year later. Out went the affluent lifestyle. I ended up in a council flat, on the dole, with banks and creditors hounding me for money borrowed on personal guarantees. It hadn't bothered Sam that I was broke.

I slept a little better the second night, although my stomach turned and rumbled constantly. The next morning, we went through the same routine, but later the steel door opened and the guard shouted, '*Inglés*!' That was me! I scrambled up, straightened myself out and waited by the door. Some of the locals slapped me on the back. '*Libertad*! *Libertad*!' they chanted. Some fucking hope of that, I thought, as I was taken back down the corridor towards the entrance to the police station.

The first person I saw was Sam. I breathed a sigh of relief. She looked tired and grubby, and I searched her eyes for a sign she hadn't been mistreated in any way. The policeman who'd taken my watch two days before returned it with a flourish. I kept looking at Sam as I tightened the watch strap, looking for signs of forgiveness. Her eyes met mine. I could see the sadness; she was putting on a brave face.

'Are you all right?' I whispered to her.

'Yes, I'm OK. I could do with some food, though, I'm bloody starving.'

'Me too. How did you go on in the women's bit?'

'It was filthy. A bit scary too, everyone arguing and waving their arms about. They were OK with me, though. Someone gave me some food the first night, but last night nothing.'

I'd let her down. I wanted to hold her and make her feel safe, but I knew I couldn't.

'Perhaps they'll feed us later.'

What a mess we looked and that was after only two nights.

'What happened to your clothes?' she asked. 'They're all wrinkled, and you smell awful. Sorry, but you do.'

'Just got a bit wet yesterday,' I told her.

After a few minutes of welcome fresh air, we were handcuffed and herded into a different vehicle. It was similar to the guardia jeep but painted white and blue; the word '*policía*' adorned the side panels. It

43

was the same inside. Familiar smells returned, the interior of the jeep again reeking of stale sweat and urine. Sam pulled a face and held her nose.

Nobody so far had explained anything to us.

I looked up. 'Where to now?' I asked no one in particular.

# 3

# A GLIMMER OF HOPE

Embarking on yet another roller-coaster ride through the town's narrow streets, we held hands during the 20-minute journey and spoke briefly about our stay at El Cinco. Not to alarm her, I toned down what had happened during my interrogation on the day of our arrest. Then, without meaning to, a slip of the tongue brought a dart of fear to her eyes. They reached into mine, asking for the truth. I turned away and stared at the floor. Minutes passed in silence, after which she expressed concern about how people could do such things and not be punished. I was to learn later that we'd got off lightly, as killings and torture were commonplace in Venezuela. There was a British consul on the island, although we'd not seen hide nor hair of him since our arrest.

Arriving back in Porlamar town, we screeched to a halt outside a single-storey building. The letters PTJ, painted in white a foot high, adorned the wall outside the entrance. Beneath it read Instituto de Medicina Forense. Still handcuffed, we were let out of the jeep and climbed the tier of stone steps leading into the building. We were soon settled in front of a clinical, efficient-looking female in her mid-40s and subjected to a series of forensic tests: skin was scraped from our fingers, blood samples and fingerprints taken. Most telling, and of greatest concern, was the scraping of skin –

fleeting eye contact left me in no doubt Sam was equally troubled at the unexpected procedure. We'd handled cocaine in the hotel room, having broken up solid blocks of the crystalline drug to render it manageable. The Institute of Forensic Medicine, I found out some days later, was part of the PTJ (pronounced *pay tay hota*), the Technical Judicial Police, and they were prone to manufacture any result they wished. Corruption inside governmental bodies was rife and payments to certain officials (which we could not afford) would ensure favourable results.

All this took a couple of hours, and by 1.30 p.m. we were back in the jeep and on our way again. It was only a matter of minutes before we ground to a halt in the middle of town. People milled about in the street, everyone going about their daily lives. A smartly dressed couple embraced passionately a few yards away. A young boy stumbled and was gently lifted by his father and comforted. A dog barked. A car hooted its horn. Someone shouted across the street. Sights and sounds that would normally be viewed with a lack of interest now came to the fore. A few people stopped to take in the handcuffed foreigners as we made our way some 20 or so yards from where the driver had been able to park.

Three policemen flanked us as we walked towards the steps of an old colonial building. I had a good idea where we were going because it actually looked like a court building. We passed through an ornate double doorway of old carved wood and heavy dark glass. Inside was a hive of activity, people toing and froing with bundles of files, the police presence very noticeable. We were led through the hustle and bustle and down a series of corridors, then locked in a holding cell.

The next two hours were spent with several dubious-looking characters who tried to beg cigarettes, of which we had none. It only reminded me again how badly I wanted one myself. Eventually, we heard footsteps. A guard appeared and opened the cell door. He called our names, struggling to pronounce them as he did so. Still handcuffed, we were led to a small office in the centre of the building where we came face to face with a middle-aged woman sitting behind a desk that was absolutely covered with folders and files, some of which were inches thick.

Our escort stayed in the background as the woman jabbered away in Spanish, oblivious to the fact we sat there not understanding a word she was saying. No lawyer was present, nor an interpreter, so we had no way of communicating our dilemma to her. It was painfully obvious things were done a different way in Venezuela.

With little clue to what was being said, I began to detail the woman's appearance when suddenly she got up, opened the door and spoke with a colleague in the adjoining office. She wore a total mismatch of clothing: a bright canary-yellow blouse, purple trousers and lime-green shoes. Sam had noticed too. A smile forced itself to her mouth as we looked at each other momentarily.

The situation was ludicrous. There we were, our fate hanging on a thread, and it was all we could do to stifle our smiles. Back home it would have been impossible to take this woman seriously. She was, according to the sign on her desk, the judge's secretary. When she'd finished her little speech, she passed over what I recognised to be the statements we'd made two days earlier. Placing a pen on top of the files in front of us, she said with authority, '*A firmar.*'

Sam and I looked at each other again. 'Not yet,' I said to her.

Neither of us made a move to pick up the pen. Thirty seconds passed. The secretary's face remained impassive. Eventually, she stood up, picked up the statements from the table and said something to the guard standing behind us, who laughed aloud and prodded us into movement. We stood and were unceremoniously escorted out of the office. Sitting in the holding cell for the rest of the afternoon, our moods changed somewhat as I expressed my feelings about it all. It was still very surreal and frightening, yet in the back of my mind there lurked a tiny assurance that help was just around the corner.

We were taken outside and back to the jeep around six in the evening. We were starving hungry and had no idea what would happen next. Darkness had not yet fallen when we pulled up outside a building that looked very similar to the station in which we'd spent the last two nights. This place turned out to be another police station serving the barrio of Los Cocos on the outskirts of Porlamar.

We very much followed the same routine as before, only this

time I refused to part with my watch. Strangely enough, the police weren't the least bit interested. The layout at the back of the station was slightly different from El Cinco, an L-shaped corridor with cells running its length with the one cell making the L-shape adjacent to the end cell.

There was obviously no separate provision for female prisoners like there had been at El Cinco, as Sam and I were locked in adjoining cells. I was in the end one, Sam in the crook of the L-shape. The cells were made up of three solid walls and fronted with bars (again, painted the same garish blue). Because of our positioning, we could see each other, talk easily and hold hands. These were the only good points about our temporary home, as it was a filthy, stinking, cockroach-ridden shit hole and smelled just as repulsive as El Cinco.

We couldn't see any other prisoners because of the walls separating each cell, but we could hear them clearly. The place sounded full, jabbering voices echoing in the confined space, all competing with one another. I was in a cell on my own, for which I thanked my lucky stars. It measured three yards square. The gate had no lock and was held closed with a thick chain and heavy-duty padlock. Sam's cell was bigger, at least by the size of the barred gate, and secured by the same means.

We'd been in there half an hour when a policeman entered the cellblock through an open doorway directly opposite my cell. In his hand he held our travel bag, which he passed to me after going through the unlocking procedure. He secured the gate and left. I opened the bag and was amazed to see everything seemed to be intact. I found sets of keys, Sam's purse and, most importantly, two £20 notes. The rest had gone. Obviously, someone along the way was 'in the know' and had helped himself. Still, it was something, and I held the notes up for Sam to see.

'Look,' I said excitedly. 'At least we can get something to eat.' We'd been without food and water for two days and nights. I was immediately faced with the problem, however, of changing those bits of paper for food. I decided to play it by ear and rattled the padlock and chain against the cell door until a policeman appeared.

'*Que paso?*' he queried.

I held up one £20 note and made gestures, rubbing my stomach and putting my hand to my mouth. He got the idea instantly, nodding his head in acknowledgement, which egged me on to play-act smoking, shaving and washing. He nodded again and held out his hand for the money. I called to Sam, asking if there was anything she desperately needed. Food and water was her only reply. I passed the note to the policeman and he disappeared.

Eventually, he returned with two plastic carrier bags, which he squeezed through the bars rather than go through the rigmarole of unlocking the gate. In one bag was a whole roast chicken with arepas. The smell alone made our mouths water with anticipation. I quickly split the chicken into two portions, burning my fingers in the process, not caring, not stopping to check the contents of the second bag. We gorged ourselves on the succulent meat, eating noisily with bare hands.

Meanwhile, the smell wafted through the cellblock, causing the locals to begin shouting, '*Gringos! Comida! Gringos! Comida!*'

'What are they shouting?' asked Sam.

'I think they want our food, but they've got no chance,' I replied. 'We don't know when we're going to eat again.' Bare arms appeared from the cell next to mine with hands outstretched, fingers opening and closing. I felt small pangs of guilt but not enough to move me. When we were full, I collected what was left and placed it in the bag.

Sam asked eagerly, 'What's in the other bag?'

I wiped my greasy hands on my jeans and opened the other carrier.

'Water,' I shouted back. 'Two litre-bottles of drinking water.' I passed one to Sam, opened mine and almost emptied it in one go. Up until then, I hadn't realised how dehydrated I had become.

I pulled out a carton of Marlboros – the seal had been broken and two packs were missing. No matter, two cigarettes were quickly lit with the cheap lighter provided and I passed one to Sam. We sat, inhaling deeply, exhaling noisily. Heaven, I thought, my head swimming with the effect of nicotine. It wasn't long before the locals whiffed the smoke and with renewed vigour began to chant, '*Gringos*! *Gringos*! *Cigarro*.'

'Give them some,' said Sam. 'It might shut them up.'

I was reluctant at first – no one had given us a damn thing so far, so why should we share what little we had with the others? Then I felt a little mean-spirited. Under normal circumstances, I would have shared my possessions with or helped anyone. To placate Sam, I placed a full pack into one of the outstretched hands. It disappeared swiftly. There was much squabbling, then all went silent for a few minutes. We enjoyed our cigarettes in comparative peace.

At the time, I didn't realise what a big mistake I'd made because after a few minutes, the hands reappeared and the shouting began once more. It angered me. Weren't we in the same predicament as they were? I learned very quickly no matter what you gave, they always wanted more. The shouting continued. I checked the rest of the contents of the second carrier. There was a small bar of soap and two razors of a make I'd never heard of.

'I knew I'd forgotten something. There's no toilet paper in here.' I went on to explain what Eric had told me about using a plastic bag or newspaper. Sam screwed up her face. I felt for her. Back in England, her home was kept meticulously clean. She would often take two baths a day and always smelled so fresh. It must have come as quite a blow to find she'd been dropped into a pile of shit, so to speak.

I didn't feel too clean either. I'd had one half-decent wash with grubby water and the three days' growth of beard on my chin was beginning to irritate. My clothes were smelly and wrinkled, and my mouth tasted like a sewer. I felt a surge of pride for Sam: she was holding up extremely well considering the deplorable conditions, and I told her as much. Don't get me wrong, she was a tough girl and she'd had her fair share of ups and downs. Like me, Sam had grown up on a tough estate and could hold her own.

I decided to check the travel bag and emptied the contents on the floor. I'd forgotten that inside were toothbrushes, toothpaste, two spray cans of deodorant and my electric razor, along with various knick-knacks that make up a person's holiday toiletry. There were also two large hand towels we'd unashamedly stolen from the hotel as souvenirs, a bottle of suntan lotion and a hair dryer, plus a couple of magazines, a Walkman and tapes. I tried to shave, but the battery was as dead as a dodo, though at least we could brush the foul taste from our mouths using some of the drinking water we had left. With nowhere to rinse and spit, even that simple exercise was a problem in itself. Struggling to carry out this everyday task brought me the realism I needed. This was just the beginning. I wondered what the hell was in store and how Sam would cope. One thing was for certain: we would need to adapt drastically to survive in such a barbaric environment.

I totted up roughly how much the chicken, cigarettes, soap, water and razors had cost, and it didn't take much calculating to work out the £20 note hadn't gone very far. I presumed the guard had kept the change.

It was getting late. A close, sticky heat had come with the darkness, the only light coming from a bare bulb hanging from the ceiling in the corridor. The bare concrete floor was uncomfortable and cockroaches had come out in force. The locals settled somewhat, and I became a little accustomed to the smell. Perhaps Eric had been right, maybe I would get used to it. Tiredness came over me as fast as the light had faded – it had been a long, hot, exhausting day.

'Are you OK, Sam?' I asked.

She replied with a sigh of defeatism in her voice. 'Yeah, I'm OK.'

'We'd best get some sleep if we can. Let's see what tomorrow brings.

'Tomorrow! I don't even want to think about tomorrow,' she replied.

'Try and keep your chin up, eh, Sam.'

We settled down the best we could on the floor. It was difficult with all the creatures crawling everywhere, the occasional cockroach bravely finding a path across bare skin, making us jump and swipe it off. Eventually, tiredness got the better of us and we dozed off. During the night, the guards turned the volume of their television so high we were woken with a start. It was difficult to sleep after that, canned laughter echoing through the building all night long.

I woke at seven o'clock the following morning having managed only a few hours' fitful sleep. The locals were already awake. I stood and stretched my aching limbs, my mind reflecting on the previous days' events. Sam stirred, opened her eyes and gave me a weak smile. My heart missed a beat, remembering so many mornings we'd woken and made love. With two sets of bars between us, we were a long way from the cosy bed we used to share. What the hell had we done? What the hell had I done to Sam? I cursed inwardly and vowed I would do all I could to get us out. By now, people would surely know of our arrest and would contact us in some way. There was a look of sadness on her face.

'You all right, Sam?'

'Yeah, I'm just thinking what's going to happen today, that's all.'

We sat and smoked in peace for a while, blowing the smoke towards the open slatted windows, hoping to lengthen the time before it was noticed. Soon, though, several hands appeared from the cell next to mine.

'*Gringo*! *Cigarro*,' they shouted repeatedly.

Losing my cool, I shouted back, 'Go and fuck yourselves, you scrounging bastards!'

'Leave it, Frank, you're inviting trouble,' Sam pleaded with me.

'Fuck 'em,' I replied.

She looked away. I'd upset her. I hadn't intended to, I just wanted to protect her, and I was finding it harder and harder. I didn't know how long we would be together – we could be separated at any time.

Within the hour, the guard from the night before came through the doorway and gave me a slimy smile. I heard clunking as he opened the cells one by one. Voices became louder as several brutish faces appeared around the edge of my cell wall. All eyes veered towards Sam when they approached her cell. Their distraction didn't last too long before they returned their attention to me. '*Cigarro, gringo*,' they chanted.

More of them congregated and joined in the chorus. That one word, 'gringo', raised the hair on my neck, reminding me of the interrogation at the guardia post. I exercised a gesture I'd seen one of the guards use. They understood perfectly what I meant because they began to shout, making ape-like actions and underarm-stabbing motions with imaginary knives. I smiled; they never came closer, it was a psychological game. Soon they drifted away, the odd one calling back an obscenity. I gave the finger, and by the looks on their faces they understood that too.

Fifteen minutes later, the guard came back and locked up the other inmates. He came over to our cells, opened the gates and made washing gestures. We got the picture. I quickly bundled towels, soap and a razor together. The guard turned, and we were left to our own devices. I ventured out and walked past two overcrowded cells. The shouting began again. I ignored them, walked past the second cell and saw two open cubicles side by side. The stench was horrendous. There had been tiles on the walls at some point, but now most of them were missing and the ones that had survived were cracked and filthy. Further down the corridor lay four more cells.

The first cubicle housed a toilet pan. It was an exact copy of the one at El Cinco, full to overflowing with excrement. The floor was littered with plastic bags and paper parcels and covered in a blanket of flies. The smell was so overpowering it made me retch.

'Don't come this far, Sam,' I warned.

'But I need to pee. I've got to wash anyway, I feel so dirty.'

'Wait there, I'll check the next cubicle.'

Next to the shit pile was another cubicle a yard and a half wide and three yards in depth. Several cut-off plastic bottles littered the floor. Above them at waist height was a pair of taps. I turned each one in anticipation; water trickled into the gutter below.

'Come on, Sam, but hold your nose.' She looked at me apprehensively. 'I'm not joking, come on.'

Passing the crowded cells, Sam was greeted with a barrage of monkey grunts. With her hand clasped to her mouth and nose, her voice was barely audible. 'I know they can't get at me. It's the smell, I can almost taste it from here.'

I beckoned her forward. She hesitated slightly, then came on, still clutching her face. 'Quick, Sam, get in there. The sooner you get done, the sooner we get out.'

Dropping her hands to strip her clothing, she bent double and retched. I stood guard as she stripped and washed down. At the sight of her naked body, I thought how the world could turn itself on its head. Normally, the sight of her trim figure would have quickened my pulse – but not today.

She dried with the hotel towels. It was my turn and I washed quickly. Though refreshing, the water was ice cold on my hot skin. I shaved by feel, using the soap for lather, while Sam helped with the parts I'd missed. We washed through our underwear and brushed our teeth, and for the first time in days we felt clean. Now we faced the ordeal of walking past the overcrowded cells. The hoo-hooing began again. Outside the cell, we had time to hold each other and kiss momentarily, and then, as if on cue, the guard appeared and we were locked up.

The rest of the morning passed uneventfully and we settled down as best we could. I felt very tired and fell asleep almost at once, the incessant chattering fading to a hum and I was gone.

I awoke with a start, hearing the clattering of the chain being dragged through the bars. Another guard I hadn't seen before shouted, '*Vamos, cónsulada!*' I jumped up. Sam's door was already open.

We followed the guard into the main station, where a smiling woman invited us to sit at a table. She was from the British consulate and had flown over from Caracas. She seemed very sympathetic to our predicament and the conditions in which we were being kept. She promised to phone our respective families later that day and said the local honorary consul, a 'Mr Mellor', would contact us very soon and speak with officials regarding our treatment. Unfortunately, the consular services could not be directly involved with our case.

She lent us £50 in bolivares and changed the £20 I produced from my pocket. All in all, we had a total of 50,000 bolivares. Now we had the right currency to buy the things we needed. She had retrieved our suitcases from the guardia post at the airport, although she was not able to return them at that moment. She had brought a full change of clothing for Sam and me, however. We returned to our cells with somewhat lifted spirits.

'I feel much better,' said Sam, changing out of her grubby clothing.

'Yeah, me too,' I agreed.

Maybe it was premature, but we celebrated with a smoke and ate the rest of the food we'd saved from the night before. The locals started begging again, but by now we were mindless to it. Nothing was going to spoil our mood. We held hands through the bars and chatted for what seemed hours.

Our conversation was interrupted when a man and woman were escorted through the doorway opposite. The guard put the man in my cell, the woman in Sam's. Neither of them spoke English, but it didn't stop us communicating. Their names were Salvador and Ana. They had been arrested that morning at Porlamar airport with eight kilos of cocaine between them. Apparently, Salvador had been carrying most of it strapped to his legs and thighs and around his waist. Ana, who was three months pregnant, had only been carrying a small amount. They were friends, partners in crime; Salvador wasn't the father of the child. They had flown from Spain to earn extra money and had actually been on the plane waiting to taxi when officials boarded and arrested them.

I couldn't warm to Ana. The fact she had risked her freedom carrying an unborn child gave me a strong feeling of distaste towards her. Salvador, on the other hand, was a tough silent type and only spoke when he needed to say something. I took to the guy immediately and was relieved to have an ally in camp.

Unfortunately, they were in the same boat as us after having been arrested. They had no money and only the clothes they stood up in. Both were smokers and were extremely hungry. It didn't bother me to share what we had with them, as they seemed appreciative of everything. Sal, as I started to call him, was a great help when it came to ordering food. That evening, he negotiated a price with the guard to go and buy food and bottled water from a local takeaway restaurant. It felt good to be somewhat organised.

As we sat smoking, the locals went crazy. Even Spanish people were gringos. Sal shrugged and dismissed them with a wave of his hand.

'*Locos*,' he said, screwing his finger close to his head, as if to imply they were crazy. The guy had a conquistador attitude and saw the local inmates as nothing more than savages who needed a good thrashing. He was a stocky five foot eight and packed with pure muscle. He had a typical Spanish face, with a trim moustache and dark, short, curly hair. His eyes were alive and a smile came readily to his lips.

By this stage, it was getting late. '*Voy a dormir. Hasta mañana*,' he said.

'*Hasta mañana*,' I replied.

We settled down on the concrete floor. It was hard and unyielding, but I was so worn out with the heat and excitement of the day's events I fell asleep within minutes.

I awoke the next morning feeling more refreshed than the day before. It was our fourth day in custody. We'd eaten our fill the previous night, and there were no leftovers, as we'd shared with Sal and Ana. After a while, the guard unlocked the locals for their morning ablutions. To my alarm, he unlocked our cells too. We were outnumbered by ten to one. Would we be attacked? I need not have worried. No one came near. We waited until they were finished before venturing out.

I stood guard with an open towel while Sam did her thing. Ana didn't come out of the cell at all. Sal and I washed and returned to our cell and spent the rest of the morning teaching each other words from our respective languages, using gestures and signs. I was picking up phrases pretty well and by early afternoon I was able to say a few sentences and at least 50 words. A guard walking through the doorway interrupted our lesson. On opening up, he called out, '*Inglés!*' My questioning look prompted him to add, '*Teléfono*.'

I followed the guard to the telephone and picked up the receiver. It was my ex-wife Chrissy. The embassy official from Caracas had given her the number to call. She told me my arrest had come as a terrible shock to everyone at home. My father was in bad health and the news had affected him seriously. My 12-year-old daughter, Josie, was so devastated she wouldn't even talk to me. There had been many tears all round.

The guilt weighed down on me heavily. Chrissy promised she'd send some money to help out before she hung up. When I returned to my cell, I told Sam briefly about the call, then sat in a corner where I let the tears flow freely. Sal knew to leave me alone and busied himself. Sam had a call within the hour from her family, and it was equally upsetting for her. Later in the afternoon, the guard appeared again. 'Cónsulados,' he said this time.

'It must be that Mellor guy we were told about yesterday,' I said.

'I hope he's got some good news, Frank,' Sam said hopefully.

As we walked through the open doorway, I stopped in my tracks. Two men and a woman stood facing us. I recognised two of them at once. The woman, whose back was turned to the guards, put her finger to her lips to signal I should stay quiet. With quick reaction, I said to Sam, 'Don't say a word. I know these people.' They stood amongst a pile of carrier bags some distance from the guards' desk.

'How the hell have you got in here?' I whispered to the woman. She and one of the men were the Latin American couple I'd dealt with during my transactions. Both spoke excellent English. The other guy I'd never set eyes on before. We were to see a lot more of this fellow in the months to come; his name was 'Joe'. They were members of the local drug cartel.

The guard came back into the room after relocking our cells. The woman waited until he'd passed before she spoke. 'We gave the police a carton of cigarettes and told them we were from the embassy. So, what the hell happened at the airport?'

'I haven't a clue,' I said. 'They just pulled us out of the queue and that was that.'

'I don't understand, it's normally very relaxed. Anyway, the thing for us to do now is get you out of here and home to England.'

'How are you going to manage that?' I asked, the words 'England' and 'home' buzzing inside my head.

'You just leave it with us. Someone's talking to your judge right now; we should have some answers pretty soon. Meanwhile, we've brought you some things.' Pointing to the second man, she said, 'Joe will come and visit you soon, OK? Oh, by the way, the results from the PTJ will be negative, that's been arranged already.'

'That's fantastic, thank you so much,' I said relieved.

'Yes, thank you,' echoed Sam. 'Please try your best to get us out of here.'

We talked a further five minutes or so at the end of which the woman pulled a wad of notes from her jeans pocket and passed them to me. 'That should keep you going for a while. We'll try to sort it out quickly. We have to go now.'

I put the money safely in my pocket, and Sam and I picked up the bags. By the weight of them, it appeared they'd bought out a supermarket. On seeing the booty, the locals went absolutely crazy. '*Nada!*' I shouted at them. A new word I'd learned from Sal. It meant 'nothing' and that was exactly what they were going to get.

Checking the contents of the carriers, we found bread rolls, sliced cheese, ham and more cooked chickens. Milk and orange juice, three cartons of cigarettes, soap, shampoo, razors and toothpaste. Writing pads, pens, envelopes and two rolls of toilet paper. We ate well and finished off the milk – in the heat, it wouldn't have stayed fresh anyway. Sal kept saying gracias, while Ana just ate, drank and smoked without a word of thanks.

Later in the evening, a guard came along and spoke with Sal. He returned a minute later dragging a grubby-looking mattress behind him. '*Treinta mil,*' he said.

I looked at Sal quizzically. He held up his hands, and opened and clenched his fingers three times. Thirty-thousand bolivares?! Ridiculous, I thought.

'No, no, no,' I said, opening and closing my hands twice in the same fashion as Sal.

'*Veinte mil,*' said Sal.

After a moment's hesitation, the guard replied, '*Está bien.*' The deal was done.

I pointed to Sam's cell and immediately the guard went off in search of the keys. I used the time to count the wad of notes the woman had given me: it came to 100,000 bolivares. I peeled off two 10,000 notes and passed them to Sal; the rest I tucked in my pocket. At least Sam wouldn't have to sleep on the floor. The mattress was battered and grimy, the stuffing bursting out, but it was better than nothing.

'It's for you, Sam. If you want to share it, it's up to you,' I said.

The guard came back with the keys, pulled the mattress through the gate and took the proffered 20,000 from Sal. A huge grin lit up his face. As he left, I wondered how many times that old mattress had been sold to people in similar situations, as there was no way we could or would have taken it with us when we left.

I woke the next day with flies buzzing around my head. There were always flies, but somehow there seemed to be swarms of them that morning. In my mind's eye, I pictured the toilet pan and jumped up quickly, swatting at them like a man possessed. Sal was already awake and laughed at my antics. '*Que paso?*' he managed to say at last. '*Muchas moscas hoy, no?*'

I looked across at Sam. The girls were still asleep, laid top to tail on the mattress. I decided it had been a good buy despite its condition. A lump formed in my throat as I watched Sam, remembering the countless times I'd woken before her at home and sat taking so much pleasure from just looking at her peaceful face. Today, it wrinkled and twitched as flies buzzed around it. She was still asleep when a guard came along and spoke to Sal.

'*Vamos, tribunal.*' He opened the gates. Ana stirred and got up stiffly; Sam woke too. Ten minutes later, they were gone. The guard hadn't locked the gates, so I said it would be a good idea to clean up before he came back and released the jail's population. We hastily washed and returned to our cells.

Fifteen minutes later, the prisoners were done and most of them were back in their cells. I suddenly remembered the two five-litre bottles I'd converted into makeshift piss pots. I made my way to the washing area and had almost emptied the first pot down the drain when Sam shouted, 'Frank! They're in your cell!'

I dropped the pots, came out of the cubicle and saw one of the locals standing by my half-open cell door. Without a thought, I ran towards him. On the run, I jumped and extended my right leg. All went into slow motion: the local's eyes popped open, his jaw dropped and my foot hit him smack in the middle of his chest before he had time to react. He crashed back into the bars of Sam's cell and collapsed in a heap on the floor. One down! Turning, I saw four more inside my cell, rummaging in the food parcels. As one they spun around, mouths agape, caught in the act. Again, acting on pure reflex, I swung back the gate and grabbed the chain draped over one of the gate's crossbars. It weighed a good two pounds and was just under a yard in length. In one motion, I swung it up and brought it crashing down on the nearest inmate, striking him squarely across the shoulders. He let out a yelp like a wounded animal.

Then I totally lost it, swinging the chain in a criss-cross pattern amongst them. They scattered and ran through the opening of my cell as I continued to swing the chain wildly after them. Disregarding any possible threat from their countrymen, I followed and left them cowering in semi-darkness at the far end of the corridor.

I slowly walked back down the corridor, the adrenalin pumping, my chest heaving from the exertion. Not one of them made a comment, let alone retaliated. Sam stood with her hand over her mouth, eyes wide in fright. Just then, a couple of guards came in to see what had caused the commotion. They took in the scene, the chain still hanging in my clenched fist. To my surprise, they burst into laughter, guffawing and shaking their heads.

'*Tu loco gringo*,' one of them laughed.

'*Vamos*,' said the other, pointing to my cell with his chin.

The locals were subdued for an hour or two but soon forgot the episode, returning to their constant chattering. Sam looked across from time to time. In her questioning look, I saw that she was calling to mind the man she had known just a few days earlier and measuring what was about to come of him. OK, I'd completely lost it, but I'd proven a point: with the odds stacked against me, I could stand my ground. If we should serve a sentence in a prison, the chances were that it would be a lot tougher than this place. I sat in the corner of my cell. Sam never said a word and the only sound I could hear was the thumping of my heart. I knew I had to fight back, otherwise I would be at their mercy.

Eventually, I lay down and fell asleep. The next I knew I was woken by the sound of Sal and Ana being let back into the cells. A guard brought a holdall belonging to Ana in the early evening.

As we got into a routine, the days and nights passed quickly. The locals kept their distance, although the begging didn't stop. They just didn't give up. New prisoners came, old ones went after being processed at the courts. Apparently, in those days the maximum length of time a person could be held before being charged or released was 16 days – I calculated Boxing Day would be our 16th in custody. Would the courts open that day, I wondered?

A couple of days after being taken to court, Sal and Ana were visited by the Spanish consul. Sam and I thought they would have some money to pay their way, but on their return they said not. We were doubtful about their statement. Although it wasn't the right thing to do, Sam made a quick search of Ana's holdall while they were washing and found a purse containing 100,000 bolivares! It disheartened me greatly; they had eaten our food, smoked our cigarettes and drunk our water. They were taking the survival instinct a little too far in my opinion. I played it cool with Sal for the few remaining days Sam and I were there. He queried many times what was wrong with me, to which I replied, '*Nada, es personal.*' Which it was, I took it very personally. Joe visited, bringing more food and water two days before Christmas. At least we hadn't been forgotten.

At exactly eight o'clock on Christmas Eve, midnight in England, a strange thing happened – the electricity went off. In the inky blackness, cockroaches came out in force, crawling over us, though they ran for cover when I flicked on my lighter. The lighter gave me an idea and Ana was soon rummaging in her bag for baby oil. Sal and I quickly fashioned a makeshift lamp using tin foil from the chicken and strips of cloth, and in no time we had a smoky light that confused the flies and mosquitoes and scattered the cockroaches.

Later in the evening, we heard screams coming from the main police station. As they grew louder, we could hear the thwack of something accompanying them. A guard appeared in the doorway, dragging a young man by his bare foot, another beating him mercilessly with a thick belt, the buckle cutting into the flesh at every swipe. In the flickering light we saw blood oozing from dozens of cuts, leaving a trail of crimson on the floor. The man thrashed and screamed as they dragged him down the corridor. With every swing of his arm, the guard with the belt shouted words I didn't understand. I looked at Sal, horrified. It turned my stomach.

'*Que paso?*' I asked. Sal explained the man had held up a couple of tourists at knifepoint. On an island dependant on tourism as its main source of income, it was a crime not tolerated. My horror slowly turned to indifference.

The guards tossed him in a cell at the far end of the corridor. I looked over at Sam; she'd covered her eyes from the spectacle, equally horrified. As the guards returned, I saw the one with the belt smiling in satisfaction.

It was silent: all we could hear were the sobs coming from the end of the cellblock. About an hour later, another guy was dragged in. This one had a bleeding hole in the calf of his leg. It looked very much like a shotgun wound. More blood spilled onto the corridor floor. It was turning out to be a busy night for the Los Cocos police station. He was similarly dragged to a cell at the bottom of the corridor and left there to fend for himself.

We sat quietly for sometime, not knowing what more to say to each other. At midnight, I sang 'Amazing Grace' to a silent audience. The electricity came back on a minute later. It was the strangest night during our two-week stay at Los Cocos.

We passed Christmas Day in a sombre mood, all busy with our own thoughts. I felt the start of a fever coming late in the afternoon and by the evening felt very ill. Fearful dreams haunted me through the night and I woke the next day feeling abysmal.

At around nine o'clock, a guard came for us. We were taken out, handcuffed together and hustled into the back of a police jeep. I felt weak and disheartened. But at least we were on the move again.

# 4

# THE PAVILIONS

Sam tried her best to comfort me as the jeep bumped and swung from side to side out of Los Cocos. I was in a cold sweat, unable to think clearly. Everything was spinning around dizzily. The journey was horrendous. 'We're here,' she said eventually, her voice seeming to come from miles away.

I was sure I couldn't have walked very far in the condition I was in, so thankfully the jeep pulled up close to the courthouse doors and we were let out. I was still handcuffed to Sam as a police guard helped me through the doors and down a series of corridors. I was in such a state I couldn't quite grasp where I was or what was about to happen. We ended up in an open room three yards square with concrete seats all around. We were directed to sit on one of the seats and were uncuffed.

'*Que paso?*' said one guard to Sam, pointing at me. She shrugged her shoulders, not knowing how to answer.

'*Fiebre,*' I managed to say with some effort. Sal had used the word the previous day when the fever had taken a grip on me.

I lay down on the seating, lowering my left cheek gently onto the cool concrete. It eased the burning sensation slightly. From where I lay, I could see the open doorway. Everything was still topsy-turvy, people passing in both directions, all appearing as a jumble of colours. Two policemen, who had placed themselves across the room by the

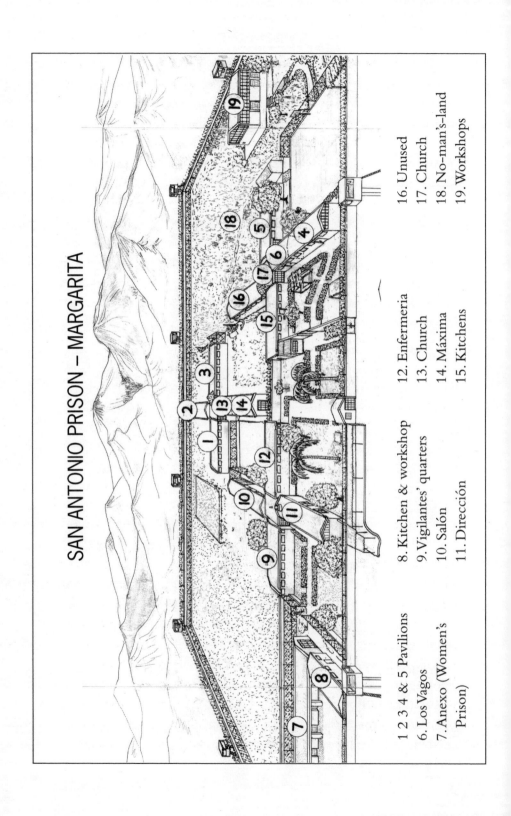

# SAN ANTONIO PRISON – MARGARITA

1 2 3 4 & 5 Pavilions
6. Los Vagos
7. Anexo (Women's Prison)
8. Kitchen & workshop
9. Vigilantes' quarters
10. Salón
11. Dirección
12. Enfermeria
13. Church
14. Máxima
15. Kitchens
16. Unused
17. Church
18. No-man's-land
19. Workshops

doorway, appeared to be talking to someone. I heard voices, one was female. I looked again, trying to focus. I could make out three figures just inside the entrance and from somewhere in the distance I could hear my name being spoken.

I felt Sam shaking me. 'Frank!'

'W—what?' I managed to say.

'It's your friends from before,' she said.

It took a few seconds for it to sink in, then it dawned on me who they were. 'Got fever – tell them,' I panted.

'He says he's—' started Sam.

'Yes, I heard him,' came the woman's voice in the distance. She spoke briefly in Spanish, turned in our direction and said, 'I've sent Joe to get some medicine. I'm going to speak with various people now, we'll talk later, OK?'

The doorway cleared and back came the dizzying mishmash of colours. I closed my eyes to it. I could feel Sam's hand resting on my hip; it felt good she still cared. I lay there in a chaos of spinning visions that made me nauseous.

Sam shook me again. 'Frank, Joe's back with the medicine.'

Sam helped me to sit up, and passed me two capsules and a bottle of water. After swallowing the pills, I barely had enough strength left to ease myself down onto the cool concrete again. All other thoughts vanished.

I lay there quite a while and by the time we were summoned I felt slightly better, managing to get up unaided and walk into the next room. My head throbbed like a serious hangover, but at least I could make some sense of things going on around us. Sam was at my side as we were ushered into a large room. At the back and in the centre was a huge, oblong ornately carved table. Behind it, sitting on an equally ornate chair, sat a plumpish woman with a heavily made-up face that was creased with a deep frown. Her clothing was as colourful as her secretary's, whom I recognised sitting to her right at a separate table. Both were busying themselves, shuffling bits of paper, and didn't even acknowledge our existence. The rest of the room was filled with tables behind which sat clerks and other court workers, all busy with their duties. The clack-clack of a dozen typewriters made my head want to burst.

A policeman told us to sit down at the first table we came to just a couple of yards inside the doorway. Behind the desk was a grumpy-faced woman, who readied herself at an aged typewriter in front of her. To the left side of the desk sat a young man with Latino features. He introduced himself with a handshake. 'I am here to act as interpreter,' he said. His voice lowered a notch. 'I am also a friend of your friends, so I will guide you correctly. First, you must plead not guilty. There is still a small chance we can get you away from here.'

'What do you mean a small chance?' I interrupted. He took a deep breath. I watched his blank expression. Oh no, I thought.

'There is an investigation on the island at the moment,' he continued. 'People from Caracas are looking into corruption among the judges here, it's something to do with Interpol. I don't know any more. Anyway, we may be overheard.' He looked about cautiously. Sam and I sat stunned by what he'd just told us. 'I've read your *declaraciónes,*' he said, reverting to normal volume. 'If you like, I'll read them to you. They seem OK.'

'Yes, but if we're to plead not guilty,' I interrupted again, 'how can we sign the statements?'

'It's just the way it is here,' he said. 'If you don't sign, they can't start the process.'

'What process?' I demanded. Lowering my voice, I added, 'We should be on our way home now; what the hell's going on?'

'I told you, there are complications,' he replied. 'Your friends will explain it to you better.'

Just then, a rotund, middle-aged balding man in a dark suit appeared at the desk. Under his arm he carried a leather document case. Our conversation came to an abrupt end. The rotund man introduced himself in barely passable English as Pablo Diaz, public defender. He and our interpreter spoke at length in Spanish.

Sam and I sat bewildered, looking at each other for encouragement. Finally I said, 'It doesn't look good, love, but maybe there's still some hope.'

'No, Frank,' she replied. 'We're in the shit here, I can feel it! We're going to be locked away in some black hole for ever, I know it.'

'No, Sam, that isn't going to happen,' I tried to reassure her. 'Be a bit more positive, eh?'

There was exasperation in her voice. 'Positive? Yeah, right!'

The court worker turned his attention back to us. 'You're going to be charged with *tráfico de drogas* right now. You have to sign your *declaraciónes* too. *Señor* Diaz here will represent you. I'm sure it won't be for long if your friends work things out for you.'

He excused himself and left through the open doorway behind us with our lawyer in tow. The typist had finished her work and pulled sheets of paper and carbon from her machine with a flourish. She placed them on the table, our statements alongside. A pen was offered. Sam and I looked at each other again.

'What are we going to do?' we said almost simultaneously. There was a moment's hesitation.

'We'd better sign and trust people are trying to get us out of here,' I said at last.

After giving our signatures and two thumbprints, one either side of our names, a police guard took us back into the room with the cool concrete seats. I lay down again, my mind in turmoil, my banging head trying to make sense of things. Sam was silent, not touching any more.

The three figures appeared in the doorway again. This time I was ready. I sat up quickly, my head exploding with pain. 'What's going on?' I shouted at the woman. 'You told us we'd be out of here!'

'Yes, well,' she began, 'we've got a small problem.' She went on to explain that a month previously a German woman who was caught with several kilos of cocaine had 'bought' her freedom after only ten days in custody. She'd returned home and foolishly told her story to a magazine. Interpol had picked up on it and through the authorities in Caracas were demanding investigations into corruption on the island. Everyone was keeping a low profile. 'So, you may have to go to San Antonio jail for a few weeks until the dust has settled. You can't stay in police custody any longer. There's nothing we can do at the moment, I'm sorry.'

'What's it like, this San Antonio?' I asked.

'It's not too bad, I think,' she said. 'When you get there, make sure you go to *pabellión cuatro*, pay someone if you have to. Look for Paul, a French Canadian. He's known to us and he'll look after you. Meanwhile, we'll keep on trying. Don't lose hope, OK?'

'OK,' Sam and I said, almost as one, but neither of us sounding like we meant it.

Worried for her safety, I asked, 'What about Sam?'

'We don't know anyone too well in the women's section, but I'm sure she'll be OK. You'll be able to see each other. We have to go now.'

Sam and I looked at each other, knowing the moment had come: we were about to be split up. The woman saw our despair. 'Joe will keep visiting you, don't worry.' And without another word, they were gone.

I took two more capsules. The medicine was working fast. I now felt just a throbbing in my temples and a light dizziness in my head.

'What's going to happen to us now?' asked Sam.

I hadn't got a clue. What could I say to her? That glimmer of hope was fading fast. 'We just have to go along with things, love. What else can we do?'

She sighed deeply and looked at the ground, not answering.

Soon, we were handcuffed again, taken out to the police jeep and were back in Los Cocos before we knew it. Not one word had passed our lips on that journey. It was 2.30 in the afternoon and we'd been gone for nearly six hours. It felt more like six days. We ate the remainder of our food in silence. The time of our reckoning was fast approaching. Afterwards, I lay down again. The drugs had made me drowsy and before too long I was fast asleep.

I awoke to the sound of the chain being dragged across the bars of the gate. The guard shouted, '*Vamos!*' I looked at my watch: it was seven in the evening. Sam and I bundled our things together quickly. I said goodbye to Sal and five minutes later we were cuffed and back in the police jeep on our way to San Antonio.

'I suppose we'd better sort our things out before we get there,' I said to Sam. 'Let me have the carrier bag, you take the holdall.' We shared out the things we each needed in the darkness.

The journey took around half an hour. I looked through the

window grilles: pinpricks of light dotted the landscape. For a time, I had the feeling we were travelling inland, as huge silhouettes in the mountainous region became visible. We turned off a long stretch of road and came to an abrupt halt after 100 yards or so. Looking around as I stepped down from the jeep, I saw directly in front of us a small concrete building with a barred entrance similar to those of the police stations. It was set into a high wall topped with barbed wire. The wall stretched away into the darkness in both directions with guard towers rising up into the night sky. Inside each tower, the silhouette of an armed guard was made visible by the glare from mounted floodlights. In semi-light, it was an eerie sight to behold. My first impression was that of a concentration camp, and I said as much to Sam. She made no comment; she didn't have to, I could see the bewilderment in her face. I felt a mixture of fear and apprehension in my gut. This was the real thing.

We were ordered to the gate and handed over to a couple of soldiers of the Guardia Nacional. Sam and I stood around for a couple of minutes not quite knowing what to say to each other; it was an awkward moment to say the least. I wanted to say how sorry I was and how much I loved her, but I'd said it a hundred times over the previous two weeks. A female guard dressed in a blue shirt and dark-blue slacks appeared through the far door – she'd come for Sam.

I took Sam's hands in mine and gently kissed her on the mouth. 'It's going to be OK, love,' I said. 'We'll find a way to keep in touch. Take care.' Sam looked at the ground in answer, then went off with the guard, her head down, not a spoken word. The inner door to the prison closed behind her. She was on her own.

A soldier shouted, '*Mira tu, gringo!*' I turned around to see an ugly, distorted face a foot from my own. He took my right hand and raised it to waist height. In my stupor, I foolishly thought he was going to frank my hand with a rubber stamp. A split second later, he brought a short length of wood from behind his back and rapped it hard across my knuckles. Yow! That fuckin' hurt. Where was my head at, holding my hand out like a fool? The soldier grabbed my shirt and tugged it violently.

'*Quita la camisa negra!*' he shouted in my face, making unbuttoning gestures with his other hand. '*Rápido!*' I took my shirt off as fast as I could. The soldier snatched it from me and threw it into the corner a couple of yards away, where it landed on top of several other garments that resembled old dishcloths. I fleetingly thought of the hundred-and-twenty quid's worth of Ted Baker that just went down the pan, then the soldier was back in my face. '*La bolsa!*' he shouted, pointing to my bag on the floor. I reached down, picked it up and passed it to him. He snatched it from me. After rummaging around for a moment inside the bag, he came out with two packets of Marlboro, shoved the carrier back in my hands and threw a pack of cigarettes to the other soldier. '*Vamos!*' the soldier said sternly, but at least a little more quietly. The cigarettes must have calmed him some.

He took me through the same steel door Sam had gone through. It led directly into the main prison. At first glance, it looked quite tidy, with neat rows of hedges either side of a concrete area some 15 yards wide. Behind the hedges stood palm trees, their fronds waving in the breeze. We walked towards a concrete building, turned left and walked alongside it until we reached a barred wall with a gate. Of course, it was painted bright blue! The word '*DIRECCIÓN*' was painted across the concrete above the gate. Above that was a sign made of wire, crudely shaped into the word '*Bienvenida*' with Christmas fairy lights fastened around the letters. Although the lights weren't on, I could clearly read the word. How bizarre, I thought. What was I being 'welcomed' to?

On the other side of the bars, a lone man sat behind a table, his attention focused on a small black-and-white television positioned on a chair some yards away. On the table lay a short-barrelled pump-action shotgun with a pistol grip. Noticing our presence, he picked up the firearm and opened the gate. The soldier pushed me through, handing a file to my new captor.

The guard was a short, stocky guy with a crew-cut hairstyle dressed in a white short-sleeved shirt and blue pants. He stuttered as he talked to the soldier. He turned to face me. '*Por a-a-allí,*' he said, pointing towards the TV set with his shotgun. I went in the direction he pointed out to me – I wasn't about to argue with what was basically a sawn-off shotgun. When the soldier had gone, the new guard locked the gate, turned to me and said, '*Vamos, g-gringo, pabellión uno.*'

'No, no,' I said to him as he guided me towards another gate opposite his desk some ten yards away. At right angles to the barred entrance was a gate crowded with people. This gate obviously served the building I'd walked alongside and opened into the dirección. I later learned this was called the *enfermeria*.

The guard stopped. '*C-c-como no?*' he shouted.

'*Pabellión cuatro*,' I remembered at last. 'Paul, *el Canadian*,' I pleaded.

A voice came from the gate to my right. 'Hey, man, I'd take your watch off if I were you; they'll chop your hand off for it where he's taking you.'

My mouth dropped open, partly in surprise, mostly in horror. Remembering what the woman had said, I fumbled about in my pocket for what I knew was a 10,000 bolivar note. 'Pay someone if you have to,' she'd said. I turned to see a tall, slim black guy with a big toothy grin.

'Do you speak good Spanish?' I asked him.

'Yeah, of course I do,' he replied in perfect English.

'Tell this guy I need to go to pavilion four, I have to meet a French Canadian guy named Paul.'

'Oh yeah, man,' he replied. 'I know Paul. *Mira* Gargo. *El señor quieres irse a pabellión cuatro a su amigo* Pa–ool, *el Canadiense.*'

The guard looked at me. 'Pa-ool?' he asked.

The black guy piped in, 'You got money? Give him some money, man.'

I pulled out the note I'd loosened and gave it to the guard. As he pocketed the money, his eyes lit up. '*Ah, s–si*, Pa-ool, *pabellión c-cuatro. Vamos, g-gringo!*'

Before going any further, I took off my watch, tucked it in my pocket and put on the spare T-shirt from my bag. 'Thanks, mate, I owe you one,' I shouted back at the black guy.

'It's OK. My name's Terry.'

'Mine's Frank.'

'I'll see you,' shouted Terry, as Gargo opened the gate. We headed back the way I'd come, crossed the concrete stretch in front of the entrance and walked down another path to a chain-linked gate made of heavy tubular steel. Once through, Gargo waved me on with his gun towards a long concrete building, then to a steel door. '*C-cuatro*,' he said.

My nerves were jangling, my adrenalin pumping. I could hear a lot of shouting and laughing from where I stood; Latin music boomed from somewhere inside. As soon as Gargo put a key to the padlock, a dozen voices rang out. '*Agua, agua!*' It must have been their password for a guard because all went quiet.

Gargo gave the door a good bang with his fist and it flew open. Inside I saw a sea of people, inquisitive faces staring at the opened doorway. I braced myself, took a deep breath and walked right into the middle of a madhouse. The door slammed shut behind me. The first thing to hit me was the overpowering odour of unwashed bodies. Fighting for attention was the pungent smell of marijuana hanging in the air. The heat was incredible. Everyone started shouting at once, a few grabbed my arm and one went to check my pockets. I lashed out violently and they backed off. '*Gringo, regalo*,' some were saying. '*Gringo, cigarro*,' said others.

I'd walked into a space 30 feet by 15. It was full of the types I'd seen in the police cells, a filthy bedraggled bunch. To my left was a corridor, which I assumed ran the remaining length of the building. Up high to my right was a barred window. The walls were bare cinderblock, a single bulb hung from the ceiling. At the entrance to the corridor stood two unsavoury characters. The one on the left was short and stocky, shirtless and covered in tattoos; he wore a red headband on his shaven head and a gold earring in his right lobe. In his hand, he held an enormous knife. It was crudely made with cloth wrapped around the hilt, the blade at least nine inches long. Crudely made or not, it looked very dangerous. The guy on the right was similarly dressed, his crazy eyes darting everywhere. He too had a huge knife in his hand.

People still pestered me as I made my way over to the corridor. I sent them scattering with a swing of my arm. As I neared the corridor, the knife wielders puffed up as if in challenge. '*Que quieres?*' asked the one on the left, his blade rising to within an inch of my gut. I looked down at the knife, trying to stay cool. It was hard work, my stomach was on a fairground ride and my heart was pounding.

'*Amigo de* Paul,' I said. I pointed at myself, trying my best to appear confident.

His face screwed up nastily. '*Amigo de quien?*' he quizzed.

Then I remembered what Terry had said to Gargo. 'Pa-ool, *el Canadiense.*'

A reaction passing as a smile crossed his lips. '*Ah* – Pa-ool!' He turned to walk down the corridor, motioning me to follow. '*Ven con migo,*' he said.

Thank fuck for that, I thought. I followed him down the corridor; it was full of prisoners milling about. They stared, and I glared back at each and every one of them along the way. There were three doors either side of the corridor, all of which were open. The prisoners I passed were somewhat better dressed than the flotsam in the entranceway. I could feel the evil all around; it surrounded me like a black cloak and closed in on me until I felt I couldn't breathe. But this wasn't the time to show the fear that gripped me. Some made comments as I passed, not pleasant ones either, judging by the heinous looks on their faces. I noticed most had knives: some had them tucked in their waistbands at the hip, others simply toyed with them.

During those first moments in pavilion four, I realised why I'd become so violent in the space of just a few weeks. Ethereal helpers from the dark side had been preparing me for *this*.

A sudden babble of raised voices turned my head as I neared the last door on the left. An argument had broken out between two prisoners at the far end of the corridor, others egged them on. There was a great deal of arm-waving and shouting between the two. Suddenly, knives were drawn. I watched, dreading their next move. My guide looked on with interest, his eyes wide and bright.

The two circled each other while people backed away to give

them space. I could see everything quite clearly as I was taller than everyone else. One stamped his leading foot, made a desperate thrust, but missed the target. The other guy, using the moment, brought his knife down on his opponent's arm, opening the flesh like an overripe fruit. This brought a sudden roar from the spectators. They began shouting feverishly, like bloodthirsty animals, the noise deafening in the confined space. People came out of doorways to watch and joined in with the shouting. Blood ran from the open wound and dripped to the floor. It went unheeded. They continued to circle each other. Fucking hell, I thought, I passed that very spot just half a minute earlier.

My guide left me and pushed his way through the crowd. '*Ya, basta!*' he shouted at the two men. They obeyed without question. The knives were put away, but the inmates still glared hatefully at each other. I stood open-mouthed as they went their separate ways and the crowd broke up. My guide returned. '*Ven,*' he said.

I followed him through the doorway. After the squalor I'd been living in for the past 16 days, it seemed at the time as though I'd walked through the dingy cinder block corridor into a five-star hotel. The room was heavy with marijuana smoke. On the right was a toilet pan, hand basin and tiled shower cubicle. There was even a curtain! Directly in front of me was a tubular-framed bed on which lay a middle-aged balding man of slight build wearing a striped T-shirt and jogging trousers. He sat up as my guide and I entered.

Inching further in, I noticed several other people in the room who had been obscured by the cubicle wall. There was also an old fridge in the corner and on top of it sat a small black-and-white television. Four pairs of very stoned eyes left the screen and quizzed me intently. I spoke to the man on the bed, 'If your name is Paul, then I'm in the right place. My name is Frank, we have mutual friends.'

'You are in the right place,' he replied in excellent English tinged with a heavy French accent. 'You must be the English guy I was told about. Welcome.' Paul motioned me to a small stool by the side of the fridge. 'Take a seat,' he said.

He introduced me to the four men in the room, all of them very serious-looking individuals. There was Ivor (pronounced EE-BOR) from Valencia on the mainland, serving 15 years for armed robbery. He was head honcho and controlled pavilions four and five. José from Barcelona and 'Ricardo' from Puerto La Cruz were partners and still awaiting sentence also for armed robbery. Last was Chivo Loco ('Crazy Goat'), Ivor's sidekick and right-hand man. He was halfway through a twenty-year sentence for four counts of murder. We shook hands – better to be friends with these guys than not, I thought.

Ivor stood to leave. In broken English, he said to me, 'Escuse me.' I was meant to be impressed, judging by the expectant look on his face. I must have appeared suitably affected because his face lit up with a huge grin. I was a little more impressed when Ivor reached to his waistband and brought an automatic pistol into view. Looking at the gun, I nodded in admiration. My apparent appreciation encouraged him further. He held out the pistol to show me closely. All the time I was thinking, how the fuck has he got a gun in here? How naive I was in those days.

'I think he likes you,' said Paul. 'You look like you've never seen a gun before.'

'It's not that,' I replied, 'it's just the last thing I expected to see right now, that's all.' My reply sounded laid-back, but my head was reeling.

'Everyone has a gun in this room,' said Paul. He reached under a folded blanket and pulled out a snub-nosed revolver.

Ivor left the room chuckling. Paul went on to explain the hierarchy in the jail. Ivor was the top man on our side; he'd been in San Antonio for five years already. He ran drug sales and gambling in pavilions four and five. With the money he made he bribed civilian guards, known as *vigilantes*, to allow the odd party with girls and booze. He bought footballs and basketballs so other prisoners could play sport. I said he seemed a pretty fair guy. 'Yes,' Paul replied, 'but don't be fooled, he's a ruthless killer if you ever cross him.'

Ivor was around 30 years old, well muscled, with a boyish Latino face. I learned he had been a serious boxer in his home town ten years earlier, winning trophies and medals for his efforts. José and Ricardo were joint chiefs-of-staff and dealt with a small army of lieutenants, such as the two knife-wielding henchmen at the entrance to the corridor. They had only been in San Antonio a month or so and, on entry, had been taken to pavilion one where members of a Margarita gang led by two brothers, Oscarlito and Mario, immediately robbed them at gunpoint. They weren't the bosses over there but had a strong following. José and Ricardo had lain low for a week, obtained weapons and came out of nowhere one day with a vengeance. José took a huge chunk out of the side of Oscarlio's head with a machete while Ricardo had stabbed Mario through the heart with a knife, killing him instantly.

Oscarlito, however, by some miracle, survived the attack and was recovering in Porlamar hospital. José and Ricardo were moved to pavilion four to 'keep the peace'. It hadn't worked out that way. According to Paul, the two sides of the jail were on the brink of war. The Jordan brothers, who controlled the other pavilions, were furious and wanted blood. So did the rest of Oscarlito's gang.

And Chivo Loco? He was Ivor's executioner, just a pure assassin. My throat tightened; I sat stupefied. It was all too much to take in: a knife fight in the corridor only minutes after I walked in; killers with guns and knives; people at war, murdering one another! What the hell was this place I'd landed in? Hell was the right word to use. The atmosphere all around was charged with violence and evil.

Babbling voices filtered through the open doorway. Raised voices in a tongue I couldn't understand. I was way out of my depth. 'Hey, man,' said Paul, 'I was like you when I got here five years ago. You've seen nothing yet, my friend. It's a crazy place, that's for sure, but you get used to it.'

Get used to it – that's what Eric had said. And I had seen nothing yet, according to Paul. The three remaining men returned their glazed eyes to the television screen as Paul explained in detail what was happening in the jail, who was who and what was what. Pavilions one, two and three were situated 100 yards from where we sat, with a patch of open ground between the two sides. Their population was all local to Margarita, 200 at least and most of them crazy. Pavilions four and five were made up of a mixture of foreigners (Colombians were classed as foreigners) and men from mainland cities, such as Caracas, Puerto La Cruz, Valencia, Cumaná, Maricaibo and Barcelona. They seemed better educated than the locals and had connections on the outside that helped finance a better lifestyle in jail.

Tribal warfare was big in Venezuelan jails and there was constant unrest, not only between the two sides but also among the men from different areas of the mainland. Paul was convinced a clash between the two sides was imminent. There had been sporadic firing across the rooftops for several days. He had seen the slow build-up to such clashes many times in the five years he'd been in San Antonio.

'What about the guards?' I asked. 'Don't they do anything about it?'

Paul laughed. 'The vigilantes won't do anything. They wait until the guardia come in, and they won't bother till someone's killed and the siren goes off.'

I sat there horrified by what I was hearing but knew I couldn't let it show, not in this macho dreamland. It would make me look weak, and I was amongst people who would take advantage. I'd made up my mind after the episode with the chain that no one would intimidate me.

'Where can I sleep tonight?' I asked Paul.

'Well,' he said, 'you'll have to find a space in the passage for a while. You have to understand, I've been here a long time and I haven't always had this room. I like my privacy at nights, to shower and things, you know?'

I didn't know, but I understood where he was coming from: you had to earn the things you got. Paul gave me a thick blanket. 'If you have any valuables or money on you, leave them here with me. It's safe here, but they'll cut your pockets off in the night if they think you have anything worth stealing.'

I hesitated, unsure. He could sense it. 'This isn't a kindergarten, Frank. There are some real live motherfuckers out there – but suit yourself.' I had to trust the guy. His eyes sparkled when I pulled the wad of notes and the watch from my pocket and handed them to him; this prompted his friends' eyes to deviate from the TV. 'Nice watch,' he said, admiringly, opening the drawer under a bedside table and placing it and the money inside.

'What about my bag?' I asked. 'It has clothes and cigarettes and some things I need.'

'Just leave it under my bed, it'll be OK.'

I made my way out after saying a few *hasta mañana*s and *bon nuit* to Paul. Luckily, there was a space just outside the door. Doubling the blanket lengthways, I laid it out on the floor ready to settle. But the noise in the corridor was too much – how was I going to sleep? I turned around to take in my new home and noticed I'd attracted a small crowd. Evil faces surrounded me, staring – some had knives, others not. I turned my back on them, got down on the blanket and closed my eyes, making as if to sleep. A second later, I felt a shadow pass over me, then a touch on my arm. I could smell him before I saw him. I opened my eyes to see an ugly, dark face inches from mine.

'*Cigarro, gringo*,' he said. His breath was foul, his teeth rotten and his rancid body odour filled my nose.

'*Nada*,' I said, patting my pockets for emphasis, but he didn't appear to be convinced. A few others gathered around, one crouched next to me and reached for my pocket. I swatted his hand away. He stood up and pulled a crude-looking knife from his waistband. I was up in a flash and in a fighting stance. It took the guy by surprise because he stepped back; the others backed away too. I was at the dead end of the corridor with nowhere to run. I returned his stare, not backing down an inch, breathing deeply, ready to go.

'*Mira! El gringo es un amigo mio!*' Ivor appeared a second after his booming voice. My would-be tormentors virtually scurried away. The guy had my immediate respect.

'*Gracias*,' I told him.

'*De nada*, my frien',' he replied in broken English. 'Dey crazy!' he added as an afterthought. Although a very dangerous man, it was difficult not to like him. He'd saved my hide, now I owed him – the trouble was I could see he knew it too. 'Goodnigh',' he said, walking into Paul's room.

'Fuck,' I said out loud settling on the blanket, my head still pounding from the close encounter. I didn't close my eyes for a while. I sat up and watched the activity in the dim light of the corridor. Guys were huddled in groups smoking crack on pipes, the sweet, sickly smell of it filled the air and mingled with the pungent aroma of the marijuana others were smoking. Music pumped from doorways.

I sat in a daze, my eyes heavy with fatigue. I had not yet fully recovered from the fever. I was trying to figure out what was going on, yet couldn't make any sense of it. I felt drunk yet sober, floating yet grounded, hazy but focused. It was like some vision from hell before me only without the flames. I desperately needed to get some sleep, but I couldn't. By the time sheer exhaustion finally took over and I lay down, most people were asleep. Slumbering men covered the floor of the corridor and beyond, nearly all lay on bare concrete using their arms as pillows. A few had tatty, wafer-thin foam mattresses.

Even in the semi-darkness the crack heads, having long since smoked their last rock, crept about searching for white crumbs someone might have dropped, wetting their fingers and touching any white specks on the floor that could be their next hit. One hovered near me. I readied myself, but there was no need: the glazed look in his eyes told me he didn't even know I was there. One thing was on his mind and one thing only: finding a rock. He wouldn't have much success near me, but who was I to speak up and invade his head space? Wherever that may have been.

I fell asleep, too tired to hold my eyes open any longer. I slept fitfully, swatting cockroaches from my hair and neck throughout the night, waking to the sound of babbling voices. People were up and about, moving around. What happens now, I wondered?

Just then, I heard someone shout, '*NÚMERO!*' The outside door banged open and people were moving quickly in that direction, bottlenecking at the end of the corridor as the mass of prisoners tried to squeeze through the single doorway.

What's all the panic about, I thought?

Paul appeared behind me. 'Stay with me and you'll be OK,' he said. As the crowd thinned, we made our way through the doorway. 'Now run!' shouted Paul, and he was gone like a greyhound.

A scary sight greeted my eyes as I passed through the doorway and ran after Paul as fast as I could. There were two lines of soldiers all the way round to the back of the pavilion. '*Corre! corre!*' some were shouting, swinging long bayonets as if to hit us with them. It was a frightening way to start the day. I reached the open yard, where I caught sight of Paul. I ran over to him, breathless by the time I'd reached him on the outer perimeter. The prisoners formed a line all the way around. Two Guardia Nacional soldiers walked along the line.

'*Uno, dos, tres, cuatro, cinco,*' shouted the prisoners in turn.

'Oh fuck!' I said to Paul. 'We're right at the other end. What happens if you don't know your number?'

'You get beat,' he replied nonchalantly.

I racked my brains to remember the numbers I'd learned with Sal back at Los Cocos. As the soldiers got closer, I strained to hear the numbers being given. When they reached Paul, he shouted, '*Sesenta y siete.*' I had to think fast.

'*Sesenta y . . .*' I stumbled. One of the soldiers glared at me. '*Ocho!*' I finished, and they walked on.

I let out a breath through pursed lips and looked at Paul, who was smiling. 'You learn fast, Frank, you'll be OK.'

When the count was done, everyone ran back into the pavilion, following the perimeter of the yard, and once inside the door was locked. As we made our way down the corridor, Paul asked if I'd like to join him in his room. I hadn't noticed the night before, as my eyes had been full of guns and knives, but in one corner of Paul's room stood a table with a small two-ringed cooker on the top of it and next to it a small percolator. Paul switched on the cooker by hanging two bare-ended wires on to two equally bare loops of cable protruding through the wall just above the table.

'It's all a bit primitive,' he said, 'but we make things work.' The coffee was thick, strong and sweet; the caffeine gave me a jolt.

We smoked and chatted for a while. I explained Sam was in the women's section and expressed my concern. He assured me he would talk to someone he knew over there, a girl called Mirelle, and she would make sure Sam came to no harm. He knew his way around and I began to trust him.

The main door was opened half an hour after número. 'Come,' said Paul, passing me a plastic bowl. 'Breakfast.' I followed him to the side of the building adjacent to ours, which he told me was the kitchen. Breakfast would be an experience in itself. Two vigilantes with shotguns were trying in vain to push and shove the prisoners into line. '*LA COLA, LA COLA!*' they shouted. No one seemed to take any notice: it was like a stampede, men arguing and fighting to get in front of one another. One vigilante stepped back and fired a few shots in the air. It quickly got their attention, and eventually they formed some sort of queue. Paul and I waited until the crush had gone. Breakfast was a bowl of watery porridge and a bread roll.

'It's not bad,' I commented to Paul.

'It's the only decent meal you get here, man. The rest is *merde!*' he replied.

He was right. Disgustingly sticky cold rice with tiny pieces of luncheon meat was served at eleven o'clock. It looked like it had been scraped off the ground! Again, the stampede. Again, shots and mayhem. The same slop was served again at 4.30; it made me heave to eat it.

During that first day in San Antonio, I was summoned to the dirección several times. Induction, questions, fingerprints, a medical (of sorts), etc. Paul accompanied me each time to translate. On one trip, Terry shouted over to me from the gate of the enfermeria. I returned his greeting. Paul quizzed me as to how I knew Terry. When I explained what had gone on the night before and how Terry had saved me from a fate worse than death, Paul burst into fits of laughter.

Somewhat perplexed, I asked, 'What are you laughing at?'

'Man, they saw you coming,' he managed to say at last. 'They're a team, those two. Terry has to be the biggest con man in the jail!'

I was hurt. Angry too. I thought I was plenty streetwise, but I'd have to smarten up or I'd be lost in this place.

'Don't worry over it,' he said, 'you're not the first!'

It was some consolation at least.

During the first day, I introduced myself to several other foreigners. There weren't many. I met 'Tammier', an English guy from London of Egyptian decent. His girlfriend, 'Sarina', was in the women's *anexo*. At least Sam would have found her and had someone to talk to. My gut feeling towards Tammier was that I didn't trust him. He was a young, fast-talking trickster and asked immediately if I needed any coke or marijuana. I decided to avoid him. There were two Dutchmen, Franz and Cornelius, both doing ten years for smuggling. They were amicable, well educated and spoke good English. Paul introduced me to Chino, a Portuguese ex-mercenary who worked in the kitchens. He and Paul had a food chain going: Chino would drop a parcel through the slats of Paul's window every morning at 4 a.m. when he started work. I was invited to sample a meal later in the evening after lock-up, which I gratefully accepted.

In the afternoon, I decided to explore the place a little. Paul advised me against going off on my own – I should have listened. I walked around the pavilion and on to the yard. Scores of prisoners were outside, standing in groups, some shooting baskets, others exercising. I walked along the back of pavilion four towards another building, which I took to be pavilion five. Nearing the gate, two men stood up and barred my way. One wagged a finger from side to side; it was plain to see I wasn't welcome. I made a quick right turn and followed the perimeter. Dozens of eyes locked onto me and I became a little nervous as hateful looks accompanied their macho posturing. I walked on, determined not to turn back. Some made comments as I passed, lightly stroking the handles of knives protruding from their waistbands.

'Fuck! Get me out of here,' I muttered under my breath. Nevertheless, I carried on. I crossed the yard and reached a stone path weaving its way up to a large building. Either side was skirted by rocks and large pebbles. Making my way along, I saw two prisoners coming in the opposite direction. They saw me and stopped, said something to each other and blocked my path.

'*Cigarro, gringo,*' one said, making an obvious display of his knife.

'*Nada*,' I replied, trying to push past them. He placed his hand around the hilt of his knife and started to pull it out.

'*Cigarro, gringo*,' he said again.

Not considering the consequences, I raised my arm, clenched my knuckles and jabbed his throat with a punch that took him off his feet. He fell to the ground gasping. I bent down quickly and picked up a couple of handy-sized rocks. The other guy didn't hang around to help his friend; he was gone before I stood back up again. The guy on the floor got his breath back, muttered all sorts of obscenities at me and got to his feet. He didn't hang around either once he'd caught sight of the rocks.

Turning around, I saw a lot of people had watched the incident. Shit! Had I opened a can of worms? Would there be retaliation? I decided I'd done enough exploring for the day and made my way back, following the edge of the yard closest to the outside wall.

Walking back, the same thoughts went through my mind as every prisoner during their first days of incarceration, namely how difficult would it be to escape? To the side of me ran a six-foot-high chain-linked fence and a ten-foot wall topped with barbed wire. The buildings were only made of concrete and cinder block. Those obstacles wouldn't present too much difficulty to a determined escapee. It was the guard towers placed every 100 yards that would be the stumbling block to any plan. They stood like grey boxes atop concrete columns, an armed soldier in each one. From where I stood, I could see five towers. There would be more, so the odds weren't favourable.

I made my way back to Paul's room. He laughed as I told him of my escapade. 'I told you, didn't I?' he said, smiling. His face turned serious. 'It's good you did what you did, though. Word will be around already that you're not a pussy. It'll get you respect from these motherfuckers.'

We chatted for the rest of the afternoon. At five o'clock, the door was locked and everyone was back inside after the day's activities. The pavilion was heaving with bodies, people without rooms having nowhere to settle.

'What happens now?' I asked Paul.

'Another número in a minute. Then lock-up until tomorrow.'

Another número! My nerves began to jangle in anticipation. Then it came. I ran out and through the lines of shouting soldiers to where I'd stood that morning, or so I thought. When the soldiers reached me, it was a totally different number. I mimicked the first word Paul said and added one. '*Cincuenta y siete,*' I managed. I held my breath. The soldiers moved on. I had escaped a beat yet again through quick thinking.

That evening, Paul cooked eggs, tomatoes and canned meat. It was a feast compared to the gruel they handed out from the kitchens. I was very grateful. (I'd dropped lucky. Eggs and canned meat were a rare treat, even for the bosses.) In the evening, I practised my numbers with Paul's help. He let me shower, shave and use his toilet, and I felt almost human again. Within minutes, though, I was sweating profusely; the heat was oppressive.

Paul's friends from the previous night came in during the evening. Ivor brought out a big bag of grass and made a long joint using brown paper. He lit it, took a few deep drags and passed it over to me. Should I, shouldn't I? I'd endured a stressful couple of weeks and longed for some sort of release. I took it from him, drew deeply on it and inhaled. Ivor's boyish face lit up in a big smile as I choked on the smoke. My head went numb after a few seconds, my body relaxed. By the time the joint came back to me, I was in never-never land with not a care in the world. It was an escape of sorts and one I welcomed.

I didn't relish the thought of sleeping in the corridor again, but as I grew tired I said my goodnights, retrieved the blanket from under Paul's bed and made my way out. The noise echoed in my head, yet I could pick out each individual sound if I chose to. Laughs, conversations, even several different types of music. The grass had been strong and I was still in a daze from its effects. It appeared everyone was high on something. I fell asleep almost immediately despite the noise. It all blended into a dark nothingness as I drifted away.

# 5

# RUNNING THE GAUNTLET

I awoke the next morning only minutes before número still feeling a bit muggy from the night before. I'd slept reasonably well – Ivor's joint had done the trick. Slowly, the tightness in my throat returned as the realisation of where I was crept into my consciousness. I gave my head a good shake, jumped up and followed the rush. I ran through the lines of bayonet-swinging soldiers. '*Corre! Corre!*' they bellowed repeatedly.

On the run, I had decided I would make an effort to learn to stand on my own two feet and not rely on Paul so much. I squeezed into a space between two nasty-looking characters quite close to the beginning of the line. They turned and glared at me. I'd practised and practised my numbers the previous night, and I stood there praying to get it right. Numbers were spinning around in my head. I looked across the yard and spotted Paul. He'd been watching me and gave the thumbs up. Please don't let me get it wrong!

Suddenly it was my turn and the two soldiers glared at me hatefully. I hadn't been listening. One lifted his bayonet and held the blade with his other hand; the body language was obvious. Starting to panic, I looked for help. There was Paul in the background frantically making shapes in the air with his arm: a one then an eight, over and over. '*Dieciocho!*' I shouted. A second or two passed in silence, the soldiers continuing to stare at me. Then, without a word between them, they walked on.

'*Diecinueve! Veinte! Veintiuno!* . . .'

I looked around at the other prisoners from my pavilion. Broad daylight and the early hour gave them a look that was hard to put into words. Never in my life had I seen so many cut-throat pirate lookalikes. I let out a deep sigh. Maybe it had just been in my head, but I could have sworn I'd seen disappointment on some of the faces around me. These thoughts weren't fresh, nor were they a surprise to me. Everything and everyone around me pulsed with evil and violence: I could feel it, taste it, it was a feeling that could suffocate you if you let it.

I shook my head and looked over at Paul, who was smiling at me. He wiped his fingers across his forehead and flicked his hand in the air, telling me I'd only just got away with it that time. And I had, too, but it had been very close – I needed to get a grip.

Back inside, over strong, sweet coffee and cigarettes, Paul enlightened me somewhat as to the number of prisoners who couldn't read or write, or even count to 100, hence the mad crush to get out of the pavilion at número – so they could get a low number, one they were familiar with. 'But give them a 1,000 bolivar note and they know exactly what they can get with it,' he laughed. I found it hard to believe, but he insisted it was true.

The next two days were to be visiting days. On Saturdays and Sundays, prisoners' families and friends were allowed into the jail. The locals got busy after breakfast, scrubbing up and pulling out their best clothes, getting ready to receive their families.

After breakfast, and against my better judgement, I submitted to the itchy-feet syndrome and started to feel adventurous. I wasn't about to sit inside day after day, and I needed to walk, to breathe fresh air and find space to think. I went around the back, giving pavilion five a miss, this time walking across the yard to the path that I'd walked halfway up the day before. Most prisoners ignored me this time, but there were a lot that didn't, following me with malevolent looks. The hairs on my arms were standing on end, tingling with static. I'm not ashamed to admit the feeling that gripped me was one of fear. I would have had no chance if a few of them decided to set about me.

Nevertheless, I carried on, and I reached the path. I wasn't alone. Two guys were walking towards me. Oh no, not again, I thought. To my surprise, I got a nod from both of them as they passed. Further up as I reached the workshops, a crowd of five or six prisoners emerged from one of the gates.

'*Hepa*!' said a couple of them, smiling. It was prison slang for 'Hi', Things were looking good. I smiled and walked on around the back of the building where the concrete path ended. In front of me lay a stretch of open land covered with grass patches, shrubs and wild flowers of every colour imaginable. There was a huge patch against the inner fence no more than 30 yards from where I stood. A crazy thought entered my head: Sam would love some flowers, they were sure to cheer her up. There was no one else in sight except a guard high up in a tower to my right. No one's going to shoot me for picking flowers surely!

I made my way along the fence, looking around me as I went. The guard in the tower frowned as I pointed at the flowers. I walked on. When I'd picked a dozen or so, something told me it was time to go. I could never explain this intuition. As I turned and started to walk back, I heard a distinct pffft-pffft pass where I'd stood a second before. Two shots rang out a split second later, the bullets hitting the concrete wall behind me. The shooters were firing from behind a barricade of sorts made of rocks and other things I couldn't quite make out. They were on the rooftop of the pavilion opposite. Two more shots rang out from our side this time. The guys on the roof opposite ducked and stayed there.

I ran like the wind back to the safety of the workshop building, still clutching the flowers I'd picked. I slumped against the wall, panting, not so much from the sprint but from the nearness of it all. Those bullets had been fucking close. What had possessed me to do such a crazy thing? Of course, I wasn't fully aware at that time just how caught up in the madness I would become.

After calming down, I made my way back to Paul's room. Crossing the yard in a daze, I was greeted with whistles and catcalls. My lunacy hadn't gone unnoticed. I looked down and realised I still held the flowers in my hand – what a fool I must have looked. Paul made a big fuss of me when I walked into his room and told him what I'd done, then called me all the crazy bastards under the sun after which he put the flowers in a plastic tumbler of water.

With Paul's help at the gate, I paid a runner from the dirección four cigarettes to take the flowers to the gate of the women's anexo along with a note I'd written. As we turned to walk back, I mused aloud, 'I wonder if she'll ever know I risked my life for those flowers?' Paul just smiled. I never did tell her.

The visitors came in at nine, and I spent the rest of the day with Paul while, outside, couples wandered, children of all ages ran around playing and a general party atmosphere settled on the place. Paul spoke several languages fluently and had an endless supply of tales to tell of his many escapades during his life as a drug smuggler. He admitted there were people who had bought their freedom. He, unfortunately, at the time of his arrest hadn't even had the chance. His supplier had been a high-ranking political type and the media coverage had made it impossible. The high-ranker spent two years in a jail called Los Teques in Caracas, a model jail used for political prisoners, corrupt officials, police officers, etc., before he was released back into public office. Paul meanwhile had served more than five years and was coming towards his first eligible release under the benefit laws. He planned to do a runner the moment he could.

I'd always had a talent for drawing and in between conversation I doodled on a piece of scrap paper. Paul was impressed with my work and asked if I could draw a picture of his son from an old photograph. I replied that I could, providing I had decent paper and pencils. He got up and left the room. A few minutes later, he returned with a sheet of drawing paper, a ruler, two pencils and a rubber! The guy was a star. I began straight away; it was good to have something to occupy my mind.

I was lost in my work when Paul told me it was time for evening número. I found my own space again, a little further up the line.

The number came easily: '_Treinta y dos._' The drawing had somehow calmed my mind.

I entered Paul's food chain for a small fee, although there weren't many provisions to share around because Rufini, the kitchen vigilante, had usually stolen and sold most of them before they even got into the prison. After lock-up, we cooked an omelette with tomatoes. I was famished. I'd only eaten a few mouthfuls of the _rancho_ food given out that day. We were savouring the treat when a shotgun boomed somewhere in the distance. Paul shrugged his shoulders and said nonchalantly that it came from the dirección and not to bother about it. We passed a peaceful evening. A few visitors popped in, mainly to scrounge cigarettes. Paul always obliged, but I found it difficult. Some looked at my work. '_Ah, artista?_' they said, feigning interest. The next line was usually '_Cigarro, gringo._'

The next day, número presented no problems but, as breakfast finished and the vigilantes withdrew, a handful of gun-carrying prisoners mounted the roof, climbing the bars that fronted the evangelist church. From behind a barricade of rocks, they fired several shots across the rooftops to the other side. Return fire came back immediately. Nothing more happened. It was only a show because it was another visiting day.

An unwritten truce reigned during visiting hours; however, once the visitors were gone at three o'clock, it was '_Plomo_'. I stayed inside and read _The Guns of Navarone_. Over the years, Paul had acquired a good selection of books. I was to discover visiting hours were the only moments of peace and calm.

Later that afternoon after visits, there was a serious stabbing outside pavilion five. Four prisoners carried the victim to the chain-link gate and dumped him there, a trail of blood leading all the way back down the concrete path and on to the yard. A guy called Valdomero was summoned to clean it up. This was his regular job apparently: whenever blood was spilled, it was down to Valdomero to wash it away with buckets of water. He was kept busy most days. He was a remarkable sight: bald-headed, tall and gangly with skin like cracked leather. Only one of his eyes functioned; the other was white and twisted grotesquely upwards. This, combined with his almost toothless mouth and stubble-covered chin, gave him a hideous look.

The victim had been stabbed several times in the chest. He was carried by dirección orderlies over to the main entrance and left slumped against the wall to await an ambulance. He lay bleeding for 20 minutes before it arrived. He actually bled to death. The thing that struck me was that no one seemed to care.

In the evening, more gunshots were heard in the distance, echoing as if in a confined space. 'Dirección,' said Paul in answer to my look. There was a sudden commotion in the corridor, followed by shouting and cheering: it was another fight. I made to stand but Paul waved me down with his hand. 'Don't get involved in their problems, Frank. There's enough tension here already.' The cheering eventually died down, followed by an unexpected quiet. Then came a thunderous banging on the inside of the pavilion door. It echoed through the building.

'What the fuck's that?' I blurted out. Paul said they were banging a rock on the door to get the attention of the vigilantes. They would open up and carry one away.

'What do you mean, carry one away?' I asked stupidly.

'A dead one,' Paul replied without emotion. This news didn't help when it came time for me to go out into the corridor to sleep that night.

Sporadic firing could be heard across the rooftops through the next day. I asked Paul where they obtained all the ammunition. He laughed in reply. 'Just about anywhere,' he said. 'Vigilantes, soldiers, visitors. They always have plenty of bullets.' He went on to explain that a number of inmates died from stabbings each month, it was part of the accepted norm, but gunshots and shootings were a different story. In those instances, the Guardia Nacional would enter the prison. 'Be ready for that day, my friend,' he told me.

That evening the soldiers were a little agitated at número. As we ran through, some of the bayonets connected. Thwacks followed by yelps. I barely managed to escape, as I ran and dodged the swinging blades.

'What the fuck's the matter with them?' I asked Paul.

'There will be a *raqueta* tomorrow, I can feel it,' was all he said in reply.

'What's a raqueta?'

Paul didn't answer.

Later that evening, Paul explained that the *comandante* of the garrison outside the jail had only a certain amount of patience and when it ran out he sent his troops in. The warming-up tactic was an obvious sign the soldiers knew something we didn't. A raqueta was imminent, he insisted. He'd seen it countless times before.

'Will the women be OK?' I asked.

'Yeah, sure, they will come to no harm.'

Sal, my cellmate from Los Cocos, turned up that evening, but we didn't have time to say more than a few words before he was whisked away by a couple of Spaniards, no doubt to take him under their wing and introduce him to the delights of San Antonio. It was good to see a familiar face despite the circumstances. I went to sleep that night with my stomach in a knot. I slept fitfully, haunted by bad dreams and never-ending cockroaches.

I woke the next day and could immediately feel the tension in the air. I cringed as shots were exchanged between the two sides after breakfast; my mind was on full alert. Paul had been sparse in his details of raquetas. 'They come in and beat everyone, wreck everything, then go,' he'd said. I had no real idea of what to expect or what to do.

At 10 a.m., a runner called me to the gate. The vigilante let me out and told me to go to the dirección: the British consul was there. Once inside, a vigilante pointed me down the corridor. Walking towards an open doorway, I spotted Sam. My heart jumped as I entered the room and we embraced. It was then I noticed other people in the room. Tammier, the Brit I'd already met, and a black girl in her early 20s who I took to be Sarina. At the back of the room stood a civil service-looking character who was, of course, Mr Mellor, the local consul '*honorario*'. In his own words, this meant he wasn't a real consul, but a part-time one since he ran an import business on the island.

He made it very clear from the start that it wasn't actually one of his duties to visit the prison. Consular visits were every three months. He would bring any mail or monies sent by our families as and when he had time. He went on to say he was doing all this as a favour to the embassy in Caracas! His speech got us off to good start. I was busy holding Sam and only half listening anyway.

He actually did us a great service that day. He spoke with the prison *director* on our behalf in beautiful Spanish and arranged for Sam and me to be able see each other once a week. We would be allowed to meet every Friday at 11 a.m. We also signed paperwork, which made us eligible to receive Prisoners Abroad benefits – money, books, etc.★

Sam and I made the most of the next few minutes as Mr Mellor readied himself to leave. I left Sam at the gate to the anexo and followed our only contact with the outside world to the main entrance. As we neared, a shot rang out from the rooftops behind us.

'Wh-what was that?' he stammered, crouching down and looking around him.

'Didn't you know, they shoot real bullets at each other in here,' I replied sarcastically.

'Right, I'll be off then,' he said, rushing for the door. He left me with the strong impression he hadn't wanted to be there in the first place. Who could blame him?

Thoughts of being released were fading slowly. I walked back to the pavilion somewhat downhearted. I'd been back in Paul's room for half an hour when out of nowhere a low hum built up in the distance to an awful wailing sound that filled the air. A dozen shouts followed.

'*AGUA VERDE! AGUA VERDE!*'

Paul turned to me. 'Get outside quickly! I need to put something away. I'll see you out there. Go! Go!'

---

★Prisoners Abroad is a British-based charity that helps Britons incarcerated in foreign countries. They play a magnificent role later on in this story and I cannot thank them enough for all their help over the years.

As the word *agua* warned of vigilantes, so *agua verde* signified the soldiers coming in. Running down the corridor, I heard shotgun blasts outside, people shouting. Prisoners were desperately squeezing through the doorway. I waited nervously for a few seconds, hearing people getting beaten outside while shotguns fired constantly. It ripped my nerves to shreds; it was the most frightening experience. I threw myself at the door and went with the flow. Squashing through the door with two other prisoners, I missed the beat. The guy on my right got it across his back, the blade's tip landing inches from my face. The soldiers were positioned well. It turned into a stampede on the path towards the yard, bodies jostling round one another on their way to the *cancha*. With everyone trying their best to avoid the bayonets that flashed in the sunlight every couple of yards or so, the task looked impossible.

Soldiers' faces were filled with rage as they beat anyone that was close enough. I managed to dodge the swishing blades along the way, but just as I thought I'd made it onto the yard . . . whack! I felt a searing pain spreading across my buttocks and shooting up my back. Fucking hell! It hurt so much I cried out with the pain. I ran on to the yard, looking for a familiar face: there were none. Every prisoner was face down, following orders from screaming soldiers. Boom! Whack! Yelp! Boom! Some soldiers carried semi-automatic rifles and fired into the air: Tat-tat-tat! BOOM! The noise and the heavy smell of cordite was sickening.

I managed to look around me for a few seconds, taking in the madness, then a soldier grabbed my shirt and literally threw me to the ground: he was a big guy and stood on my back with one foot for several seconds before moving on. My backside burning, throbbing with each heartbeat, I cursed the soldiers inwardly. Now the heat of the concrete was burning my head, elbows, chest, and every other part of me that made contact. Once everyone reached the cancha, the shooting stopped.

Every prisoner in pavilions four and five was face down with hands on heads. '*Silencio!*' the soldiers shouted. We lay in the burning sun, my ears still ringing from all the shooting. It was an eerie moment. If a prisoner was seen talking to another, he got a beat. I kept my head down – if I took another beat, I knew I'd cry like a baby. After half an hour, an order rang out. '*Levantarse!*' Everyone got to their feet quickly. Another order, this one I didn't understand at all. There was chaos as prisoners ran in all directions, bumping into each other in their haste and confusion. More shouting. Boom! Boom! Shotguns blasting again, bayonets flashing. I hadn't a clue what was going on.

I spotted Paul's striped T-shirt not too far away and ran over to him. At least I would be in the right place. Bayonets hit flesh and order came as eight neat rows of prisoners stretched out across the length of the yard, four rows for each pavilion. I began to take things in. Mean-faced soldiers stood a couple of yards apart around the perimeter of the cancha. Others milled about the lines of prisoners, stopping here and there, doing their macho staring bit before moving on. Some had guns, others carried bayonet-type swords called *planillas*. More searched the grounds and found hastily hidden knives. A handful of soldiers stood along the path leading to pavilion four.

'*Desnudarse*,' came an order from my left. I looked over. An officer had delivered it. I had no idea of his rank. He commenced counting from ten down to one. Once I realised what people were doing, it didn't take me long to undress: I wore only a T-shirt, shorts and sandals. Some were quick, but despite the intense heat others wore layer upon layer of clothing. They were slower and took the beatings. I could only assume those prisoners were frightened they'd get what little ragged clothing they possessed stolen if it wasn't fastened to their bodies. Whack! Yelp! The soldiers moved in and out with menace, crazed looks in their eyes as if they wanted to beat everyone to death.

Naked, with neat piles of clothing to our left, we were ordered to sit with our hands behind our heads. I sat down, unthinking, and the severe heat of the concrete on my recently bruised skin racked my body with pain. This was insane. I creased my face, tears of pain flowed from my eyes. Fuck! The pain was unbearable. I noticed how many of the locals were squatting rather than sitting. It was their natural way, of course, so I tried it. The relief was noticeable, but how my feet burned on the concrete. The sun beat down relentlessly. I realised how tough some of these guys around me really were. Or maybe they were just plain stupid: to willingly create and provoke this degradation and torture was way beyond my comprehension, but that's what they'd done, knowing this would be the outcome! I had little knowledge of the workings of their minds at the time and was to be left scratching my head in wonder on many occasions to come.

As we waited, soldiers picked at the clothing on the ground with their bayonets, searching the odd pile here and there. '*Cuchillo!*' one soldier shouted. He'd found a knife and its owner was sent to the fence. '*Drogas!*' another shouted. Overall, 14 prisoners were sent to stand naked facing the fence, hands spread clasping the wire. They each received three more beats with a planilla in full view of everyone. There were a few shrieks as the blade swished down on them. It was a painful sight to behold; blood oozed from wounds as skin was broken with the repeated thrashings.

I looked to my left and saw two vigilantes I'd seen many times on my visits to the dirección. One was named Salazar. He was the *jefe de régimen*, the man in charge of all the vigilantes; a sly, corrupt little fox of a man, according to Paul. The other was his sidekick Flores, a tough, black, beefy-looking no-nonsense thug. They each held a pistol-gripped shotgun and appeared to be enjoying the show. On reflection, I'd seen them before at número. They were talking to a Guardia Nacional officer. As I watched, a dozen or more soldiers came around the corner, walked across the front of us and into pavilion five. Two of them carried buckets. Paul turned to me and said, 'They've searched our pavilion. All is well.'

Twenty minutes later, they came out of pavilion five after much crashing and banging. The bucket carriers took their spoils over to where Salazar stood with the officer. From where I was, I could see odd lengths of piping protruding above the lips of the buckets. Some minutes later, we were ordered to dress. '*Vestirse!*' shouted the officer. A count was taken, then we were herded back into the pavilions, bayonets swinging and soldiers screaming. I learned later that the guardia had found many weapons secreted around the pavilions: mainly home-made knives and 'one-shot' guns called *chopos*, handmade from odd parts of piping and scraps of metal. Although they only fired once, they were crudely effective at close range. Some pistols had also been found. The knives and chopos would be made again quickly; the pistols would soon be made available for a price from Salazar, the chief vigilante.

What greeted my eyes when I ran back inside stopped me in my stride. It looked like a bomb had exploded in there. People's possessions littered the floor. Mattresses, clothes, shoes, books, bedding, tins, bottles, food, toiletries, things were strewn everywhere. There was instant chaos. The men fought amongst each other as they collected their belongings, some snatching things from others in anger. Raised voices and lots of arm-waving added to the mayhem. I picked my way through the debris, being careful not to tread on anything, and made my way down the corridor. Paul was already in his room, head in hands, standing in the middle of what looked like the aftermath of a barroom brawl. Taking a deep breath, he said, 'OK, let's get on with it.'

Within 15 minutes, we had the place back to how it had been and the coffee pot was on. My backside hurt like crazy. Paul produced a cactus leaf and told me it had amazing healing properties. It was, in fact, aloe, a plant that was grown on the grounds behind the cancha. Paul pulled out a knife from its hiding place and sliced the leaf lengthways. I scraped out the jelly and applied it to my burning backside. Never before had I experienced such a soothing relief. It was no wonder these guys actually cultivated the plant on prison grounds.

'Fuck! That was insane out there, Paul,' I said.

'I've seen worse,' he replied with a wry smile. 'They found nothing.'

Either the soldiers in the search party were brainless or Paul was blessed with an amazing amount of luck. In his room laid flat on a shelf covered with a piece of lino were two machete blades – the soldiers had thrown all the crockery on the floor but hadn't lifted the lino. His gun was hidden inside the fridge door behind the mouldings with my money and watch. A four-inch blade was stuck under the corner table on which sat the two-ringed stove. When I mentioned this to Paul, he shrugged. 'They don't really look that hard. They just like to destroy and steal.'

I wondered where the rest of my cigarettes had gone, as I'd helped tidy up and found my few possessions amongst the jumble. I was beginning to see the benefits of travelling light in this environment. It was quiet that night as people nursed their aches and pains.

Wednesday was another visiting day. There wasn't a shot fired from either side, and it was a welcome relief. Something else that left me scratching my head was the fact that visitors were allowed inside the jail to walk around freely with their menfolk and friends. Even the vigilantes were smiling. What a total contrast it was to the previous day.

Standing outside the pavilion watching people coming and going, I saw a familiar face coming down the path towards me, laden with carrier bags. It was Joe. I relieved him of some of his burden, and we greeted with a handshake. 'Pa-ool?' he asked. I motioned him to follow me to Paul's room, where we found him reading a book. His face lit up when he saw Joe, and they greeted each other like old friends. There were bags of food, cigarettes too, and just in time; I was as hungry as an ox, having eaten only a few decent meals since my arrival.

I tucked in to bread rolls and chicken, while Paul and Joe spoke in Spanish. I didn't understand any of it, but I got the idea from Joe's occasional glances that things weren't going too well for us. Paul confirmed my thoughts, telling me there was no news of us getting away as yet. Joe didn't hang around for very long; half the bags were for Sam and he was on his way over. Before he left, I gave him a note and told him to tell her I couldn't wait until our first meeting. We ate well that night. It was my birthday that day, but I kept it quiet. What was there to celebrate anyway? There was a fatal stabbing in pavilion five late in the afternoon, a sign that the visits were over and things were back to normal.

My second week in San Antonio didn't go so easily. Sam and I had kept in touch by sending notes to each other daily. Meanwhile word had spread about Sam and how lovely she was. I could understand how their minds worked: she was like some TV starlet to them. It seemed every male prisoner (and possibly some female) was in love with her, even though the majority hadn't seen her. Many comments were passed by the wannabe macho types that she was their woman or that they loved her, which meant I had more than my fair share of fights that week. I didn't carry a knife at the time, so they would not fight me with theirs (it wouldn't be seen as fair), which was a big mistake on their part, as many of them didn't have a clue how to fight without them.

On the Thursday, a prisoner died of gunshot wounds on the other side. My heart was racing as I heard the siren revving up towards its piercing shriek. '*AGUA VERDE! AGUA VERDE!*' came the shouts, people scattering in all directions to hide weapons and drugs.

'Oh fucking hell, not again!' I said aloud. I was outside at the time and could see the soldiers coming through the main gate on the run. A vigilante unlocked and opened our gate. I ran with every ounce of strength I could muster into the yard and over to the far corner and got down on the ground ready. I wasn't going to run through the fuckers again!

Boom! Boom! Tat-tat-tat. Swish. Thwack. Yelps and shouts. Mayhem again. I didn't escape totally; one soldier kicked me in the ribs as I lay face down. I hadn't done anything to provoke him, I hadn't moved a muscle. More pain, more terror. I hated them for their brutality. I was angry with the prison population, too. If they lived peacefully, there would be no reason for this terror, and the soldiers wouldn't have an excuse to maltreat us. But this was their way of life, they'd grown up in poverty surrounded by violence and evil, and they knew nothing else. The primitive tribal thing still played a major role in their way of thinking. Groups from certain areas would stick together, which meant if you fought one you fought them all.

My ribs ached as I ran back to the pavilion. Same bombsite inside, same squabbles going on. Paul and I set about putting right the mess. When we were done, we sat and smoked a joint to calm down. Paul had taken a beat this time.

'It still hurts after all these years,' he said. 'But not so much now, you get used to it.'

Those words again! My mind drifted away with the smoke and thoughts of my first visit with Sam the next day.

At número the next morning, the soldiers were still in a semi-rage. One or two locals got a beat, but the soldiers' efforts were only half-hearted. I perked up some when I saw Sam later that morning during *entre vista* in the *salón*, part of the main dirección buildings. We sat on the concrete floor and were allowed to sit close and hold hands, but not to kiss. Sam told me of her time in the anexo. She'd claimed a space with Sarina in one of the large cells that housed six girls, each partitioning off their space with string and a bedsheet. She had a half-decent mattress. Their food was edible unlike ours, since food was delivered to their kitchens and they cooked it themselves. I told her of the madness on the men's side. She'd heard all the shooting and expressed concern for me.

'These people are evil,' I said.

'They're not so bad,' she replied. She teased me by saying she'd received streams of letters and had been chatted up several times. Sam was very much her own woman. Outwardly, I smiled, but inside my stomach churned.

Glancing around, I took in the salón. A dozen couples sat around the room at a spaced distance. Two sour-faced female vigilantes ran the proceedings and were quick to admonish anyone who broke the rules, which was every couple of minutes. Time went quickly and the hour was up before we knew it. We parted with a kiss and a hug and went our separate ways.

The salón was the size of a pavilion. At the far end, the whole wall was taken up with a mural of Christ in agony with thorns around his head. On Sunday mornings, two local priests came in and performed Catholic rituals to a handful of believers. Evangelists had the religious stronghold in San Antonio; they had churches inside the prison. The pastor, though a convict, would lead his followers into song after screaming a sermon. They sang and danced every day, sometimes starting before dawn. The drum beats reminded me I was in the jungle and far, far away from home.

Three weeks in and the daily madness continued. Visiting days were peaceful between the hours of 9 a.m. and 3 p.m. One morning at número, Salazar beat every single prisoner in our pavilion across the buttocks with an aluminium baseball bat because one guy was caught pissing through the wire fence. That's how it was, everyone paid for the actions of others. Later that week, two died in a gang fight on our side. The vigilantes locked everybody up, set off the siren and opened up again so we would be forced to run the full gauntlet through a horde of waiting soldiers.

As I dodged around several swinging bayonets, a soldier some yards ahead made eye contact with me. I saw a gleam in his eye – I was to be his next victim. I tried my best to swerve past him, but someone got in my way. He'd marked me out well. I put my hand out automatically to defend myself just as the blade came swishing down and slapped into the small of my back, gashing my wrist.

The pain was unbearable, it was all too much. I lost my head. While people were getting on the ground all around me, I stood like a lunatic, fists raised in the air. 'You fucking bastards!' I screamed over and over, tears filling my eyes. I didn't think of the danger. A soldier appeared from nowhere and brought the stock of his shotgun crashing down into my chest. I fell to the ground gasping for air. That's what I got for losing my head; it was a quick and painful lesson.

As things worked out, the following day I was waiting by the salón door for my visit with Sam when Terry came to the gate of the enfermeria. We talked. I'd forgiven him for the little trick he and Gargo had pulled on me that first night. After all, three weeks of San Antonio, witnessing rife homosexuality, told me if I had gone to pavilion one that night they would have raped me for certain and smoked my cigarettes while they did it. He invited me to share his room in the enfermeria. It was rare they had raquetas, he told me.

I was wary of him but at the same time wanted to get away from the violence in the main jail. The thought of peace prompted me to accept his offer.

I had my visit with Sam. She seemed OK, eating and drinking well, making friends and getting used to the routine. We both agreed it was unlikely, barring a miracle, that we would be released, and parted on a sombre note.

After being strongly advised by Paul not to do so, I moved into the enfermeria that afternoon. Paying Salazar 10,000 bolivares, I was set up in Terry's room within minutes. Evening número was taken in a fairly orderly fashion outside along the path. Ten rooms accommodated the sixty people living in the enfermeria. More than half of the population slept in the corridor. One toilet served everyone and a length of bent plumbing pipe with a valve attached was the shower. It stank to high heaven and cockroaches ran the place.

Terry had a cooker of sorts: a bare cooker ring held onto a paint tin with bits of wire. He cooked up rice, fried potatoes and garlic. As I lay on the mattress Terry had procured for me, I mused that things had got off to a pretty good start. The whole jail was a shit tip really, but this was as good a place as any to rest my head.

Wrong again.

It wasn't long before I realised I'd left one kind of madness and walked into another. The inmates of the enfermeria were always fighting amongst themselves. One might think the name suggests a connection to a hospital. Not so. Maybe years ago, but not any more. There was loud music booming. People shouting. Terry had many visitors, all wanting to meet the new gringo to see what they could get. Whenever a fight broke out in the corridor, which was almost every night, it was only a few strides for the vigilante on duty to let off a round of plastic through the bars of the gate. The first time it happened, it made me jump. Then I realised what I'd been hearing in the distance from Paul's room all those times. We weren't allowed out during the day and took one hour's exercise each night on the land in front of the building. I soon missed the freedom to come and go.

I met Freddie one night. He'd invited Terry and me to his room to eat with him. Freddie was a Colombian drug baron, and he had the two end rooms knocked into one, a nice bed, colour TV, mobile phone and his own shower and toilet in the corner. It must have cost him a pretty penny to live in this way. He never saw the light of day except for número and the times his wife turned up on visiting days, when he would escort her stylishly from the main gate. People cooked for him, cleaned and washed his clothes. All day he lay on his bed, smoked pot, watched inane television shows and talked to friends on the phone.

He looked every inch the drug baron. Gold-rimmed glasses, nice clothes and an air of power about him. I heard that Freddie was safer in jail than on the outside. People were after his blood over some crooked deal. Terry and I were invited to eat with Freddie on several occasions, and each time he would ask questions about England, while Terry translated. On the third visit, he asked if I knew people in England who would collect a suitcase at Manchester airport. He would get it there, no problem.

He'd been priming me, and Terry was part of it too. What was I about to be caught up in? There was no fucking chance I would get involved with the guy, and I had to let him down gracefully. For a man to live like he did, he had to have plenty of money to grease the right palms. He had influence and I didn't want to make an enemy of him. I told him I would make enquiries.

In early February, Mr Mellor came with letters and money from home. As I sat and read the letter from Chrissy, my heart sank. Someone had broken into her house on Christmas Day while she was out at lunch and robbed the place, taking many valuables and all of Josie's presents. How despicable, I thought. It was yet another blow to my already low morale.

I carried on seeing Sam on Fridays, while the raquetas continued in the main jail. Soldiers would run past the gate to pavilions one, two and three. The prisoners there suffered the same fate as in four and five. One Saturday, Joe came to visit. He'd asked Paul where I was. He brought food and cigarettes as usual. There were things I would have liked to ask him but didn't want Terry to know my business. He went off to see Sam and was gone.

After six weeks in the enfermeria, I'd had enough. It was as manic as the main prison only with fewer raquetas. I'd taken a beating a week before after someone was shot in the passageway. They never found the gun, but the guy's head was all over the wall. We were made to stand naked hands up against the wall in the midday sun for an hour while they searched. Each person in turn got a beat and was sent inside. I was shaking as the soldiers came up the line. I heard the swish and tensed my muscles. Fuck! There was no escape. Then it was over. I ran inside, carrying my clothes, my arse burning like it had been lashed with a hundred stinging nettles. For me, that was it.

Some days later, I began to consider how I would get back without Terry getting to know my plans beforehand. Paul turned up the very next day and called for me at the gate. He asked how I was faring. A coincidence? I told him of my wishes.

'That's good, man. I miss your company,' he said.

Another 10,000 for Salazar – the bastard was doing well out of me. I'd hated him since the morning of the beating with the bat. That afternoon, we sat in Paul's room and he told me what had been going on during my absence. There had been a few minor skirmishes on no-man's-land during February, groups of rival gangs fighting with knives and machetes. Several had died each time. Paul told me all this in a matter-of-fact manner. Another change was that the Jordan brothers, who ruled pavilions one, two and three, had received a 'benefit' after five and a half years and were now working away from the prison and sleeping outside the walls in a rehabilitation unit. Hernandez had taken their place, and Oscarlito didn't have the manpower to go against him. This was a new twist.

There had been no shooting for a couple of days. Ivor and Hernandez parleyed. There was to be a trial ceasefire supposedly. The two sides would attempt to live in harmony.

# 6

# ARMED RESPONSE

The tension eased slightly and, in a lot of ways, life in the prison became more manageable for a while. There was talk of a united hunger strike in sympathy with prisoners in the Casa Amarilla (the Yellow House) at El Dorado, a jungle prison camp in the south of Venezuela near the border with Guyana. Inmates there were protesting against torture and human-rights abuses carried out by prison guards. Paul was keen on local news and always watched the nightly programmes on his tiny TV.

I'd heard about El Dorado, or rather read about it. Henri Charrière, author of *Papillon*, had spent some time there before his release. Charrière, nicknamed Papillon because of a tattoo of a butterfly on his chest, was a member of the Parisian underworld who was sentenced to life imprisonment in 1931 for murdering a pimp. Charrière always maintained his innocence and swore vengeance on the people who sent him away to the penal colonies of French Guiana. During a string of daring escapes, he traversed the northern coast of Latin America, finally ending up in Venezuela after his break from Devil's Island. The Venezuelan authorities, unsure what to do with him, sent Charrière to El Dorado, a remote jungle penal camp in the south-east of the country, where he spent over a year before being released into the community as a free man. He settled in Caracas, where he wrote his famous story. Charrière himself described the conditions at El Dorado as the roughest and most savagely inhuman he'd witnessed during his penal servitude. The situation hadn't improved much since his day by the look of it.

It seemed that every news programme I saw reported at least one story about violence and deaths in prisons. It was a major problem all over the country: ten die here, twenty-five there, fourteen in another place. Paul assured me that because Margarita was the 'pearl' of Venezuela, a tourist attraction, San Antonio was quite tame in comparison to the jails on the mainland. In those places, gang wars, riots, protests, killings and torture went on endlessly. Death tolls were high. 'Lucky old me,' I said to Paul, with a touch of sarcasm in my voice. 'Thank God I'm not in El Dorado then.'

Raquetas became less frequent because of the ceasefire, though inmates carried on killing one another over what seemed minor personal grievances. They were replaced with new prisoners every week, so it became a never-ending cycle. I still got into fights, mainly with new guys, macho types who mistakenly demanded my worldly goods; they received violence for their trouble. A great number of the locals began to call me '*Señor* No'! Most were crack heads who, although they had money to buy rocks, were loath to purchase matches and cigarettes to make ash for their pipes.

Days rolled into weeks. It was almost April when Mr Mellor visited, bringing letters and money from home and a little money and a few books from Prisoners Abroad. After the visit, I walked back to Paul's room to share the paperbacks and read my mail in privacy. Two letters were tucked inside one envelope, one from Chrissy, the other from Josie. I read them repeatedly. How precious those letters were to me.

I called home the next day to thank Chrissy for the letters and money. The 'public' telephone was situated in a small cubicle to the side of the main entrance. It rarely worked and was usually locked. On the days it did work, however, hordes of prisoners would fight and squabble outside it, nobody wanting to queue, people pushing to the front to join their friends. I paid 1,000 bolivares to the vigilante staffing the gate to allow me through. It then took an hour or more to make my way to the front of the queue. I called collect, as I did not have a phonecard; it was something I needed to get hold of. When I finally got through, I could barely hear anything, as half a dozen locals jabbered in my ear to hurry up. Using the phone at San Antonio was a nightmare.

Sam and I had now been incarcerated for three months. Our weekly visits had been amicable, and we were getting along considering the circumstances. Joe visited every couple of weeks or so laden with bags but never carrying the news we were so desperate to hear. Something should have happened by that stage and we were gradually losing hope of getting away.

A few days into April a young German guy by the name of Alexander was brought into pavilion four. Lost amongst the rabble, I befriended him immediately. He spoke good English and I considered him another ally. Alex found a spot in the large entranceway among the locals. There was nowhere else for him to go – the corridor where I slept was littered with bodies at night. To my left slept a quiet guy who went by the name of Jesus (pronounced *Hey-zu*). He never bothered anyone and I was lucky to have someone so mild mannered sleeping next to me. He was serving 12 months for stealing a car radio and was due to be released soon. I introduced Alex to the world of San Antonio. Being European, he had gone through the same horrors as Sam and I. It seemed strange that after only a couple of months I was guiding a newcomer. The Dutchman Eric had been right: I was getting used to it.

One morning a week later, Tammier and I were summoned to the dirección. People were there from the embassy. We were sent to a room at the end where we usually met with Mr Mellor. On entering the room, at first glance it looked very much like a consular visit. Sam and Sarina were chatting away amicably to a couple of smartly dressed men who spoke with slight cockney accents. They wore fastened ties, which seemed strangely official in the tropical heat. Two leather briefcases sat on a table nearby. My suspicions were aroused.

Sam greeted me. 'Hi, Frank. These men are from the embassy in Caracas.'

I shook their hands in turn, taking them in as I did so, that little voice telling me to be wary. 'You're not from the consulate,' I said accusingly.

They argued that they were, but I wasn't convinced. Sam stared at me in disbelief.

'Do you have any letters or money for us?' I continued.

They began to stumble.

'You're police, aren't you?'

They reddened slightly, and then finally admitted they belonged to a special drugs force and were working from the British embassy.

'C'mon, Sam,' I said, taking her hand and walking out of the room, 'we've got fuck all to say to them!'

Tammier and Sarina stayed behind. They must have had something to discuss was all I could think at the time, and it made me more wary of them. Sam and I chatted at the gate to the anexo for a few minutes until a vigilante let her through. I was furious at the men for abusing our trust in such a sly way. It wasn't just them: I was getting angrier as time went on. I was changing and I could see it clearly at odd moments, although there was nothing I could do to stop it. Sam had seen it too and mentioned it on several occasions. I'd become violent, mean and angry. Hateful, in fact. What was happening to me? It was a question I asked myself over and over.

San Antonio was the society in which I lived and breathed, a society that engaged in staggeringly abnormal behaviour. Outer chaos really does reflect inner turmoil. I was caught up in a storm and no matter how much I fought it collective negative energies overwhelmed and engulfed everyone, including me. Marcus Allen once said, 'Within our darkest moments our brightest treasures can be found.' Famous words of wisdom, yet I couldn't see any treasures at all from where I stood.

I arrived back in Paul's room in a foul mood. I was seething and told him what had gone on. Soon after, a guy named Pescado ('the Fish') came to the door selling a bottle of cough medicine. I'd seen him around; he was one of the many who bugged me constantly for money, matches and cigarettes. Thinking the medicine would come in handy at a future date, I paid Pescado 1,000 bolivares and thought no more about it. An hour later, I met up with Alex, who was wild with anger. Despite his vigilance, someone had stolen several things from his holdall.

'Was one of them a bottle of cough medicine?' I asked.

'Yes,' he replied. 'How did you know that?'

'Hang on a bit.' I returned a minute later and handed the bottle to an astonished Alex.

My back was up. I'd been conned out of 1,000 bolivares by a sneaky, thieving rat. It just wasn't my day, and it wasn't Pescado's either because an hour later he appeared at the door with more goodies in his hand. I tried my best to retrieve the 1,000 bolivares from him, but he made out he didn't understand. I screamed at him. Paul warned me to leave it be, but I ignored him and flew at Pescado. He didn't have time to react, my momentum taking us through the doorway and into the corridor. My hand tightened around his throat as his back slammed into the wall.

'*Darme mi mil!*' I yelled at him. It wasn't good Spanish, but he knew what I meant. His left hand dropped as if to go for his pocket. I followed his hand – the bastard was reaching for a knife. I dropped my hand slightly, pressed my thumb in the hollow of his throat and pushed with all my might. He went limp, eyes and mouth popping open, and it wasn't long before he began to lose consciousness. In a haze, I continued to squeeze the life out of someone I didn't even know, someone who'd cheated me out of just over a pound sterling.

Hands tugged at my shoulder. I turned my head and it was Paul. Something snapped inside me and I let go. Pescado dropped to the floor, gasping for air, crumpled up like a rag doll. I was still frenzied and kicked him for good measure. I noticed lots of people in the corridor, but no one was cheering. I turned and followed Paul to his room. Instantly, there were raised voices in the corridor.

Once inside, Paul said, 'Do you know what you've just done?'

'What have I done?' I asked, shaking my head free of anger.

He went on to tell me the guy I'd almost killed in the corridor was a cousin to Carlo Pino, the tattooed character with the red headband who'd brought me in on my first night. Pescado also had a highly placed brother in pavilion five. My temper had me in a fix, and I became worried because I'd have to sleep in the corridor that night.

Just then Ivor came bowling into the room, shouting, cursing and waving his arms theatrically. I got the idea it was about the trouble with Pescado. I sat like a frightened rabbit, startled into frozen stillness. Everyone was in awe of Ivor, myself included. After a minute, he ran out of steam. With Paul's help, I explained the full story of why I'd attacked Pescado, and as quickly he became quite calm about the whole thing. I was glad for Paul interpreting and backing me up. Without him, I would have been on a stretcher on my way to the hospital.

Ivor said he would see to it that there would be no retribution from anyone. True to his word, no one came near me that night, but it didn't stop the hateful glares as I settled down. I stayed awake for as long as I could, waiting, ready for anyone that came. No one did. Late in the night, fatigue got the better of me. I dreamt of being attacked, waking with a start just seconds before they called número.

I had no problem with numbers by this time and could stand anywhere in the line. After breakfast, Paul allowed me to sleep on his bed for a few hours while he did his thing outside. I dropped off within seconds. Pescado and his friends avoided me that day. In the afternoon, Paul introduced me to a dark-faced, dangerous-looking character named Peco. A bandage covered the whole of his right calf. Peco had been transferred back from a prison on the mainland after taking part in a blood strike. This is when prisoners gash their flesh open as a protest. Peco and Paul had been friends for years.

He had come with a story that Terry from the enfermeria had offered him 5,000 bolivares to stab me in the side. He knew Paul and I were friends, so wanted to inform us. I sat there aghast! Paul laughed. 'C'mon, we'll teach Terry a lesson.'

He explained what we were going to do, and Peco clapped his hands together with glee. Between us, we made it look like I had a bleeding wound on my side just above the waistline by soaking a piece of cotton wool in red oil paint and taping it to my side. By the time we'd finished, it looked very realistic indeed. It would fool anyone at a distance.

I dropped my T-shirt and made my way past the vigilante on the gate, Paul telling him I was wanted in the dirección. I went through to the enfermeria gate. Salazar and Flores were on duty, sitting at their table in deep conversation. Perfect!

'*Mira*! *Llama* Terry,' I shouted into the corridor.

'Terry, Terry,' a few locals shouted. He appeared a few seconds later and started to walk towards me.

'Don't you fucking come near me, you bastard,' I shouted, lifting my T-shirt quickly and pointing to the red mess underneath. 'This is down to you. I'm gonna get you sorted good, you twat,' I added, pointing at him through the bars. Terry's mouth dropped open.

I left him like that and made my way past Salazar and Flores, who looked at me curiously as I walked through the dirección gate. When I got back to Paul's room, I washed the mess off and told them it had gone well. Peco was delighted. He could now draw his 5,000 from Terry.

But that wasn't the end: we would have a bonus laugh out of it. An hour later, Salazar stormed through Paul's doorway, shotgun in hand. Flores was right behind him, towering menacingly. Salazar demanded to see underneath my T-shirt to which I obliged. Paul asked innocently what it was all about, acting dumb, with expressions to suit. Salazar said Terry had told him I'd been stabbed. It was rare for a foreigner to be stabbed, so he'd come over personally to check it out.

There was nothing for him to see. He went away disappointed and very angry. The outcome, we heard next day, was that Terry received two beats with a planilla for wasting Salazar's time. I had no idea why Terry wanted me stabbed; I'd done him no harm. Looking back, it may have been an order from Freddie, as I'd let him down. It could have been Paul and Peco dreaming the whole thing up. I never did find out.

The following week, Mr Mellor turned up at the main gate with our suitcases. They'd finally been sent from Caracas. He wouldn't come in, so we took each item out and placed it on the floor in front of two Guardia Nacional soldiers and awaited their approval. After a while, they lost interest, whereupon with a fleeting glance at Sam we put everything back. Clothes were thrown on top of a small portable radio cassette player, a set of binoculars, a pair of nine-inch kitchen scissors I'd brought along to make the waistcoats and a large, brown paper bag containing £1,000 worth of assorted pearls I'd bought at a wholesalers in Porlamar. They would have been worth many times that amount in England.

I was surprised to see everything intact. Sam was pleased to have extra clothing. I took the Samsonite back to Paul's room amid many stares from the locals: such a smart suitcase to them meant lots of nice, expensive gringo things for the taking. I showed Paul the radio. It functioned on 220 volts or batteries, whereas the system in the jail was 110 volts – would it work? Paul said he'd get round it. I placed my watch inside the case, closed it tight and spun the numbers, then pushed it under Paul's bed, where it would be safe.

Or so I thought.

The following Friday at midday, I returned from a visit with Sam. It was her birthday the next day and I'd given her a beautiful card I'd drawn. We'd enjoyed a pleasant hour and, feeling good, I walked into Paul's room smiling. He gave me a grim look. 'I think you'd better check your suitcase.' My smile faded.

He told me while he'd been waiting in the telephone queue, someone had snapped the lock on his door. Strangely, nothing of his was missing, but the case had been pulled out and was open. Paul was livid. Checking and sorting things out, a strong feeling of sadness overpowered my anger. They'd taken the pearls, an expensive pair of sunglasses, binoculars and scissors, but most upsetting of all was they'd taken my watch.

My daughter had bought it for my 42nd birthday. I was stunned for a minute or two, my head reeling with a mixture of emotions. At that moment, I hated everyone and everything. I wanted to find out who was responsible and maim them, but no one would tell me anything. I was the gringo.

I provoked an argument in the corridor that night; the guy only asked for a match. People looked on. They knew why I was so mad, but they kept the secret to themselves. I felt myself slipping deeper and deeper into the shadows. I withdrew from people for a while, preferring to sit on my own during the day. It became harder and harder to switch into a smile during my visits with Sam. Things became strained between us. I was disappointed with Paul, too. He'd said my things would be safe. I couldn't show my true feelings to Paul, though; I was still sharing his hospitality during the evenings. I became almost vicious with the locals, sometimes taking on the occasional knife fighter, although I still didn't carry one myself. If I had carried a knife, I would surely have used it, I was so angry.

During May, Mr Mellor visited with long-awaited letters and money from home. He brought me an old, battered guitar, as I'd told him during our last visit that I missed playing. It had been in his garage for years, he said. The bridge was broken and three of the strings were missing. I thanked him nevertheless, confident it could be repaired.

After reading the letters, I went over to the workshops to talk to a guy called Cardoso about the guitar. An accomplished woodworker, he ruled the roost in the workshops and made a steady living making chairs and tables and selling them through a contact on the outside. Always ready to help anyone, he gave advice and lent his tools out freely. A mild-mannered black giant, he shared a room next to Paul's and was serving 25 years for hacking his wife to pieces over a breakfast argument.

I had no problems with Cardoso. New strings were bought with his help through a vigilante and the guitar was ready and working within two weeks. It was my first treasure. I played it most nights to relax, always fearful that the soldiers would destroy it during one of their 'searches'.

Paul and I had run a length of single cable to a distribution box inside the evangelist church, the separate phase link giving us 220 volts. The bare wires were dangerous but, with care, we got the radio working. Among the myriad Latin music stations on the FM band, one shone like a star above the rest, playing Anglo-American rock music 24 hours a day. It was an absolute blessing. My second treasure.

At the end of May, the relative peace we'd been enjoying came to an abrupt end. A prisoner from pavilion five was shot and killed while visiting his cousin in pavilion one. The killer was one of Oscarlito's men. He'd provoked an argument out of nothing and shot the guy point-blank in the face, killing him instantly. Oscarlito wanted nothing but war between the two sides and vengeance on José and Ricardo for the attack on himself and his brother seven months previously.

Ivor was beside himself with rage. The killing had provoked things to the point of no return. Prisoners on our side were baying for blood. Ivor asked Hernandez for the killer. Hernandez tried to parley but wouldn't give up the troublemaker. Talks fell apart. White rags flying on the rooftops came down, and Ivor vowed there would be bloodshed.

The raqueta that followed the killing had been ferocious: everyone was beaten, kicked repeatedly, and prone naked bodies were used as stepping stones, the soldiers sometimes leaping from man to man. The pavilions were totally ransacked. Property was stolen and belongings destroyed. My radio had been thrown across the room but still worked, and by some miracle, my guitar was safe.

No-man's-land was once again out of bounds to everyone, with shots exchanged between the sides daily. The madness was back. Camaraderie grew amongst the prisoners of four and five – maybe because Ivor had given strict orders that we weren't to fight amongst ourselves on pain of death. If we wanted blood, he said, we would get it very soon.

People spent every available moment making new weapons, servicing others, sharpening knives and machetes. The noise of stone on metal filled the air. Ivor came into Paul's room one night and asked if Paul and I were going to join them in the attack on pavilions one, two and three. Paul bowed out graciously, saying he couldn't this time as his early release on *confinamiento* (compulsory residence) was due in the next few weeks and he couldn't risk it. Ivor looked across at me with raised eyebrows, as if to say, 'You owe me one,' daring me to back out too. It was payback time. What could I do? Although handy with my hands and feet, I had no idea how to fight with a knife or machete. After telling Ivor this, he replied, '*No problema.*' He would have somebody teach me.

The next day, my teacher turned out to be Ricardo. Using pieces of wood, he painstakingly went through moves with me for an hour or two each day in the yard. We weren't the only ones practising on the cancha. Scores of men were warming up for the battle ahead. I was filled with a mixture of dread and excitement. I got to know Ricardo quite well during those days of instruction. He was very serious about his teaching and extremely proficient with a knife. His pale European features, blond hair and sharp blue eyes, set him apart from his fellow countrymen, giving him a less threatening appearance. But Ricardo's fast hands did the talking and woe betide the man who crossed him. Macho types who had glared at me before nodded and smiled. This was the way to gain their acceptance and respect. They were drawing me in deeper and deeper.

After careful consideration, the machete became my weapon of choice. The two hidden in Paul's room turned out to be part of Ivor's cache, and he told me I was welcome to take one. I could see he was happy I was getting involved, but deep down I wasn't too sure about my feelings. Part of me still held on to peace and tranquillity. That side of me didn't want to go, but I'd gone so far it would have been impossible to back out.

That night, I sat and sharpened the machete with a stone; the wooden handle had long since been discarded in order to render it concealable. On Ricardo's instruction, I wrapped cloth around the hilt, then fashioned a loop into which I could slip my hand for better purchase. Paul could tell I was having misgivings. 'Stay on the edge and let the crazy fuckers go first and you'll be all right.' It sounded like good advice and I intended to heed it.

I hadn't told Sam about the attack. For one thing, it was top secret; for another, she would have gone crazy. She knew little about what really went on in the main jail. She heard the shooting and screaming and had been told about the raquetas, but there was no corporal punishment in the anexo and, although the living conditions were atrocious, the women were treated with respect. Searches in the anexo were infrequent and carried out in an orderly fashion. I'm not saying she had it easy; on the contrary, life was tough in there also. Many of the girls were female equivalents of the men, tough and violent. She surprised me by telling me she'd fought with a girl, punched and head-butted her, and said it had been a matter of instinct. I understood where she was coming from, but it saddened me. She'd met Paul's friend, Mirelle, after which she was left in peace.

The corridor was alive that night: guys reliving old fights and skirmishes, showing each other their moves. They were raring to go, laughing, joking, play-fighting, lunging and stabbing with their fingers. They were up for it, excited by it. So was I but in a different way. Although the thought of it was unnerving, it had now become a dare, a challenge to go through with it. In my early teens, I'd been in many battles between Mods and Rockers, but this was something else. I was 43, unfit and a long way from Rhyl beach. This was life or death. I struggled with these thoughts until I eventually fell asleep.

I awoke early, before dawn, and saw many were up and moving around. All weapons were hidden. We were to go after breakfast when the vigilantes had left the area. Somehow, my head cleared of worries and doubts. It wasn't talk any more, it was going to happen. For a second or two, I likened myself to a warrior, calm before the battle. In truth, I had one thing in mind: I was to run across a patch of ground, waving a machete like a savage, and try to kill someone. Then make it back so the soldiers could beat me up. Was I totally mad?

Número went uneventfully. Back inside, men gathered their weapons, putting them on show, proudly displaying their handiwork, while many tied strips of coloured cloth around their calves: a tribal sign that meant they'd killed before and were about to kill again. Breakfast came and went with its usual disorder: people squabbled, the vigilantes fired shots; nothing changed. I didn't eat breakfast, feeling it would spoil my clarity of mind. Ivor walked around like a born leader organising his men.

Within five minutes at least one hundred combatants from the pavilions congregated on the cancha. The array of weapons astounded me. People carried knives, machetes and chopos. Others held pistols and revolvers. Many brandished long hardwood sticks. Where the fuck did it all come from? Where the fuck did they hide it all?

I didn't have time to wait for an answer. '*VAMOS, CABALLEROS!*' came the cry from Ivor, as he took the lead down the side of pavilion five.

Others I knew were right behind him: José, Ricardo, Carlo Pino, Chivo Loco, Peco, even Pescado. Before breaking onto the open ground, Ivor gave a signal to someone behind me. I was positioned somewhere in the middle, my heart racing. The next moment, a barrage of shots rang out from the rooftops on our side. Fuck! I struggled for breath and trembled with anticipation. The bitter taste of bile bit at my throat.

The shots continued. Ivor ran forward into no-man's-land. Everyone followed. My adrenalin pumping, my head tingling, we squeezed through the buildings and fanned out on the run. We moved fast before the guard in the tower overlooking the cancha could alert the *comando*. I had a feeling he didn't even bother, preferring to watch the show from his ringside seat. With my heart in my mouth, I struggled to catch up with the others, gathering speed over broken grassland towards pavilion three. Shots still continued from our side, keeping the guys on the opposite roof busy and giving us cover.

In that instant, hordes of prisoners came out to meet us from all directions, and it appeared they were as well prepared as we were. My body took another jolt of adrenalin as we closed on each other. People on both sides opened up with their guns. The war cries began: screams and shrieks, some were even howling, their weapons glinting in the sunlight. I weaved over to the left flank to get away from flying bullets, the shooters concentrating mainly on each other. We were 20 yards away when the enemy swarmed through the broken fencing. People from both sides fell as bullets hit their mark. Nobody faltered. There was so much noise, men screamed and cursed as we clashed head-on.

I was screaming too, looking for a victim. And there he was, coming right at me with a foot–long knife. Working on pure instinct, I reversed my hold, with the blade facing outward, and swung the machete in front of me in a very fast criss–cross fashion, keeping him at arm's length as we circled each other for a few moments. The distinctive tat-tat-tat of a Fal echoed out from a nearby guard tower, slicing into the fray like a knife. My opponent was momentarily distracted. I took the opportunity and brought the machete down, glancing it across his upper arm. It wasn't a mortal blow by any stretch, but blood poured from the open wound.

The Fal rang out again, taking potshots at people in the crowd. In the distance came the low hum of the siren as it wound up. Everybody scattered, making their way back to their own pavilions. Weapons were discarded along the way, thrown into clumps of foliage. I did the same, knowing I would be subjected to a beat but wasn't about to invite another three lashes for the machete. Not many made it back in time. A mass of Guardia Nacional soldiers burst onto no–man's–land with shotguns booming and planillas flashing.

The soldiers ran amongst us like men possessed, beating everyone wildly with a fury I hadn't seen before. The shotguns this time weren't fired into the air, they were aimed at people's legs as they ran. Although riot pellets were being used, at close range the plastic tore away clothing and left open flesh wounds four inches in diameter.

As the crowd bottlenecked by pavilion five, I positioned myself behind and slightly to the left of a guy. We came out slowly onto the cancha. A soldier shot him in the lower thigh. Stray projectiles gave me a passing glance, taking the skin off both my shins. I hobbled on to the yard and was struck across my back by a blade. Somehow it didn't seem to hurt; I was too busy concentrating on the pain in my shins. I found a space, dropped to the ground and thanked God I was still alive.

Soldiers moved about, lashing out at people randomly. Laying face down, I took another beat on my backside. We lay prone on the yard for hours; it was almost midday by the time we sat naked in neat rows under the blistering hot sun. By then, every prisoner on the yard had been punished brutally in one way or another. Then silence as an officer walked through the ranks of naked prisoners giving his speech of admonition, striking people across the back occasionally. I made an important decision that day: I would do all I could to stop this brutality.

After cleaning up the mess in the pavilion, Paul was kept busy helping to sew wounds. He was quite an expert. I watched in fascination. Paul said there was always an abundance of suture kits. In a place where knife wounds were an everyday occurrence, I wasn't at all surprised.

Despite the wounds and beats, there was jubilation in the pavilion that night. Ivor had killed Hernandez with a shot to the head, José had shot and wounded Oscarlito, and Ricardo had stabbed someone in the chest twice. We'd lost a couple, with 20 or so wounded, and many of their men had fallen. Those with bullet wounds had been taken to Porlamar hospital after the raqueta and returned that evening. Men nursing their wounds swathed in blood-soaked bandages were everywhere. The air was electric. Many weapons had been lost, but those that mattered would soon be on the market again. Others were hidden and many more would be made.

Later that evening, I wrote a letter to the British ambassador at the embassy in Caracas. I went into great detail about the diabolical conditions and physical maltreatment by the guards and asked respectfully if there was anything they could do. I decided I would give it to Mr Mellor on his next visit. When that would be, I had no idea; his visits had become irregular of late.

The next day, Ivor took charge of the whole jail. He quickly organised his men and placed them strategically. Oscarlito must have had the luck of the devil: he was told to stop his nonsense or he and all his friends would die. It was that simple. The whole jail was open again, people coming and going as they chose. I smoked a joint that night to celebrate and slept like a top for the first time in months.

In early July, Paul received confirmation of his confinamiento benefit. He said he was off to live on the mainland, and then escape. He only had a month to serve in this hellhole. Confinamiento was a benefit not automatically given to foreigners, as they lacked the necessary documents and identity card to live in the community. Paul had paid several people quite substantial sums of money to arrange his release, along with all the paperwork needed. He was on his way and I would miss him. Paul promised me his room once he left. I accepted gratefully, but deep inside I wasn't sure I wanted the responsibility.

Still, that was a month away. I decided to wait and see.

# 7

# TO TOUCH AND HOLD

The following month brought a dramatic decrease in hostilities between the warring factions. They began to live peacefully. White rags tied to sticks fluttered in the breeze above the rooftops; the *garitas*, the lookout posts, were left unmanned. The heavy mood in the prison lifted noticeably.

Over a period of time, my drawing of Paul's son, displayed proudly above his bed in a frame made by Cardoso, attracted a lot of attention, prompting a few of the better-off prisoners to ask me to sketch for them. They were quite willing to pay my asking price of a carton of cigarettes, and I was more than willing to oblige. It worked out well because against my better judgement I broke my pledge and gave cigarettes away to people I trusted and those who didn't persistently bother me. In turn, new friendships had been brokered.

The prison calmed down so much that the *director* allowed a few women from the anexo to sit and sell wares they'd made or cooked outside the wall of the enfermeria on visiting days. It wasn't long before artisans on the men's side joined them. The talent came out of nowhere: men produced and sold intricate wooden carvings, bracelets and necklaces, and sculptures made from old tin cans; one even went round selling doughnuts!

Sam got on to this little twist right away. She began to make cuddly toys with materials bought outside the prison through a *vigilante*. Within a week, she'd acquired a little spot outside the *enfermeria* on visiting days. I wasn't quite ready to trade, but we sat and talked until a sharp-eyed *vigilante* spotted us and moved me on. After all, it wasn't *entre vista*, he quickly pointed out.

By the end of the following week, I'd sketched several drawings, pencilled from photos I'd received from home. Among them was a portrait of Simón Bolívar copied from a 500 bolivar note. As the country's saviour, pictures of him adorned walls in official buildings everywhere. I asked permission to speak to the *director*. He expressed interest in my work, but especially the drawing of Simón Bolívar, holding on to it longer than the rest. I knew he wanted it and realising I had a bargaining tool, told him he could keep the picture, that it was a *regalo* (gift). I asked permission to sell my talents on visiting days. He held the portrait at arm's length, scrutinised it for a moment or two and smiled. I was in business.

By that time, I'd acquired drawing pads, an assortment of pencils, a sharpener and a small, flat board to rest on my knees. Sam and I were soon enjoying each other's company for several hours each visiting day. Unfortunately, there was no shade where we sat. Sam loved the sunshine, but I'd always found the intense heat uncomfortable. While we chatted, I asked about Sal's partner Ana. Sam told me she had given birth to a baby boy named Franklyn. I shuddered to think what kind of environment the boy had been born into.

During July, with the prison open, Paul took me over to the other side – pavilions one, two and three – a couple of times to see his friends. I didn't relish the idea at first but being curious, I went along. Paul had spent two years in pavilion one before moving over to four. As we rounded pavilion five and stepped onto no-man's-land, an eerie feeling came over me: a shiver ran down my spine. Walking across, I pondered on how many people had died on that patch of ground over the years. Passing a broken chain-linked fence, I saw that from the outside the buildings looked as dilapidated as any other in the prison; however, inside the living quarters it was another story. Each pavilion housed over sixty men, with one tap and a toilet to service them. The electricity supply consisted of odd lengths of different coloured cable twisted and joined together, suspended in the air like a giant spider's web.

The pavilions resembled long-disused cattle pens and smelled like them too. Here and there, small areas were partitioned off with cleverly strung lengths of wire and bedsheets. The locals called these 'boogaloos' and for those who could afford the expense, it was the only form of privacy available. Eighty per cent of the prison population at San Antonio were hopeless crack addicts, vagrants and vagabonds, and every last bolivar they earned, stole or scrounged was spent on rocks. They wouldn't dream of spending money on a bedsheet to sleep in, let alone the four it needed to make a boogaloo, much preferring to smoke crack and sleep on bare concrete.

I'd experienced the drug, having tried it with Paul after a painful raqueta some months before. He'd mixed it with marijuana into what the locals called *rusos*, and the combination took me to a place inside myself that was so peaceful I wanted to stay there for ever. It wasn't too long before I found an excuse to smoke a 'special' after every raqueta; it became an easy way to escape pain and sorrow. After the skirmish some weeks before, I'd broken the habit, not wanting it to get the better of me: it was tough enough getting through each day without becoming a drug addict as well.

On my second visit, I was introduced to Ciro, an old friend of Paul's. When he'd entered the prison five years back, Paul had been sent to pavilion one, where Ciro had rescued him from murderous gangs. Ciro liked foreigners; he didn't call us gringos, preferring to use the word *extranjero*. Both laughed and joked about old times. By now I'd grasped bits of the local language, so I was able to join in their conversation here and there. My input of prison slang amused Ciro, causing his beaming, jolly, round face to explode into bursts of laughter. Short, grey, curly hair crowned his head, with grey bushy eyebrows above his shining eyes. A thick moustache topped his lips, which were set in a permanent smile. At first, it was difficult not to stare at Ciro because both his ears were horribly deformed and scarred, as though made of melted wax. But he was obviously accustomed to people's stares, as he appeared to pay no heed to mine.

Ciro was the main independent drug dealer on that side of the jail, giving commission to whoever ran things, which ensured prompt payment from his customers. He was well connected on the island and liked among the prisoners. His operation was smooth and ran like clockwork: vigilantes were paid off, and no one ever troubled or searched him. He was happy the jail was open and was already negotiating with Ivor to expand his business and extend his percentage. He lived in a very basic boogaloo, with knick-knacks here and there, a paint-tin cooker and a mattress on the floor. But in the corner sat a 20-inch colour television with remote. Once again, the total contrasts of the jail had me guessing. Outside the thin walls of his place, men slept on bare concrete floors with little more than their arms to rest their heads.

Still, it seemed to work. Ciro wasn't fazed by it. He took their money with a grin. There seemed to be something emanating from Ciro that made me smile: he didn't give a fuck and was happy whatever they threw at him. I liked his cavalier attitude. I didn't imagine at the time that he and I were to become good friends for years to come.

During that month, there were three raquetas. Even though white rags flew from pavilion rooftops, people continued to give vent to their personal grievances, which would inevitably lead to someone's death. Crack heads caught stealing from the wrong person would usually die for their addiction. It had been quiet for so long that gunfire was unusual, except when vigilantes restored order at meal-times. In my opinion, the odd raqueta seemed worse, because it came so unexpectedly. The calm breaks in between meant no one knew when it was going to happen, they just knew it would. It was a nerve-wracking time.

Once I was actually on the phone talking to Chrissy. It had taken a maddening hour and a half in the hot sun to get to the front of the queue. We'd only been talking a matter of seconds when shots rang out, echoing around the buildings, followed by a barrage of shotgun blasts, their distinctive boom that of the vigilantes. My senses fired up immediately. Chrissy heard the shots quite clearly over the phone.

'What's going on there, Frank?' she asked, her voice barely audible as shots and then the hum of the winding siren filled the air.

'Oh no!' I bawled into the receiver.

'What?' she shouted.

'Oh fucking hell no, not now!'

'What's happening to you there?' she asked, panic rising in her voice.

'Raqueta,' I shouted out. 'I've got to go . . . I hate this fucking madhouse.'

I turned to a see a ranting soldier delivering a blow to my shins. The receiver fell from my hand as the boot struck my arse for good measure. I ran, forgetting everything, through the gate and down the path, soldiers all around. Boom! Whack! Boom! Whack! I took two beats that time, all for being in the wrong place at the wrong time. I remembered the time I thought I'd cry like a baby after two beats. I didn't cry. I hadn't cried for a long time. I'd become hardened like the rest.

Paul was released in the first week of August. Friends on the mainland had arranged a job, and many people came out to see him off. He was a very popular guy. His face glowed with happiness, and I felt a little envious. What a feeling it must have been to be leaving that awful place. In no way did I begrudge his freedom. If he could walk away unscathed, after more than five and a half years in that brutal environment, he had my total respect. The moment came, the door opened and we shook hands.

'*À bientôt!*' I said.

'I hope not,' came his reply with a laugh, as the steel door slammed shut behind him. He was gone. Lucky Paul.

I went back to my new home, closed the door and sat alone with my thoughts. I had mixed feelings about taking on the room. There were downsides: the devastation after raquetas and the responsibility for weapons hidden; people in and out all day using the fridge, others borrowing pots and pans, never returning them; and the endless stream of toilet users and scroungers. However, it was a base; somewhere I could close out the noise of the night and be alone with my thoughts.

A couple of days later, Ricardo came to see me. We'd become quite good friends since I'd been his pupil out on the yard and even with the language barrier we understood each other perfectly. He asked if he could share my room – it would be somewhere private where he could be with his wife on visiting days. I agreed without a second thought. The next day, he acquired a springless tubular frame for a bunk bed and we spent the day fixing it up with planks of wood courtesy of Cardoso.

By evening número, I had a new room-mate – and not just any old room-mate but the man third from the top in the prison hierarchy. It put a different slant on my life in the jail. I received nods of respect wherever I went. Ricardo moving in with me meant an unspoken protection order: no one was to hassle me.

I met Ricardo's wife, Carla, the next visiting day and spent an hour in their company before leaving to sit with Sam outside the enfermeria. Carla spoke excellent English. I was quite amazed, as Ricardo had never mentioned it to me. She worked in the tourist industry in Porlamar and promised to bring me an English–Spanish dictionary the following week to help improve my grasp on the language. I was touched, warming to her as I had done to Ricardo. They had a young child, a boy named Enrico, and as a goodwill gesture I drew his portrait, which then took pride of place on the wall in our room. Ricardo rarely slept in there. Every night at eight, he would pull his mattress and sheet off the bed and carry them into the corridor, where he spent the evenings with his *paisanos*, falling asleep wherever he happened to be. The arrangement suited me.

Ivor and José came in to watch the TV and get stoned, which was fine as we got on famously. One of Ivor's soldiers often brought in food, and on those occasions I always received a plateful. It made no odds that they were noted desperados and ruled the jail with such ruthlessness. They were on a higher mental level than the rest and that made the difference.

Now and again, Ivor made rusos. I declined at first, remembering the addictive euphoria I'd felt on the occasions I'd smoked with Paul. Those had been extremely painful and stressful times; now, I possessed a room, a bed and somewhere to wash and cook. Of course, there was always the stress of living in such deplorable conditions thousands of miles from home, but I read books endlessly, played my guitar and drew pictures. However, eventually, I thought what the hell, took a joint one night and it became routine.

Late one evening in early September, Mike 'the American' was brought to pavilion four. I could hear the commotion and went to investigate. He stood in the entrance, visibly shaken, clutching his holdall, surrounded by the flotsam. Waving them aside, I took him to my room and made a strong brew of coffee. He eventually calmed down enough to talk. Mike was from Florida. He'd been arrested at the airport with fifteen kilos of coke in his suitcase two weeks earlier. He had the same tales of El Cinco and Los Cocos. They'd thrown him in amongst the crazies. 'Goddamned monkeys!' he said in his southern drawl. I smiled inwardly, thinking back to Eric the Dutchman.

The word 'monkey' sprang to mind on many occasions in San Antonio. I am not a racist or a bigot, but there was a vast array of prisoners there – some educated but mostly not; some simple, others bright; some well dressed, others in rags – and the majority were basically jungle people: savages who spent their time waving their arms around and screaming at each other. They dressed in cast-offs and walked barefoot, used bits of cardboard from the rubbish dump to collect their rancho food and squatted down in tight circles to eat with filthy hands, swarms of flies buzzing around their unwashed bodies. They smoked crack endlessly, yet it was amazing that amongst the squalor and drug abuse they never fell ill. They were immune to it all. They even drank the muddy water that came out of the taps. I drank it once unboiled and suffered from diarrhoea for three whole days.

I invited Mike to bed down on the floor for a while until he found his feet. Ricardo OK'd it, so long as it wasn't a permanent arrangement. I fully agreed.

I was now looking after food parcels for Chino, who slipped them through the window each morning. I became a cog in the mechanism of things: Chino collecting the parcels later in the day to distribute among his customers. There was always a little something for me at the end of each day for my trouble.

Mike didn't care too much to mingle with the population, but I insisted, as he'd never get anywhere sitting in the room every day. I took him around the place a few times and during one walk introduced him to Cardoso, who offered a third share in his room for a mere 50,000 bolivares. On his fourth week, Mike's consul brought letters and money from his family, and the next day he bought a share in the room next door with Cardoso and his room-mate Victor. Victor was a strange rodent of a man, who was rarely seen and never heard, being friends with few people. He worked in the kitchens but did no favours for anyone except himself, selling the odd food parcel to feed his crack habit. Nobody liked him.

I saw Sal regularly; he'd organised daily five-a-side soccer matches on the cancha. The games generated a huge following, especially among the gamblers, of which there were many. Ciro, who never missed a moneymaking opportunity, came over to take bets. The Latinos loved soccer, and Sal was truly a remarkable sight, running rings around everyone. Pavilion four adored him, and he bathed in the glory every time he scored and the locals erupted with pleasure.

I watched on many occasions with Alexander, but he became busy when two more Germans arrived. They bought a room after Ivor ejected the occupants. Harald was a blond-haired gangster pimp from Berlin, well muscled and always ready for a fight. He'd be OK. Irwin, on the other hand, was a mild-mannered guy, balding, middle-aged and quiet, who wouldn't hurt a fly. I remember thinking, what strange partners in crime.

In the middle of September, a rumour spread that we were to have a party on the cancha in front of pavilion one to celebrate an important holy day. All over the country in towns and cities people would be in the streets partying. Ivor had organised it with the *director*. Lots of money had changed hands to fix the event, and even the girls from the anexo were allowed to participate. I thought it just a cruel joke at the time and dismissed it from my mind, but people kept talking about it. Sure enough, the next day a huge PA system was wheeled through the main gate and up through the dirección. Sometime later, speakers boomed into life. I still couldn't believe it. Then at ten o'clock, the internal gates were opened and everyone made their way over to the sound of loud salsa music. It was early, with the sun beating down, and the question on everyone's lips was where were the girls?

Sitting on a small wall in front of pavilion one, I rested back on a wire fence, struggling to take it all in. Not so long ago, these guys had been at each other's throats, stabbing and shooting, and now they chatted and partied together. To a resounding cheer, along came the women, flanked by four female vigilantes. They entered through the linked gate. It was apparent the girls had made an effort. Sam came towards me, her long, silky hair moving from side to side as she walked. My heart stopped for a moment; everything around me ceased to exist as I took in her deeply tanned legs, white blouse and black leather miniskirt. We kissed and held each other tightly, lost in the feel of each other, squeezing tighter still as pent-up emotions came to the surface. Eventually, we parted, sat on the wall and wrapped our arms around each other. Many guys began to stare at Sam and made comments. I stared back, but she took no notice. Soon we were immersed in each other, stupefied that we were actually at a party in the middle of hell.

Sarina came over for a few minutes, Ana too with her new baby boy Franklyn. Such innocence, I thought, as I held the child's tiny hand. Ivor also walked over and I introduced him to Sam. He was delighted and passed me a Coca-Cola can. Without thinking, I put it to my mouth and took a gulp, neat whisky burning my mouth and throat. The unexpected taste almost made me choke. With a gentle warmth spreading inside my head, I passed the can to Sam. She had taken a swig or two when I spotted a female vigilante rise from her seat and make her way over. She walked up to Sam and without a word snatched the can from her hand, sniffed it, gave Ivor a withering look and walked off, taking our whisky with her. As she sat, the vigilante looked around and began to sip from the can. I pulled a face at Ivor, he just burst out laughing. '*Hay más!*' was all he said – there was more! He walked away chuckling. Sam and I fell about, while the vigilante sat and glared but continued to sip.

Men and women danced on the cancha, loud music filled the air, echoing in the confined space, and most people were high on drink or drugs. Even vigilantes, sitting in pairs around the courtyard, joined in. I thought how weird it was to be so happy, knowing how much pain and suffering had been dealt out on that very same yard. It was another mind-boggling contrast. It was fantastic to be together, but we just couldn't switch into party mode like the locals. The day went quickly as good times always do.

At three o'clock, the girls were ordered back to the anexo. It was a sad moment. To be able to touch and hold each other after so long and kiss without admonition had been surreal. Sam and I had spoken of our predicament and resigned ourselves to the fact that realistically we weren't going to get away, not now, not after so long. We had been incarcerated for nine months and Joe's visits had been scarce lately. We said goodbye, and I watched quietly as Sam joined the crowd of women and disappeared through the dirección gates.

I looked at the ground, breathing deeply, then up at the clear, blue sky, maybe searching for divine help. My heart was heavy. The party continued and, letting out a deep sigh, I made my way back. It had been like a dream – maybe I dreamt the whole thing after all.

Another month went by reasonably quietly. There were always fights, that was the norm, but the death rate in the jail was down to one a week. Mike settled into Cardoso's room, and we spent a lot of time together. He'd played in rock bands in the '60s, so we had a common interest in playing guitar. Appalled at the conditions, he made notes every day until it became an obsession.

'I'm gonna write a book about all this,' he said one day.

'You ain't seen nothin' yet, pardner,' I replied in my best American accent. The soldiers had been well behaved since his arrival; he hadn't had the misfortune of running the gauntlet yet – but it wouldn't be very long before he had plenty to write about.

In some ways, the 'open' prison wasn't such a good idea: it invited many undesirables over to our side, begging and stealing. On one occasion, I was returning to my room after a particularly enraging hour spent in the telephone queue – I hadn't been able to make the call because vigilantes had scattered everyone with their shotguns after a fight broke out – when I passed Mike's open doorway and saw a troubled frown on his face. In front of him, with his back to me, stood a local, someone I didn't know, waving his arms in Mike's face. I moved closer to see what was happening and, sure enough, the guy was hassling him for money. This guy wore only tatty shorts, his back and shoulders criss-crossed with old lash wounds. He turned slightly and I saw his chest and arms were also heavily scarred, along with his black Indian face, which was hideous to look at with the gaps in his rotten teeth.

I adopted prison slang. '*Que virga es chico?*' I asked, which meant, more or less, what the fuck do you want, boy? His eyes glazed over – he was as high as a kite – and he pushed me roughly. I wasn't balanced and stumbled back, hitting the wall of the shower cubicle.

I was up and moving as he turned fully. I aimed a fast, hard jab at his throat; he moved slightly and I missed the mark. My punch, however, hit him square in the mouth, I felt his teeth rattle with the force. His lip burst open and he went down in a heap. My hand throbbed where it had connected; it felt like I'd hit a rock. He was only on the ground a second or two before he scrambled up and pushed past me.

'Thanks, man,' said Mike. 'Did you see the state of that ugly fucker?'

I nodded. I'd seen him all right, and I was to see him again sooner than I thought. Mike set the water to boil, and I decided to stay for a drink, to calm down and enjoy a good conversation. Scarface appeared in the doorway within minutes.

Without exaggeration, he looked like everybody's worst nightmare. I sat stunned for a moment, taking in the fierce face, his eyes ablaze; red froth spluttered from his bloody mouth while he pointed a foot-long home-made knife at me, shouting, '*Te voy a matar gringo!*'

My blood ran cold – wrapped around his calf was a strip of red cloth, the sign of a killer. He continued to shout obscenities from the doorway, inviting me into the corridor, goading me to fight with him. There was no way I was going to take him on with that knife. My heart raced, but I was also getting angry. The one remaining machete blade in my room was way out of reach.

'What have you got, Mike?' I asked quickly. He looked at me dumbstruck. 'A tool! A weapon!' I shouted.

'We got this,' he said, pulling a yard-long hardwood club from behind his bed. It resembled a pickaxe handle. It would have to do. I could maybe stand him off until he cooled down.

Jumping up, I snatched the club from Mike's outstretched hand and made for the door. My aggressor backed out into the corridor. I was genuinely frightened for my life; this creature from hell really wanted to kill me. Entering the corridor, everything became sharper and clearer as instinct took over. He fell silent for a moment, then slowly and deliberately said aloud, 'I'm going to kill you, *gringo* cocksucker *coño de tu madre!*'

What was that he said about my mother? Seeing red, my hackles rose. He could get away with calling me a cocksucker, but 'the cunt of my mother' was something else. Who's this fucking monkey to insult my mother? 'What did you say?' I screamed at him, gripping the club tighter, raising it up.

Lunging towards me, he shouted, '*Coño de tu madre!*'

Luck was with me. The club was in the right position, and I brought it down a glancing blow across the knuckles of his knife hand as he raised it to stab me. He didn't drop the knife but backed off again, weighed me up, and shook his head. I kept the stick upright, a voice in my head telling me to take advantage of his hesitation. In two quick movements, I struck him in the chest with the butt of the club, then swung the stick in an arc, crashing it down on his knife hand with such force I heard bones breaking. The knife fell, clattering on the concrete floor. The words 'cunt of my mother' went around and around in my head. I struck him repeatedly about his head, arms and back. It took a while for him to go down, but eventually he fell to the floor unconscious. I kicked him once and spat on him for the benefit of the spectators. They loved that sort of thing; it would be all over the jail within minutes.

'*El Santo Loco*!' said one or two who knew him. They said it with such awe I began to wonder who the hell this guy was. Crazy Saint? I handed Mike the club.

'Fucking monkey,' I panted.

I went to my room and pushed the door closed, took out the machete blade from its hiding place and placed it on my bed for easy reach. I would kill him if he came back, there was nothing surer in my mind at that moment such was my rage. Just then, the door flew open with a bang. I was so startled I reached for the machete, instinctively sweeping it in an arc with my right hand. As I turned, the blade rising, José stopped in his tracks and raised his hands in the air. '*Hepa!*' he said, with a big grin.

I dropped the blade on the bed with a huge, audible sigh. Behind José stood Ricardo and Ivor. Between them they told me who I'd beaten senseless out in the corridor. Santo Loco turned out to be one of Oscarlito's gang and very likely on a spying mission when he'd decided to do some foraging on his own. He would probably get a pistol-whipping from Oscarlito for going back beaten up.

'*Pana mio*,' said José, holding out his hand. It meant I was his good friend. I took his hand and we shook firmly. There was a fiery look of camaraderie in his eyes and I found myself returning the look, and meaning it.

'*Pana mio*,' said Ricardo. We shook, his piercing blue eyes searching mine for doubts. He saw none.

'*Alto pana mio!*' shouted Ivor, taking my hand firmly in his, holding on tightly and guffawing with laughter. It meant I was his best friend. Before long, we were all laughing. Through the laughter, a little thought entered my head: why was I being so jolly when I'd just put myself on Oscarlito's hit list?

# 8

# BITTER BLOWS

Late November brought the first raqueta in months after two prisoners died from gunshot wounds during an internal gang fight in pavilion three. It had nothing to do with our side but as usual everyone paid. Making up for the quiet period, the soldiers made a meal of it, preceded by the vigilantes, who locked us in the pavilions, letting everyone sweat for ten minutes before running the gauntlet. Those ten minutes were nerve-wracking. It had been quiet for so long it was almost like starting all over again. I double-checked to make sure things were well hidden. Mike appeared at my door in a state of panic and asked with concern, 'What's going on?' I'd already enlightened him when he first arrived, though it was impossible to explain the pain and mayhem of a raqueta in words alone.

'Stay with me, do as I do and do it quickly,' was all I had time to say as the siren began its low hum.

By the time it reached wailing pitch, shouts came from lookouts positioned at the window slats: '*Agua verde! Agua verde!*' Seconds later, the steel door to our pavilion flew open with a bang. I held Mike back until the crush eased slightly. Listening to the deafening noise of shotguns and the sounds of blades hitting flesh, his face took on a look of sheer terror.

Squeezing through the doorway, I shouted, 'Now! Run like fuck,

Mike, but stick with me, OK?' He was visibly unnerved, shaking, but he wasn't on his own; my heart was pounding too. I knew what was in store.

Running through the screaming soldiers, Mike stuck to me like glue. But by keeping us locked up, the soldiers had had time to position themselves well and the odds of escaping a beating were extremely low. It appeared there were more soldiers than ever before, each hell-bent on inflicting pain. Yards ahead, Alex's body jerked as he received a beat across his back. Mike and I, running in much the same line, found no escape, each receiving a beat as we neared the cancha. I'd learned a trick from Paul: to get in the right place on the yard before dropping to the ground. It saved running around in confusion when it came time to form rows.

'Man, that fuckin' hurts!' Mike said as we lay face down next to each other on the concrete.

'Keep your fucking mouth shut,' I hissed, 'or you'll get us another beat.'

The soldiers were particularly cruel, beating, kicking and trampling on us with their heavy boots. Many weapons were found in the pavilions, and after a couple of hours we were herded back inside and locked up for the rest of the day. I brought out the trusty aloe leaf and gave Mike a smear to ease the pain on his backside. He'd taken a kick in the ribs too. I had a feeling of déjà vu, remembering back to the time Paul had first introduced the aloe's healing properties to me. Mike was in a mess. He was quite a few years older than me, unfit and overweight, and the day had more than taken its toll on him. Within minutes, his breathing became laboured, then suddenly he doubled up in pain and collapsed in a heap at my feet. Struggling for breath, with both his hands clenched tight across his chest, he managed to gasp, 'It's my heart!'

I panicked. I wasn't a doctor, and I hadn't a clue how to deal with someone having a heart attack. Placing a pillow under his head, I ran to the pavilion door, picked up the rock that lay there for such occasions and started to bang the door frantically.

'*Que paso?*' asked one of the locals.

'*Toma!*' I replied, handing him the rock. '*Toca la puerta*,' I emphasised, telling him to bang repeatedly until the vigilante came. His half-cocked head gestured that he hadn't understood my meaning or hadn't wanted to. This was no time to argue: the half pack of cigarettes placed into his outstretched hand prompted him to strike the door furiously. I ran back to the room to find Ricardo crouched next to Mike.

'*Que tiene?*' he asked.

'*Ataque del corazón*,' I replied, still out of breath with panic.

'*Virga!*' he exclaimed, dashing to the door, shouting, '*Miren, llaman el médico!*'

A few minutes later, a vigilante showed and the door flew open; it was Terry's sidekick, Gargo. I pleaded with him to call an ambulance for Mike. He didn't seem very enthusiastic until the obligatory 10,000 bolivar note was shoved in his greedy hand, and it wasn't too long before two dirección orderlies turned up and wheeled Mike off on a stretcher. I watched him leave, praying inwardly he'd be OK. We heard no more until later in the evening when he returned and walked into the pavilion under his own steam. It had taken 20 minutes for the ambulance to arrive, and Mike said he'd almost recovered by that time. They'd taken him to the hospital in Porlamar, where he'd been administered a drip for several hours before being driven back by a vigilante.

I let out a deep sigh, thankful he was OK. 'Don't do that again, man!' I said, choking with emotion. 'I thought you were going to die right there in my arms.'

He told me he'd suffered from a heart condition for several years but hadn't taken any medication since his arrest. He would call his consul and arrange for tablets to be sent. I was worried for him: San Antonio certainly was not the place to be with a heart condition; he could easily have died. But then it wasn't the place to be with any condition.

While it had been relatively quiet in San Antonio, the TV news had shown many incidents in other prisons. In August, 29 prisoners died and numerous others were injured in a reported riot in the

Casa Amarilla at El Dorado. Overcrowding and grossly unhygienic conditions in prisons throughout the country prompted the spread of tuberculosis and cholera, and thousands of inmates had been affected. In October, hundreds of prisoners at La Planta, a notoriously violent jail in Caracas, went on hunger strike demanding improved prison conditions and an end to systematic beatings and torture by prison guards. Several died as a result.

Nothing changed. Only that month, 16 prisoners had died and another 32 were seriously injured in a fire at Sabaneta prison in Maricaibo. Prison guards had been accused of starting the blaze. The television coverage, always uncensored, showed grotesquely burned bodies being dumped unceremoniously in piles to await removal. Paul had been right. San Antonio, although a brutal and violent place in its own right, was a boy's camp compared to jails on the mainland. In a sick way, I considered myself lucky to be where I was.

In early December, two more inmates died in a gunfight between rival gangs from pavilions two and five. Despite his vigilance, Ivor was powerless to stop those spontaneous clashes. Soldiers came in and beat everyone again. Mike and I escaped lightly this time with one lash each.

A new *teniente* (lieutenant) was now in charge of the raquetas, a sadistic son of a bitch called 'Jiminez'. He was feared and hated by everyone, as he loved to dish out punishment with his planilla. The man was the devil himself.

After morning número on 10 December, a dirección runner told me that Sam and I were to face the court that morning. It was exactly one year to the day of our arrest. A year of our lives had disappeared in that awful place. Joe hadn't visited for months, my friends' promises had faded to nothing, and it looked like we were on our own. Tammier and Sarina had been to court the month before and were sentenced to ten years each. Sam and I resigned ourselves that we'd receive the same.

Eight were heading for the *tribunal* that day, five men and three women. Outside the jail stood an old American school bus to transport us to Porlamar. Men and women were kept apart, each handcuffed separately with hands behind our backs making it impossible to sit comfortably. Four armed soldiers and two vigilantes accompanied us. A vigilante drove the bus, which rattled and shook all the way. It had certainly seen better days. I was surprised it got us there at all.

Inside the courthouse, Sam and I were locked in separate holding cells. An hour or so later, we were taken to the small office where we'd seen the judge's secretary almost a year before. Nothing had changed, the room was still bursting at the seams with files and paperwork. The same secretary sat behind the same cluttered desk. Her dress sense hadn't improved, but we weren't smiling this time.

There was no ceremony. We were informed by the judge's secretary that we had both been sentenced to ten years. Even though we'd been expecting it, the news came like a bolt out of the blue. Sam and I looked at each other for a moment, then turned to face the secretary. She must have thought we hadn't understood because she held out her hands in front of her, fingers and thumbs outstretched. '*Diez años*,' she said without compassion. We hadn't even seen the judge, and there was no sign of our lawyer, Pablo Diaz. We'd had one ten-minute visit from him at San Antonio some months back. He'd done a fantastic job of representing us, I thought bitterly.

It was official. Ten years each. There was no one to speak to and no one to appeal to. We were taken back to our respective holding cells for the rest of the day. I sat and mulled over the future, and what would become of us. My head was spinning. I wasn't too sure that I could keep my sanity for much longer.

I don't remember much about the ride back, all clear thoughts obscured by the bitterness I felt towards the whole wretched system. Inside the jail, Sam and I parted in low spirits. I returned to my room and closed the door, hoping to shut out the world for ever. It was impossible. The few people I'd befriended were eager to hear my news. José and Ricardo were the first. They'd been sentenced a month before to ten years each. Throughout the rest of the day, I received a steady flow of visitors. Mike, Franz, Cornelius, Sal, Ivor,

Chivo Loco too, all bearing commiserations. Even Ciro came across, bringing a bag of marijuana to help soften the blow. I smoked myself into a stupor that night and all the next day; it helped to nullify the overwhelming despair I felt.

By the third day, I was just about getting used to the idea when Mr Mellor turned up. He'd asked to speak to me specifically and not the others, which I thought was rather odd. When we were alone, he broke the news that my father had died of a heart attack three days previously on 10 December, the very day Sam and I had been sentenced. I sat stunned, unable to take it in. It felt like someone had punched me in the stomach. I choked up as tears filled my eyes and felt the sudden need to be on my own. I couldn't sit with Mr Mellor any longer, I had to go. I thanked him for coming, composed myself and went back to my room.

My head was shot to pieces. This time my friends left me alone with my grief. I withdrew into myself for the next few days. Sorrow turned into anger, making me lash out at the slightest thing. I went to the phone to call Chrissy and thank her for informing the embassy; instead, I got into a fight outside the phone box with a big mouthy type from pavilion five who pushed in front of me. I beat him senseless; he was an excuse to vent my anger at the world. A vigilante came along and locked the phone. I wasn't very popular with the locals that day, but I didn't care. For several days, I went out of my way to provoke fights with anyone who crossed me.

One night, Ivor came to see me. He told me he understood how I felt, but it was time to stop: enough was enough, people were complaining about my attitude. The fact I was Ricardo's room-mate wouldn't save me if I carried on, he said. It was what I needed. I snapped out of my mood. We smoked a ruso together and watched a quiz show on the television; in fact, it was the Venezuelan version of *Who Wants to be a Millionaire?* I slept well that night and woke with a clear head.

Christmas would soon be upon us, and with three visiting days in a row, Sam and I saw quite a lot of each other. The shock of our sentences had worn off and I was accepting my father's death somewhat. My birthday came and went; nobody except Sam knew, and I preferred to keep it that way.

Late January brought about a complete change in San Antonio – one that would have dramatic consequences. A new *director* was appointed, though he was rarely there, leaving the day-to-day running of the place to 'Vasquez', one of his men. The man was a tyrant. He immediately put a stop to prisoners, male and female, sitting outside the enfermeria on visiting days. All internal gates were closed and manned by vigilantes, who let visitors in and out as and when they needed to pass. Vasquez didn't give an inch. If a prisoner was stabbed or injured, the whole population of the jail was locked up for the rest of the day. At the first sign of any shooting, he would set off the siren and bring in the soldiers. His tyranny provoked much unrest amongst the prisoners. He was an obnoxious character and very unapproachable. Even the vigilantes disliked him.

Vasquez and the teniente, Jiminez, were often seen together. They were a loathsome pair who conspired to make life for the prisoners as difficult as possible. It wasn't long before strip searches for visitors were implemented. It slowed things down immensely, some visitors not entering until ten or eleven, sometimes later. The prisoners soon became enraged: with no one else to vent their anger on, the atmosphere in the jail became more hostile than ever before. It surprised me that Sam and I were still allowed our visits on Fridays; though sometimes we missed out because of the regular lock-ups and raquetas.

The population became very restless – whether the tactics implemented by Vasquez were meant to cause tension, no one knew, but they certainly did. Fights broke out continuously in our pavilion resulting in at least one person being carried out every week. Raquetas, too, became a weekly occurrence. Soon, I was marked all over.

During a visit from a temporary consul in February, Tammier and I took off our shirts, dropped our pants and showed her the marks on our bodies. She made an official note but said she was powerless to do anything. She would of course write a strong letter to the

Ministry of Justice complaining of the barbaric treatment to British nationals but that was all she could do. A fat lot of use that would be, I thought.

In the same month, two wealthy Colombian couples were brought into the jail – just to prove that money does talk, the two men moved into the doctor's surgery to the side of the salón and used it as their living quarters. Their womenfolk took over a large room behind the female vigilantes' quarters in the anexo. The men spent most of their days on our side, gave out money and cigarettes freely and for fun organised boxing matches amongst prisoners, offering substantial sums of money to the victors. A shallow pit of ring size was dug out behind the wall to the side of our gate to contain the fighters. Even gloves were bought from the street to make the bouts look more realistic.

Ivor was beside himself with glee and although he was too good a boxer to compete, he made an excellent MC. The gamblers loved it. Huge crowds would gather and Ciro, who always grabbed the moment, came over regularly to take bets. Even the vigilantes came to watch and gamble. Men would beat each other senseless for the prize money. It couldn't last. It wasn't long before Vasquez found out about the fights and put a stop to them. He couldn't bear to see the men having fun of any kind.

One Friday morning in May, while waiting for Sam by the salón, I saw a sole prisoner escorted in under heavy guard, with at least half a dozen soldiers surrounding him. After an exchange of paperwork, he was handed over to Salazar, who in turn ordered him to the *máxima* with an escort of four armed vigilantes. I'd never seen that kind of security before and became curious, taking him to be an extremely dangerous prisoner.

Sam and I had barely finished our visit when the siren went off. I managed to run back to our side just as the soldiers came in. Again, it was a painful raqueta, and we were locked up for the rest of the day. News soon filtered through that the prisoner I'd seen being brought in was a child rapist. The abused girl's uncle was head honcho in the máxima, a place where uncontrollable prisoners were kept apart from the population. Inside the máxima, they'd raped him repeatedly, stabbed him a dozen times and hung him by the neck from a window slat. He hadn't lasted an hour. Child abusers were not tolerated amongst the prison fraternity. It had been a set-up: Salazar had knowingly sent the man to his death. On hearing the news, I decided it had been worth the pain that day.

Slowly, the weeks rolled by. The raquetas became so frequent they seemed to merge into one another. Jiminez was in his element. I began to smoke rusos more often, the drugs getting the better of me. It was such an easy escape route to take.

In June, I managed to phone Chrissy only to hear that my younger brother had died from a brain haemorrhage, aged 26. It had happened three weeks previously. She'd phoned the embassy, but no one had informed me. I replaced the receiver with a trembling hand, absolutely devastated. Once more, I withdrew into myself, smoking more drugs, losing control.

In July, two Danish guys, Peter and Mads, arrived in pavilion four. Both spoke excellent English, and we made friends immediately. Mads said the first person he saw on entering was Valdomero. He made them wonder where the hell they'd been brought to.

Two weeks after their arrival, Mads was peppered with plastic during a raqueta. They left his left side in a mass of red weals. The Danish consul was quickly on the scene and wasted no time, complaining vehemently to the Ministry of Justice. The official report given by prison authorities stated the soldier fired into the air and the pellets had landed on Mads from above. Incredible, but true. The Guardia Nacional could get away with anything they wished. They were untouchable.

By then, there were a number of foreigners in pavilion four. Our respective embassies complained bitterly to the authorities in Caracas, all to no avail; if anything, this enflamed the soldiers even more. Obviously, Jiminez had heard of our complaints and advised his henchmen accordingly. Although he didn't beat any foreigners personally – he was too clever for that – he beat the locals with gusto.

In the first week of August, Ivor gathered signatures on a petition to get rid of Vasquez. Every prisoner to a man signed the papers. I have no idea how Ivor got the petition to the right people or why notice was taken of it, if at all, but within two weeks Vasquez was gone. He had been transferred to El Dorado.

A new prison had been built in El Dorado alongside the notorious Casa Amarilla to house 2,000 men, and there was a rumour that sentenced prisoners from all over the country were to be shipped there over the months to come. This was not welcome news. A new official from the consulate in Caracas visited in September. I shared my fears with her but she appeared to brush them aside, saying that in her opinion no foreigners would be sent to El Dorado. I wasn't convinced.

Two days later, Ivor was transferred to his home town of Valencia on the mainland to face further charges; it came completely unexpectedly. One minute he was there, large as life, the next he was gone, leaving José and Ricardo to run a jail where peace was hanging by a thread. Another officer was appointed, who turned out to be no better than Vasquez.

Calling home was almost impossible by then, the phone constantly being either out of order or locked up when it did function. Word had it that Jiminez had ordered his men to break the connecting wires inside the main gatehouse, rendering the phone useless and causing more provocation. The atmosphere had become intolerable.

To make matters worse, Oscarlito had used Ivor's transfer as an opportunity to take over. He lived for conflict, and it wasn't long before one of José's lieutenants from pavilion four was shot dead. The white flag was lowered and prisoners manned rooftop garitas once more. We were back at war. The raquetas continued with regularity.

On 4 October at evening número, 25 prisoners from our side were called out of the line by name and kept back on the cancha. The rest of us were herded back inside. Half an hour later, they were marched out of the main gate with just the clothes they stood up in. Thirty-five prisoners from the other side joined them, making sixty in total. News spread quickly that they were being transported to El Dorado, the monstrous jungle prison that everybody feared. Of the twenty-five from our side, two were foreigners. One was Cornelius, the other I didn't know, but both were Dutch. So much for the consul's opinion.

We soon heard that the Ministry of Justice in Caracas had issued an order declaring all male detainees in San Antonio who had been sentenced were to be moved, along with others nationwide, to a central holding jail, namely the new Central Penitentiaria Oriental (CPO) complex at El Dorado. Yet more psychological torture. Everyone panicked. The tension reached fever pitch. The day after the transfer, I wrote a letter to the British ambassador in Caracas expressing my concerns. As luck would have it, Mr Mellor turned up later in the week. I gave him the letter to pass on and kept my fingers crossed.

The following week, José and Ricardo got wind of Oscarlito's plans to muster his troops and launch an attack on our side. He was still looking for revenge over his brother's death in 1996. I didn't want to get involved this time; I'd grown weary of it all. My body was covered in scars and marks from the regular beatings. Ricardo must have sensed my feelings because he said I should stay at the rear on this occasion and suppress any of the enemy that should break through our ranks. I agreed. Weapons were quickly gathered, lookouts posted and men prepared for battle once more. Out came my machete. We were ready and waiting.

And didn't have long to wait. Sharp-eyed lookouts shouted warnings the second they saw the signs, and when the attack came, all hell broke loose. José and his followers ran from behind pavilion five and across no-man's-land. I stayed on the edge with 20 or so armed prisoners as rearguard. Then came the war cries, the howling and screaming. Shots rang out as the sides opened up at close range. On the run, people fell – dead or wounded – then the main body clashed. The battle began in earnest.

A minute or so later, the siren went off. Prisoners scattered in all directions, discarding weapons as they ran. I quickly hid my blade under the concrete edging of the cancha. Soldiers burst onto the yard as men from our side made their way back. Boom! Tat-tat-tat! Boom!

Swish. Whack! I fell to the ground face down next to a guy I knew as Ramon. He was bleeding profusely from a wound in his thigh. We lay there in a spreading pool of blood with soldiers running wildly amongst us, beating and kicking, shooting plastic. Several lashes and repeated kicks left me virtually paralysed with pain for the whole duration of the raqueta. I couldn't get up when the order came to get in line. I lay curled in a ball, unable to move, my clothes soaked in Ramon's blood. Pain racked my body. When the order came to return to the pavilion, two prisoners half carried me back to my room.

The aloe gel was of no use to me that night, I just lay on my bed in agony, stabs of pain shooting through my body every time I moved. It was some days before I recovered properly. I did not leave my room except for número.

The following Friday, Sam and I fell out badly. Looking back, I must have been a real pain in the neck, raving about everything and everyone. I felt Sam couldn't grasp what I was going through, and we parted that day without a kind word being spoken. A few days later, on 1 November, I was summoned to the gatehouse: Mr Mellor had left a letter for me from the embassy in Caracas. I went back to my room to read it. I opened it and shook with relief when I read that the ambassador was distressed to hear of our predicament and that the Ministry of Justice had assured him categorically no foreign prisoners would be transferred to El Dorado. Even though it was right there in front of me in black and white, I still wasn't totally convinced. After all, two Dutchmen had been taken the month before.

On 4 November 1998, three days after receiving the letter, a mass of soldiers entered at evening número. My whole world disintegrated as 80 prisoners from pavilions four and five were called out of the line to the centre of the cancha . . . I was one of them.

# 9

# WELCOME TO HELL

A shiver ran down my spine. I felt both fear and apprehension as the reality of the situation gripped me. The nightmare scenario was upon me: I was to be transported to the infamous El Dorado prison.

As I left the line of inmates, my initial feeling was one of total disbelief. For a moment or two, I stood helplessly in the centre of the cancha with the rest. I was filled with dread but, like the others, what could I do but accept my fate? Looking along the line of soldiers, I saw Jiminez, hand on hip, smiling openly, obviously having the time his life while he scrutinised anxious faces and watched the blood drain from every single one.

Soldiers encircled the lucky ones and herded them back into the pavilions, leaving the remainder to pass another número. Then began the grim roll call with the total count of 80 men from pavilions four and five. How many would there be from the other side, I wondered? Fear had been with me constantly since the very first day but nothing I'd been through so far could compare with how I felt right then. It was as though I'd been condemned to death.

On the order, we formed a line and marched in single file to the main gate. My legs would hardly carry me; they felt like jelly. A quick glance over my shoulder to where I used to live and we were through the door. There wasn't even time to say

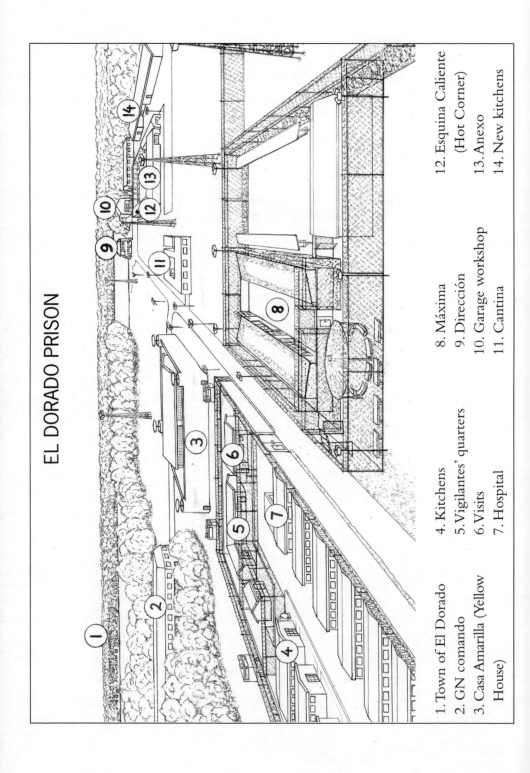

# EL DORADO PRISON

1. Town of El Dorado
2. GN comando
3. Casa Amarilla (Yellow House)
4. Kitchens
5. Vigilantes' quarters
6. Visits
7. Hospital
8. Máxima
9. Dirección
10. Garage workshop
11. Cantina
12. Esquina Caliente (Hot Corner)
13. Anexo
14. New kitchens

goodbye to Sam: how could I watch over her now? I couldn't think straight. And what would happen to the few belongings I had? More shouted orders and the process moved up a gear until prisoners from other pavilions joined us. We formed rows to the noise of shotgun blasts and the thwack of people being struck by planillas. Another count and the total came to 180, almost half the population of the jail.

We were ordered to sit, hands on heads, facing the jail. Behind us, five ancient Dodge school buses idled noisily, belching clouds of exhaust fumes everywhere. They looked unroadworthy, and I had strong doubts they would even make it across the island to the ferry, never mind deep into the Guianan rainforest. Another número, another roll call. When my name was shouted, I answered, '*Presente!*' and right at that very moment I wished to God I wasn't. Looking around, I saw other foreigners among the rows of prisoners, though in my confused state I couldn't count the exact number. The only thoughts going through my mind were 'This is it, this is the end.'

When the numbers tallied and Jiminez was satisfied, we were handcuffed in groups of three in such a way that our arms crossed, making it uncomfortable and awkward to board the bus. As fate would have it, a soldier handcuffed me to José, my right wrist to his right. José was in the middle; his left wrist cuffed to Carlo Pino's left.

Thirty-six prisoners from our party made ready to board the bus. As always, if there had been a level of order and sequence by the soldiers, we might have got off to a reasonable start but it wasn't to be. Before we had the chance to make an orderly queue, the soldiers were amongst us, pushing, threatening and inevitably intertwining groups of prisoners. Absolute mayhem followed. To make matters worse, because of the way we had been manacled together and allocated one seat per trio, one unlucky prisoner would be forced to sit in the aisle. Soldiers, eight of them in total, took up the two front and rear seats. After much cursing and pushing by prisoners and soldiers alike, we finished up bracketed together like sardines in a can. Before the bus had turned a wheel, I had already become overwhelmed by the heat and stench of sweating bodies. Daylight faded as we set off into the unknown.

José, Carlo Pino and I were placed on the left-hand side at the rear of the bus with me sitting on the floor crushed up against another guy from the three opposite. Four soldiers sat behind us, and we had gone no distance before one decided it would be amusing to use my back as a footrest. His companions laughed loudly, thinking it was hilarious.

'Get your heads down, no talking!' shouted one suddenly, all four beating anyone within reach with their planillas. With my head bent as low as possible, all I could see was the filthy floor and the back of the person in front of me. If I strained my eyes to the left, I could see a patch of unobscured window. It wasn't too long before I made the mistake of stretching to make myself more comfortable and received a beat across the shoulders for my trouble. My head went down again, and I kept very still.

Thoughts of self-pity filled my head. I felt an intense hatred toward the soldiers as they openly enjoyed the suffering around them, shouting, prodding and wafting cigarette smoke in our direction. The bastards were really making a meal of it. I thought about my family and friends, and how we could keep in touch with one another. Images of Sam filtered through the jumble in my head. We had parted from our last entre vista barely speaking, and I hadn't had a chance to say goodbye. What would she think of me being dragged away so suddenly? I felt so wretched.

We reached the port and waited an hour for the ferry to offload before the buses could board. Even then, with men anchored to one another with not the slightest chance of escape, we still weren't allowed to move. By that time, my legs and arms were sore and ached with cramp. On the ferry, four soldiers behind us decided to stretch their limbs, booting their way through to the front as if we were piles of rubbish. One soldier stood over us with a machine gun. Everyone used the time to stretch the aches and pains away as much as he dared.

As the ferry bobbed and crashed through rough waters heading out to sea, I began to feel nauseous. I wasn't a good traveller at the best of times and proceeded to retch, but my stomach was empty; only a clear spill of liquid dribbled down my chin. At the end of the four-hour crossing, I felt dreadful. Reaching the mainland, the soldiers boarded the bus, kicking their way through as they had before. The ferry berthed at Cumaná and within minutes, we set off again.

It was late into the night. No one slept, as men stirred and adjusted position to facilitate their discomfort. I rested my forehead across my right arm, which stretched awkwardly over José's right wrist. Sweating profusely, my head still feeling light and dizzy from the seasickness, I somehow dropped off and the night seemed to disappear. When I woke, it was getting light. The bus trundled along, rattling and shaking, bumping and bouncing on the poorly made roads. I was ravenously hungry, and the taste in my parched mouth was foul; no prisoner had eaten or drunk water since we'd left Margarita. My tongue was so swollen it filled my mouth. I couldn't have spoken even if I'd wanted to. The soldiers didn't go without, however. We made a mid-morning stop at a roadside filling station where a couple of them pushed their way through and came back five minutes later carrying food and water. All four ate noisily behind us, purposely making pleasurable munching sounds to torment us, then slurping from bottles to add to our anguish. The heat in the bus became torturous as the sun rose to its zenith. By then, I felt so weak I was intermittently blacking out.

The journey dragged on into the afternoon. While the bus rolled along through the countryside, I lifted my head slightly to the side and fleetingly saw the rooftops of houses as we passed village after village. Late in the afternoon, the convoy stopped and we disembarked to urinate. Three prisoners at a time were permitted off the bus, which meant wading through people to reach the door. Thirty seconds was our allotted time, but time was of no consequence, I'd been hunched up for so long I couldn't relieve myself. There was nothing to come out anyway: all the liquid had been sweated out of me, but it gave me time to look around and stretch some of the stiffness out of my legs. The way in which we were shackled made the exercise difficult. If circumstances hadn't been so dire, it would have been laughable. José freely splashed my feet, while Carlo pissed against the bus's wheel arch and received a slap on the back of his head for lack of respect to the rusting Dodge.

We were high in the hills, and in the valley below a huge lake tapered off into the distance. Ordinarily, the spectacular view would have taken my breath away, but there was no time to enjoy the beauty as we were hustled quickly into the bus and ordered once more to get our heads down. I sat and took one last look out of the window to my right. As beautiful as the vista was, it wasn't worth the crack on the head I received for my hesitation.

I tried to rest, but with my head still throbbing from the whack, the staccato pant from the engine and the rumbling prop shaft beneath it was impossible. Darkness fell as we travelled on through open countryside, leaving the hills behind and descending onto more level ground. The occasional village light flashed by the windows, each time giving the interior of the bus a short-lived eerie glow. On and on we went, without a break and still without food and water.

At last, late in the night, we crossed a bridge and stopped. I raised my head and risked a look. Up ahead, made visible in the glare of halogen lights, I saw a huge set of metal gates with a large number of soldiers milling about. The gates opened after a minute or two and the first bus went through. We were next in line. As the bus ground to a halt, a soldier carrying a clipboard came on board and took a headcount, pointing his pen in methodical fashion. A número followed after which the bus drove through the open gates and on for a good way down a tarmac road with dense vegetation on either side. Prisoners raised their heads, looking anxiously around, following the bus's headlights as it travelled through a dark tunnel beneath the jungle canopy.

The bus slowed, rounded a sharp bend and instantly the sky took on a glow. There in the distance clearly visible in the glare of a hundred floodlights was the prison. We drew closer and the sky grew lighter, highlighting a high wall topped with razor wire to our left. On our right, surrounded by two high mesh fences and raised on slightly higher ground, stood a floodlit compound. The bus stopped 150 yards further on outside a huge pair of heavy wooden gates at least 12 feet high. The left-hand gate had a small door set into it, which opened as we pulled up. A soldier walked amongst us and unlocked our cuffs, which came as such a relief everyone to a man rubbed the pain from their wrists.

Ordered off the bus and driven towards the doorway, I could hear soldiers yelling, '*Corre! Corre!*' followed by the sound of blades hitting their mark. The yelps and shrieks of pain, mingled with the shouting, brought on a panic attack, and my legs ceased to function when my turn came to enter. The prisoner behind me eventually pushed me forward. There was just enough room for one person to squeeze through and, as I entered, a chilling sight greeted me: two unbroken lines of Guardia Nacional soldiers stood beating people as they ran, planillas flashing in the bright lights from above.

The narrow corridor we were steered along curved to the left around a low building and on a further 20 yards to the doorway of another building. I have no idea how many beats I received on that short run. But it wasn't over. Once inside the building, vigilantes took over, dozens of them moving with menace, each one brandishing some sort of beating implement, using it with gusto. Their weaponry included planillas, hardwood clubs and short lengths of heavy-duty plastic water piping. With pointed directions and lashes along the way, we ran to the far end of the building where we saw small hatchways built into the wall at waist height. There, faceless people passed through metal trays from the other side. My tray contained lumps of congealed spaghetti that tasted so foul it made me heave, but I was so hungry I ate it, stuffing it in my mouth with bare fingers like a man possessed.

We ate furiously, the vigilantes running among us, beating and yelling, '*Rápido! Rápido!*' I'd never come across such evil vigilantes during my two years in San Antonio. They must have been handpicked to work at El Dorado; their brutality was frightening. Up on the wall a clock read ten minutes past midnight. Thirty-one hours had passed since the número in San Antonio.

When we had finished eating, we were forced outside and ordered to join others sitting in rows in the centre of a concrete roadway running down the middle of a dozen pavilion buildings. Once there and under the arc lights a Guardia Nacional officer ordered everyone to strip, sit with hands on heads and wait for the inmates from other buses to go through the same process.

After half an hour, every prisoner sat in the roadway naked surrounded by armed soldiers; no one dared to speak for fear of more punishment. Número was taken twice and then the roll call, during which time I didn't hear if there were others present that I knew. I couldn't concentrate: the aches and pains had taken over my senses.

A soldier called my name and I acknowledged it. To my surprise, he told me to stand and motioned me to sit apart on the kerbside ten yards away from the rest. As the roll call continued, other foreigners joined me, and then I recognised a few. It was only then that I saw Mike the American, who had been on another bus, coming towards me. He was closely followed by Alex, Harald and Irwin. Seconds passed, then Sal, Tammier and Franz joined the group. A Spanish guy named Juan Carlos, whom I'd befriended recently, made his way over. Five more I only vaguely knew were Ferdinand, a Dutch Indonesian, Carlo, Xavier, Kike and Juan, who were all Spanish. The roll call ended with 14 foreigners being separated from the main body of prisoners – so much for the British ambassador's promise.

I foolishly thought we'd been separated from the rest for special treatment. In a way, I was right. An orderly came along and gave out prison clothing, which consisted of a shirt, shorts and plimsolls, the latter being the only item that didn't itch. We dressed quickly. A Guardia Nacional *coronel* swaggered over, and surprised to see so many foreigners began to ask us individually what crimes we had committed. Everyone replied with the same answer: '*Tráfico de drogas.*' The coronel blew his top, accusing us of being an international drugs ring. In his opinion, he said, every last one of us ought to be executed on the spot for bringing drugs into the country! Fuck! His rage was such I'm certain every foreigner thought his time had come. Before any of us could defend ourselves and rectify the situation, he bellowed hysterically, '*TODOS POR LA MÁXIMA!*'

On hearing the order, we were surrounded by a group of soldiers, who ran us back to the main gate. My mind was in total confusion. On what grounds were we being sent to the máxima? Wasn't that where especially dangerous prisoners were kept? It was a spine-chilling moment. We squeezed through the small doorway and ran diagonally across the road, and there ahead on raised ground, brightly lit by a score of halogen lights, was the maximum-security compound. Two high mesh fences topped with razor wire surrounded the outer walls, which were only six or seven feet high. More razor wire spiralled on the ground between and outside the fences. As we ran up steps built into the hill and round the corner, the formidable sight filled me with uncontrollable fear.

Outside a set of gates, we were stopped by a huge black vigilante. The shotgun he wielded looked like a toy in his giant hands. '*Aha, los gringos!*' he shouted, then laughed loudly, '*Bienvenidos a el infierno!*' Welcome to hell! He entered the máxima through a door set into the gates, stooping as he did so, and motioned us to follow. As we entered, he pointed to an open barred gate in the far left corner of the yard and screamed, '*POR AHÍ, RÁPIDO!*' clubbing each one in turn with the butt of his shotgun as we ran past him. I took a blow to the top of my right arm, which knocked me sideways.

Passing through the open gate, we found ourselves in a narrow corridor housing four cells. Only the third cell door was open. On entering, the stench stopped us in our tracks. It was dark inside, but in the little light that filtered through from the floodlights outside we could see the floor was awash with human sewage. Our new plimsolls were soaked immediately. The cell door clanged loudly behind us as the vigilante slammed it shut, fastening a padlock to secure it. He also banged the outer gate and padlocked it. Through the bars, I watched the vigilante make his way back across the yard. It was completely silent until the outer door closed behind him, then it began. '*Gringos! Gringos!*' Threats of violence, death, pain and torture echoed around the yard, even coming from the cell next to ours. If I'd had any liquid left in me, I'm sure I would have pissed my pants at that moment.

'Oh, fucking hell!' I said aloud, turning to take in our new home. It was almost as if we'd been dropped into an open sewer. Several guys were retching from the awful smell and seeing them made me retch too, bringing up bits of undigested spaghetti, which I spat on the floor. Our cell measured four yards by three with two tiers of concrete bunks on either side, enough to sleep eight people. No one needed to work out that fourteen into eight didn't go. At the far end were two narrow cubicles partitioned by walls at head height. In the left-hand cubicle, four inches of plastic water pipe protruded from the wall. The other functioned at one time as a toilet of some description though the hole in the ground was full and overflowing onto the cell floor.

The concrete ceiling sloped upwards from the entrance making it approximately nine feet high at the far end with quarter-inch steel mesh covering it completely. Attached to the mesh were two small circular fluorescent lights, but neither functioned. Set into the end wall at the height of seven feet was a barred window slit, nine inches by eighteen.

Morale was low. Dazed and downhearted, we were still reeling from the shock of it all. I climbed onto the left top tier and sat there, my feet dangling, my plimsolls dripping. From where I sat, I could see through the barred window and down into the main compound below, the wooden gates clearly in view under the lights. I put my head in my hands and wondered what I'd done to deserve such treatment. I had tried to smuggle drugs, but surely it didn't warrant this.

Not wanting to stand in the pool of shit and piss around their feet, the other guys followed my lead and sat or lay on the concrete bunks. Being constantly bitten by clouds of mosquitoes and dumbstruck with the frenzied shouting of the locals, there was no need to sort out sleeping arrangements that night. Nobody could sleep. When at last the locals settled, all that could be heard were the sounds of night-time creatures. With hardly a word spoken, we sat in darkness filled with our own fearful thoughts. Our first night in El Dorado had been a harrowing experience.

As daylight came, so did the flies, thousands of them. We hadn't seen where they'd settled in the darkness, but they soon found their targets, swarming, filling the air. It became a form of continuous torture in itself. The locals woke and started to scream and shout again, at each other and at us. I was looking around, noticing in the light of day that the máxima was broken up into four segments with four cells in each, when suddenly it went quiet. A few pushed up against the cell door to see what was going on: there stood a dozen soldiers with the giant black man who'd 'welcomed' in our group the night before.

'It must be número,' said Mike.

'Yeah,' I replied, 'make sure you get it right, eh?'

As it happened, it wouldn't have made any difference: the vigilante opened up and as we came out, we were lashed. Each segment passed número separately, ours being the first. Lined up against the far wall and round towards our gate, it was impossible to miss the occupants of the other three cells glaring, each one a carbon copy of Santo Loco, the savage I'd beaten in San Antonio. Including foreigners, 38 prisoners made up our segment, and the odds were stacked against us if it came on top. We ran back inside to yet more beats, after which only the outside gate of our segment was locked. It brought an instant influx of scroungers, not begging but demanding we gave them cigarettes, money, food, just about anything. Some even came into our cell to make sure we had nothing hidden. I wanted to tell them they were welcome to the shit on the floor but thought better of it and bit my tongue.

Standing in the corridor with Sal and Alex, I was checking the headcount as other prisoners passed número when a gang of six or seven locals came out of the far cell and walked towards us. Their leader, a young, evil-eyed guy in his early 20s, was spinning a broom handle in his right hand imitating a Kendo fighter. With his men fanned behind him, he stopped a yard in front of us and demanded money.

'*No hay nada!*' said Sal sharply.

The broom handle froze in the upright position and the young thug threatened us with a violent death if we didn't hand over some cash.

'*No hay nada.*' I said it this time, trembling – not so much out of fear, more out of anticipation, ready to retaliate at a moment's notice. I sensed Sal had the same idea; he wouldn't back down, I could see it in his eyes. I was confident we could take them on between us, longing to relieve the thug of the handle and smash it across his ugly face. I clenched my fists ready, and it didn't go unnoticed. A few tense seconds passed then the young guy backed off, pointing his finger at us, telling us to watch our step and to give more respect in the future. His gang followed him, turning occasionally to glare at us. When they'd gone, Sal and I looked at each other and let out sighs of relief.

Alex, meanwhile, had carried on counting. The máxima totalled 154 prisoners, and not only were we in the most fearsome prison in the world, we were trapped with 140 of the craziest, meanest murdering bastards imaginable, each one hell-bent on making the gringos' lives as miserable as possible. I didn't have time to ponder on that blood-curdling thought, as just then the small door of the yard opened and in walked two vigilantes both carrying a shotgun in one hand and a short, stout length of plastic piping in the other. Close at their heels were two prisoners carrying a huge metal pot, which they placed down just inside the doorway.

Another prisoner carrying plastic bowls entered, made his way towards us, then passed bowls through the bars. The vigilante unlocked the gate, trying his best to strike everyone running across the yard to where the kitchen orderlies stood. I was lucky and escaped a beat. Breakfast was a bowl of disgusting, thin, watery gruel, half of which spilled to the ground as we ran back trying to dodge the vigilante with the pipe. I wasn't so lucky this time. Whack! With my backside stinging like hell from the blow, I sat and stared into the bowl, wondering if it had been worth the trouble. Bits of dead flies, insect wings and legs floated about in the watery remains of the previous day's spaghetti. I picked out the limbs and wings, and demolished what remained nevertheless. I was hungry and, looking around me, I saw I wasn't alone: there wasn't a scrap of food to be seen in anyone's bowl.

When the cell doors were locked, we paddled through the piss and shit and hoisted ourselves up and onto the bunks. The heat added a new dimension to the foul smell, which got worse by the minute. Half an hour later, we heard a gurgling sound coming from the far corner of the cell. Intrigued, a few stepped down and gathered round the short length of pipe sticking out of the wall in the left-hand cubicle. Seconds later, a muddy, brown liquid spurted from the open pipe, spat once or twice, stopped, spat once more and ended with a trickle of filthy water. It didn't look drinkable so we used the water to rinse the greasy bowls, but before we'd finished the water ceased to flow. Fuck! was the general consensus. Starving hungry with only half a bowl of pigswill for breakfast, no water to drink or wash our stinking bodies; no soap, no razors, no towels. Flies in our faces every second and 140 murderous savages for neighbours. Beats from the soldiers, beats from the vigilantes. What could possibly happen next?

The atmosphere in the cell was one of pure despair. Everyone was very demoralised. We were isolated from the outside world in the middle of a hostile jungle. What else could they possibly do but kill us?

Later in the morning, a vigilante came and ran our party across the yard and out through the door. A large concrete building stood to the left of the gates; it must have served more than one purpose as there were several doorways along its face. We were instructed to sit on concrete seats under a circular canopy close to the gates, then one at a time were called through a door into a large room, which was empty except for a single plastic chair and a trustee holding an electric hair trimmer. Our heads were shaved completely, yet another cruel form of degradation, and although I was dressed it gave me a strange sense of nakedness.

While we stood outside, Franz, who spoke excellent Spanish, managed to scrounge a couple of brushes and a container of disinfectant from a vigilante, promising him a regalo when the consul came. With the cell door open, we swept the pool of filth down the length of the corridor and through the open gate. The locals in the other cells went crazy, shouting and complaining. We couldn't understand why – after all, it wasn't our shit we were cleaning up. With no water to swill the floor, we used the whole gallon drum of disinfectant. How wonderful a smell it was. Even the flies were eradicated for a while.

Lunchtime followed the same routine as breakfast, having to run across the yard and back, dodging the vigilante and his length of pipe. For lunch, we received a bowl of cold, sticky rice. As with the breakfast gruel, the rice contained an assortment of insect parts, but by this time we were so hungry no one could be bothered to pick out the bits. There was also a strangely coloured liquid on the menu, but we didn't have a container to put it in. The locals, however, were well prepared with sawn-off plastic bottles to collect their drinks, and ever resourceful, they'd cut and shaped bottlenecks into crude spoons to scoop their rice. This inventive move gave us food for thought.

At evening número, we were lashed again. By this time, I couldn't pick out any single pain on its own, they'd all intermingled into one. After número, the evening meal came with the same brutal process and the same disgusting rice. Now that our cell was somewhat cleaner, we were thankful to be locked up again and out of harm's way. We made sleeping arrangements that evening: the four bottom bunks would occupy two men each sleeping top to tail, with two on the floor, leaving the four top bunks sleeping one person each.

On our fourth day in the máxima, a lifesaver came to see us: well, that's what it felt like. It came in the form of the Dutch consul, who had driven a great distance from Ciudad Bolívar. He also came to act on behalf of other embassies. We sat with him under the canopy outside the gate and it felt like we were a million miles away, talking and laughing with a friendly face. He had brought bars of soap, razors, toothbrushes and paste, bottles of spring water, various magazines, papers and a carton of cigarettes. We drank the water immediately, the smokers lit up and rested. For a moment, we were in heaven. The consul had no idea why we'd been placed in the máxima but promised to speak with the *director* either to get us out of there or at least arrange better treatment. When it came time to go, the consul gave Franz money to share between us.

We were on the up, but as always, we faced a problem. How would we get our goodies back inside without the locals finding out? Our newly acquired possessions were quickly shared out, stuffed into waistbands and covered with shirt tails. Only newspapers, magazines and bottles were carried where they could be seen, but the locals knew we had more. After all, we were gringos and the consul had visited. News travelled fast. It automatically meant we were rich beyond imagination and in their eyes it was nothing less than our duty to give them everything we owned.

Inside the cell, we made a pact: we would stand as one and no one would take anything from us. We agreed unanimously that the cigarettes would be rationed, and we would smoke only when the gates were locked. There were eight smokers amongst us, so the remaining six took an extra share of the money to balance things out. We allotted each man four cigarettes a day; that way we had sufficient to last another six days.

Next morning after número, the young Bruce Lee wannabe appeared in the doorway with his gang: would this be the decisive moment? I was ready to fight and so was Sal, but I wasn't too sure about the others. The thug made to step inside. I stood up, loosened my wrists and noted Sal had quickly positioned himself by my side. Juan Carlos, Xavier and Kike followed suit, then suddenly everyone was on their feet and moving forward. With a nasty edge to his voice, Sal asked, 'What do you want?'

To our surprise, the thug went on the defensive. 'You should share your things with us,' he said. 'We're all prisoners together here.'

'Nobody has shared anything with us,' Juan Carlos shot back. 'Lose yourselves.'

We represented a united front and the gang could see we were a force to be reckoned with should the stand-off end in conflict. As I thought they would, they backed away, muttering obscenities as they went.

At breakfast, half our group stayed behind in order to guard our possessions until the others returned. It worked well, and we repeated the strategy each mealtime until the locals gave up trying to sneak inside our cell. The next few days rolled by in the same routine. By this time, we'd cut our empty bottles and fashioned cups and spoons so at least we were able to drink our meagre allowance of half a litre a day; nevertheless, everyone was becoming seriously dehydrated and losing weight at an alarming rate.

Locked in the rainforest region, the heavens opened up every afternoon for a period of 15 minutes. It frustrated everyone to see the rain cascading from the roof but not be able to collect and drink any of it. One day, a flash of inspiration took me to fasten a broken toothbrush to a broom handle with a strip of cloth ripped from the hem of my shirt. Burning two holes in a sawn-off bottle, I pushed the toothbrush handle through the holes and stuck my invention through the bars, catching the rainwater as it dripped from the roof. A minute later, I possessed a cup full of fresh water. It tasted like wine. In turn, the contraption passed along the line. This trick didn't go unnoticed by the locals, who started to do it immediately. They hadn't thought of that, I laughed to myself.

On the tenth day, we ran out of cigarettes and although we had money hidden, there was no way we could possibly spend it because if the locals in our segment hit upon our wealth they would definitely attack us. We needed to get out of there. Franz and Kike suggested we should write a letter to Vasquez asking for his clemency. What did we have to lose? We still didn't understand why we'd been thrown into the máxima as no one had done anything to warrant such severe treatment. We decided that the coronel's antics on our arrival had been a sham for the benefit of the other prisoners, as the vigilante in the máxima had been expecting us because the cell door and outer gate were open and ready to receive us.

Four days later, whilst having our heads shaved for the second time, we managed to bribe a vigilante to deliver the letter. Some days later, to our surprise, we were taken outside the gate to meet Vasquez. It was an awkward moment, but we swallowed our pride and pleaded for mercy. In return, he said that although there was nowhere else he could put us, he would meet us halfway and issue an order allowing us to spend our days outside the máxima compound or on the cancha at the rear. He went on to say he didn't want us in the main prison for our own safety.

At first light the following day, we left the compound and spent a day sitting around under the canopy and chopping vegetation (under supervision) around the area with machetes. In the afternoon, a vigilante bowled me over by shouting my name and handing me an envelope, which he said had been in the dirección since the previous weekend. I recognised the writing on the envelope immediately: it was a letter from Sam. With a shaking hand, I opened it there and then. It turned out Ivor's mother had visited Margarita and asked Sam if there was anything she would like taken to El Dorado, as she would be travelling down to visit her son. Ivor had been sent here directly from Valencia after his court appearance. I hadn't seen him, so I took it he must be somewhere in the main prison. Sam had managed to save most of my things with the help of a friendly vigilante named Armando and enclosed in the envelope were photos of her and my daughter Josie. The letter gave me such a lift. I stood transfixed, reading it repeatedly, taking pleasure in the photos. Eventually, I folded it and placed it with the photos safely in my breast pocket.

As the days went by, we communicated and made friends with the vigilantes and the beatings thinned to nothing. In the afternoons when it rained, we stripped naked and showered under a stream of water that flowed from the corner of a rooftop opposite the cancha. It was luxurious to be able to bathe, shave, drink water and wash our grubby clothing, but it became a burden having to return to our cell each evening at six to face the constant abuse and threats from locals.

One morning I woke with a slight fever but still went outside with the others. As the day wore on, I got gradually worse until I eventually collapsed in a heap and lay down unable to move. A medic was quickly on the scene and transferred me to the hospital wing in the main prison where I spent the next two days on a saline drip. On the third day, feeling better than I had in weeks, I even managed to acquire a few cigarettes and smoked them in the toilet area when no one was around. That evening the medic declared me fit. I returned to the máxima to discover we'd changed cells.

The foreigners now lived in the end cell of the same segment. It was larger than our old cell by a good five feet, fitted out with an extra tier of bunk beds with two narrow window slits, one at each end. The locals had been moved out and were now residing in our old cell, and they weren't taking the arrangement kindly, ranting and cursing at regular intervals.

As we sat under the canopy two days later, a jeep pulled up on the road below and out jumped a stocky, blond-haired guy. He made his way to the fence and called out in German. At once, Alex, Harald and Irwin jumped up and walked over to him. They chatted for some time, and when he'd left, I asked Alex who he was. He was beside himself, beaming as he explained the guy's name was 'Vincent'; he was a Swiss ex-mercenary now working as an instructor and consultant for the Guardia Nacional. Apparently, a whole area within a 50-kilometre radius provided a training ground for the Guardia Nacional, and he taught soldiers basic battle manoeuvres and how to pilot helicopters. Through the grapevine, he'd heard there were Germans in the máxima. He'd promised to return the next day with drinking water and purifying tablets.

True to his word, the following day he brought a huge plastic drum of drinking water and tablets. He and Alex talked for an hour through the fence, and it was clear they'd made friends, which, of course, would be beneficial for everyone. To take the container into the máxima would have caused uproar, so we left it in safe keeping in the vigilantes' quarters sited in the large building close by.

Some nights later, a visitor to the prison took us by surprise. A military envoy from the American embassy came to our cell with a vigilante to see Mike. On seeing the conditions in the máxima, he asked questions relating to our treatment. In darkness, under torchlight provided by the vigilante, he took notes and promised he would speak with an official immediately. His high-ranking uniform had a strong effect on the vigilante, who couldn't do enough to please him. He was almost subservient. We hoped it would have the same effect on Vasquez.

The next day we discovered nearly all our drinking water had gone. We'd stupidly left it in the vigilantes' block. It was evident they had helped themselves and there wasn't a lot we could do about it. It was a chance we'd taken. The following morning, all the water had gone, so we took the empty container back to the cell in the hope the Swiss mercenary would return and replenish it.

The days rolled by, our aches and pains healed, and life became somewhat bearable in the máxima. However, it wasn't to stay that way. On the afternoon of 10 December, 34 days after our arrival, documented prison scenes from El Dorado would make groundbreaking news across the world.

# 10

# THE MASSACRE

It was daybreak, and we foreigners left the máxima compound to do menial tasks and chop weeds around the perimeter fencing. Waiting to pass número, we could hear shouting from the main prison, which grew louder and louder as the minutes went by.

'What the fuck's goin' on over there?' asked Mike. We looked at each other in turn, but no one had an answer.

The rattling of a dozen gates added to the noise, while the shouting slowly took on the form of a screaming chant. '*Rebelión! Rebelión! Rebelión!*' Just then, a vigilante rushed up, shotgun in hand. He pumped the action to gain our immediate attention, then ran our party across the yard back to the cell, the sights of his gun pointing at us continually.

Once inside, it took us a moment to regain our senses. The screaming continued outside, the sound reverberating through the window slits. '*Rebelión! Rebelión!*' The noise had grown to such a fever pitch it seemed to be everywhere at once. Crashing sounds filtered through the shouting. Franz jumped up onto the water container, which was the perfect height for looking out of the window.

'Fucking hell, man!' he exclaimed, 'they're smashing the place up!'

One at a time, we took turns to see. When it came to my turn, I saw pavilion walls here and there starting to disintegrate. The walls of the máxima had been constructed from the same materials: cinder blocks laid into a concrete framework and finished off with a coat of white paint. A bit ludicrous really having barred gates and tiny windows when walls could be smashed in minutes with nothing more than a rock.

The racket began to generate a lot of excitement around the máxima. Prisoners on our side cheered encouragement through the window slits, others shouted news across the yard to those who could not see. All the guys in the cell were stunned with what was going on but were somehow drawn to the window to observe the scene unfolding below. When I next looked, prisoners were running amok in the compound, some smashing the walls of other pavilions. Tat-tat-tat! came the sound of Fals opening up from the towers. People scattered in all directions, but it didn't stop the demolition. Tat-tat-tat! More prisoners emerged from broken pavilion walls and ran for cover, carrying on their destruction out of the line of fire.

By this time, a hundred or more were out, prowling the compound, smashing anything within reach, spinning in every direction like wild animals. Tat–tat-tat! The tower guards were using them for target practice; some fell, having been wounded, and crawled for cover, others dashed for safety. What fucking madness was this? Only five minutes earlier, Juan Carlos had witnessed nine or ten vigilantes make a dash from their inner compound to the small door in the main gates. It looked like the vigilantes were leaving them to it. They did the right thing. It would have been impossible for so few men to control the screaming rampage; they would have died in the attempt. More yelling prisoners crowded the yard, smashing whatever they could, fighting one another, some jumping from behind pavilions, hurling rocks at the guard towers, then dashing back for cover.

I jumped down, still reeling from what I'd seen, suddenly aware I hadn't been following events around me in the máxima. Shouting and chants for rebellion had started in cells close by and gates were rattling. They were nerve-wracking moments. There had been no número, no breakfast and no lunch. The máxima gate had stayed locked, no one had entered since we'd been rushed back. The shouting in the máxima reached a crescendo and the gates continued to rattle. We sat in awe of the events.

Tammier climbed on the water container. 'Fuck me! Look at this, the place is on fire!'

We scrambled up in turn to look. The pavilion walls were full of huge, gaping holes with smoke billowing from several of them. Transfixed, I watched more buildings being set alight. It dawned on me the only combustible property the prisoners had in their possession were foam mattresses, which the majority seemed to own except us. It wasn't long before the roof felt caught alight, flames licking from every pavilion. The shooting had stopped – the guards in the towers had gone and the vigilantes had done likewise. Every prisoner, it seemed, was out, screaming, running amok, smashing walls, ripping gates from their mountings. Clouds of thick, black smoke filled the air and drifted over the máxima, forcing us from the window for a while. Luckily for us. Moments later, a huge explosion shook the ground, followed immediately by a blast of heat through the window slit.

Ignoring the danger, I was first to the water container, my face smarting from the shimmering, radiating heat as I watched the flames die a little, then the dust and debris settle. I could see the whole front of the kitchen building had been blown to bits. Parts of the gas tank lay scattered around, black and twisted.

'The crazy fuckers have blown the kitchens up!' I called out to the rest as I jumped down and gave someone else a turn at the window. Roars of appreciation echoed around the máxima.

Everyone was screaming for the riot – all except the foreigners. We were in a very precarious position. In a state of shock, we realised the crazies were hell-bent on breaking out, smashing the place up and probably killing every one of us in their frenzy.

'They're out! They're fuckin' out, man!' Tammier was at the gate. We crowded round to see eight screaming prisoners in the yard. Between them they carried the heavy barred gate from their cell. They were from the next segment. No one could see how they had managed to get out; I assumed the gate must have been literally shaken off its hinges and the lock snapped in the process then used to smash through the outer barred wall. They crashed the gate into walls and moved along, helping others to escape. The place erupted with a screaming madness.

Within minutes, 25 to 30 prisoners were out in the yard. I saw a flash of someone I thought I recognised from Margarita. Prisoners were using three gates to demolish the outer walls of each segment around the máxima. The place had been poorly built, so barred sections fell from their mountings as block walls beneath were reduced to rubble. Locks were shattered on the cells inside.

A group of prisoners carrying a gate ran over to our outer wall. I seriously thought the next few moments were going to be my last. Crash! I asked for forgiveness . . . Crash! Crash! The wall caved in, broken cinder block tumbled to the floor. Crash! The hole grew bigger as piles of rubble fell into the cell. As the dust settled, ugly screaming faces appeared from outside.

'*Vamos gringos, rebelión!*' they shouted.

I couldn't believe my ears. One moment I was preparing myself for death, the next I was invited to join in a South American prison rebellion. It would be impossible to describe my feeling of euphoric relief unless you had experienced something similar. We hung back, wary of climbing through the gaping hole at the end of the cell. Sal was the first, Juan Carlos second, then Xavier, then me. Alex, Mike and the rest followed.

Outside in the yard, the whole place resembled the aftermath of an earthquake: prisoners continued to smash into walls until most of the concrete framework became visible. The máxima lay in ruins after only one hour's rioting. I became aware of the number of weapons on show; even in the máxima many had made crude knives, keeping them well hidden for times of need. I went back inside for a moment to see what was happening in the main compound. From my perch, I could see black smoke belching from the pavilions, flames licking through the broken walls. Huge crowds of prisoners darted around, ranting and raving, destroying anything they could. Some went into the vigilantes' quarters, the guards not having stopped to lock up when they left. Within minutes, black smoke billowed from the windows.

I jumped down and made my way outside, picking a path through the rubble. After a few steps, I spotted the familiar face I'd seen earlier. '*Hepa*, Psicario!' I shouted above the din. He turned his head, looked at me and frowned for a second, then a huge smile lit his face as he recognised me.

I met Psicario in San Antonio. He had lived in pavilion one with Ciro and we had become friends. He was one of the few Venezuelans, like Ricardo, to have fair skin and blue eyes. He spoke a little English with an American drawl. His father, long since gone, was from the USA, his mother a *Venezuelana*. The nickname Psicario meant that he was a paid assassin. He'd killed several men in Margarita and had ended up in the máxima there. Now he was here.

He greeted me with a huge laugh and the ritual handshaking and slapping. '*Hepa*, Frank! How are you, man?' The exchange didn't go unnoticed by the locals. We talked for a while amid the noise. He told me he'd been one of the first out; they had shaken the gate off the wall. Psicario had been thrown in the máxima three days before after killing someone in a fight inside his pavilion. According to him, the riot in the main prison had been brewing for some time. Dragging a huge number of violent men from their home prisons all over the country and dumping them together in one melting pot was the perfect recipe for disaster. It was inevitable that something was going to blow.

I then realised why Vasquez wanted to keep our group where it was. He knew this was going to happen – he most probably instigated the whole thing – but couldn't have realised that it would spread to the máxima. Walking back to our cell, I heard a local shout at me. '*Mira, gringo, ayudame!*' He was struggling to twist a cell gate off its hinges. Lost in the sudden solidarity around me, I went over to help. Two more quickly joined in. A minute or two of lifting and twisting accompanied by a few grunts and it was off, clattering to the ground with a resounding cheer. In jubilation, we slapped hands. In a way, I was glad to have done my bit, though this rioting business wasn't exactly my idea of fun.

On rooftops, men tore off the felt roofing completely and with hands wrapped with clothing tugged at razor wire and rolled it over the sides of the buildings. Amidst the pandemonium, the whole place was beginning to resemble a bombsite. Constant shouting, war cries, screams and shrieks rang out from everywhere; it was evident the whole jail was about to explode. In the main jail, hordes of prisoners were still on the rampage. There wasn't much left but the concrete frames of the pavilions. They'd torn down the fencing flanking the vigilantes' quarters, which was already burned out, and started to destroy that building and the one next to it, which was used for visits. The small pavilion on its own surrounded by wire was known as 'Sing Sing' and housed special prisoners, people like Freddie back in Margarita; people with serious money.

Late in the afternoon, as the sun began to dip over the horizon, wisps of smoke continued to rise from smouldering fires in the main jail. Prisoners were still on the rampage, bodies lay here and there, the result of either prisoner-on-prisoner conflict or shots from the soldiers before they'd left their towers. It didn't slow the routine, far from it; men just stepped over them and dispatched their rage.

In the máxima, prisoners had piled foam mattresses against the main gates and set light to them. The fire raged. With daylight fading, bits of roof felt were added and the flames grew higher, reaching 20 or 30 feet, illuminating the whole area with an eerie red glow. Against the semi-darkness of dusk and a deep red sunset, it resembled a scene from Dante's *Inferno*.

The floodlights came on, prompting the locals to shriek and dance around the fire. They'd managed to destroy the máxima in just a few hours. Prisoners were perched on what remained of the rooftops, others roamed around the yard in groups recounting the action, a few sat on piles of rubble sharing a cigarette. No one had bothered us and so far the camaraderie had been fierce in the máxima.

By late evening, prisoners were wandering about, dragging mattresses to fuel the fires, creating clouds of black smoke that filled the night sky above the máxima. A fight suddenly broke out among a group of prisoners. Others gathered round, spurred on by the imminent action. Knives were drawn and the protagonists circled each other, lunging and parrying. In no time, a huge crowd had gathered around the fighting men, erupting with cheers and shouts as the first blood was drawn. Delirious with the events taking place, they screamed for more like bloodthirsty animals. Behind the packed crowd, my view became obscured, and I could only follow the fight by ear. Cheering continued for a while and then a roar erupted around me. Hoots and whistles, shrieks and howls, every sound imaginable. Just as quickly, the noise died down. The crowd dispersed, leaving one bleeding body. Dragged by its feet, it was dumped by the side of the main gate close to the fire. As flames licked around the corpse, another argument broke out in the middle of the yard. Latin American prisoners were terrific showmen, spending minutes insulting each other, pointing fingers and waving their arms around before anything actually happened. The argument ended with sharp words and threats – it meant it wasn't forgotten. As night drew on, fighting between the locals continued. Arguments occurred here and there, and each time a crowd gathered there were screams of encouragement until blood was spilled.

None of our group dared sleep that night – too afraid of getting our throats cut, not trusting any of them. Our cell remained in one piece except for a five-foot round hole in the wall, through which anyone could walk straight in. From my position near the window slit, I saw the main jail had calmed down a little. Every building appeared to have been destroyed with the exception of the hospital, which seemed reasonably intact. At this moment there wasn't anything left on which to vent their anger – soon they would turn on each other.

It wasn't long before the roars and cheers filtered through. When I looked, crowds had gathered tightly around fighters, people shouting and waving their arms in the air. I couldn't fathom these men out: one minute they were screaming death and abuse; the next, brothers in arms. Now they were outside killing each other! In both the main jail and the máxima, the early camaraderie had turned sour, and people were lusting after blood. It was their way. I sat on my bunk for a while and leaned against the wall; all the foreigners sat about the cell, no one remotely interested in rioting or attracting too much attention from the crazies.

The night drew on and still no one dared to sleep; we were all aware that at any moment we might have to defend ourselves against attack. We all sat frozen – Sal, Tammier, Franz, Mike, Alex, me and the rest – staring at the hole in the wall. The odd person came and went, but there was no trouble. Late into the night, I decided to get some air, so picked my way through the rubble and sat on the corner of what used to be our outside corridor wall. The fire had died down, though some flames still licked here and there, and plumes of black smoke obscured patches of the starry sky. Many prisoners sat around inside their broken cells, although dozens were out in the yard taking in the coolness of the evening.

Among the many noises in the yard, I could make out grunts of pain coming from behind me and to my right. I turned to look and couldn't believe my eyes. A group of prisoners were raping someone in the remains of the second cell of our segment. One held a hand over the guy's mouth and a knife at his throat, others pinned him down, holding his arms and legs. When one finished, another took his place. It was the most nauseating sight to see. I had to move over to the corner of the yard and detach myself from the spectacle. From where I sat I could still hear the muffled grunts quite clearly, but no one else in the yard seemed to be bothered. Then the grunting stopped and was replaced by pleading shouts that got louder and louder as the gang dragged their prey on to the yard. Prisoners, who moments before had taken little notice, now became engrossed in the scene unfolding before them.

Fuck! It was one of the boys from the gang in the end cell begging for his life. I could see him quite clearly in the floodlights. His friends weren't around to help him, they were nowhere to be seen. Six men held him tightly, his head down.

'What's he done?' someone shouted.

'Stolen marijuana from Culebra [Snake],' was the reply. An accusing 'Ahhh' was the collective response.

174

'No! No!' screamed the boy, trying to wriggle free from the hold.

With one round sweep, the gang leader cut the boy's throat. Blood spurted and poured from the open wound. The naked boy stopped struggling and the gang roared with laughter. A cheer erupted from the prisoners in the yard. It had been a good show for them. It wasn't good enough for the gang though, two or three hacked away at the boy's neck until the head came off. Blood splattered everywhere. The crazies were frantic with pleasure. It turned my stomach, I was ashamed to be remotely part of it, but in some bizarre way, at the same time I was drawn to watch in fascination.

The gang members kicked the boy's head like a football for a few seconds. The spectators loved it. Then one finally picked it up and with both hands held it up like a prize trophy for all to see. The ritual over, the body parts were taken and unceremoniously dumped next to the gate with the rest of the dead.

Shortly afterwards, Sal and Alex came out to see what the commotion had been about. When I explained in detail, they both made a beeline back to the comparative safety in numbers of our cell. I wasn't too far behind them.

All night long, visions of the boy haunted me. Over and over, I saw them hacking at his head, laughing wildly at the blood. The boy was no more than 18 or 19 years of age. He hadn't stood a chance.

I was in a half-awake daze as daybreak came. Outside, birds sang their morning chorus – if only I could have held on to that tranquil moment. The sound of vehicles snapped me awake fully. I looked out of the window and from where I sat I saw several long, green buses drive past, the windows brimming with camouflage.

'A consignment of soldiers have just gone past the window,' I shouted to Franz.

He jumped up to look. 'Shit!' he exclaimed. 'Looks like we're in for a lot of trouble, guys.'

Shouting echoed around the máxima. '*Agua verde en banda!*' Prisoners responded to the call and began to mill around the yard menacingly, the fever taking them again. Back in the main jail, many prisoners wandered about restlessly amongst the destruction and dead bodies. Now what, I thought.

Down the road from the right came a column of soldiers, each fully kitted out with flak jackets, face shields, webbing and heavy firepower. They marched in perfect step. These were no ordinary prison guardia, the type that fumbled with their laces, they were the real thing; I could see the order and discipline. They stopped ten yards short of the gates, arms at the ready. Of course, no prisoners inside could see what was going on outside the walls, and they carried on as if nothing was happening.

With my sight focused between the mob in the yard and the approaching soldiers, the thumping sound of a heavy engine to my left took me by surprise. I got an even bigger surprise when it came into view: it was an amphibious armoured vehicle the size of a small tank painted dark green with a wedge-shaped front. Six mortar launchers dressed the sides, a short 50 mm cannon atop the turret. It looked strangely out of place. As it neared the gates of the CPO, it turned 90 degrees and blew a good part of them away with the first explosion. Boom! The second explosion blew the gates to pieces. The guards reappeared and took up firing positions in the towers, tat-tat-tat, aiming with purpose at prisoners running frantically for cover in the ruins they themselves had created.

The armoured vehicle crashed through what remained of the gates. The guys around me were desperately trying to get me down so they could see – at this point the eighteen-inch-diameter water tub was taking the weight of three people clinging to the short bars in the window slit. Not twenty yards away a remarkable sight was unfolding.

The gate was down. Soldiers moved in as one, fanning out as they entered, front men running at a crouch and then down on one knee. The soldiers opened fire and shot anything that moved. Nine-millimetre bullets ripped into prisoners, dropping them like rag dolls. Constant firing lasted for a good minute, so bodies now littered the compound. Soldiers continued to fire sporadically as they moved forward, stepping over corpses, killing at random. Halfway down the road, however, among the broken ruins of the pavilions, the soldiers turned their weapons up and fired into the sky. A huge crowd of prisoners were trapped like cowering dogs at the far end of the compound with nowhere to go, nothing behind them but a 12-foot wall topped with razor wire.

I jumped down and told Mike what I had seen, and we cautiously ventured outside, hoping to find my friend Psicario to get his opinion as to what would happen in the máxima. A crowd of 50 or more stood by the gate, chanting, '*Hay hambre! Hay hambre!*' They were shouting for food! Incredible! Their countrymen lay shot to ribbons 100 yards away and they were demanding food. In their bizarre way of thinking, they'd had fun rioting, calmed down and now they were hungry.

We were still looking for my friend when a sudden barrage of shots scattered everyone and forced Mike and me to the ground. We crawled left a couple of yards and took cover behind unbroken brickwork, bellies stuck to the ground, motionless, panting like dogs with the sudden adrenalin. The shotgun pellets raining down and ricocheting about us were no longer plastic but lead. There were Fals too, the steady tat-tat-tat unmistakable. The soldiers must have cut their way through the high fence and razor wire on the ground because shots were coming directly over and along the inner wall: a score of gun barrels were blindly spitting death into the yard.

The shooting stopped for a moment.

'C'mon Mike, let's get the fuck out of here!' I shouted, making to get up.

'No, wait!' He grabbed my arm. A second later, the place exploded with another barrage of gunfire. 'Fuck, man,' said Mike, 'this is just like Nam, only we ain't got nothin' to shoot back with!'

The firing died down once more and without hesitation we crawled along the broken outside wall of the first segment. The firing started again. We were trapped at the far end of the broken wall halfway down the yard. A frightening five minutes followed, bullets zipping around us, pinging here and there – the angels were surely with us that day.

When the shooting stopped, we were up and running, making it to the hole just as the first gas canister hit the yard, belching out its obnoxious smoke. A prisoner, his hand bandaged in cloth, ran from cover, picked up the burning canister and in one quick movement threw it back over the fence. More canisters landed and yet more prisoners, similarly protected, dashed out to throw them to safety. The toing and froing went on until there were so many canisters in the yard amongst the rubble and on the rooftops that it overwhelmed them. Soon we were engulfed in a burning, choking fog of dense smoke. I took shelter in the corner, crouching beneath the water pipe, holding my shirt tight to my face. It didn't help, the gas burned my eyes raw. Tears streamed out and it became difficult to breath, as each inhalation created a fire in my throat and lungs. Everyone in our cell collapsed to the floor, gasping for air. This was another of the many moments I thought would be my last. I was convinced we were all going to die in horrific circumstances.

We suffered more than half an hour of blind choking terror before the air began to clear. The smoke had been so dense I wasn't able to see my hand in front of my face. As the smoke thinned, we discovered Tammier face down on the floor between the bunks. He wasn't moving. Franz and I turned him over. His breathing was shallow and he was unconscious. Red-eyed and wheezing, we gathered round and pumped his chest. After a few slaps, he came to, choking, having no idea where he was or what had happened. Sighs of relief passed around the cell and we staggered through the hole to fill our lungs with fresh air.

Prisoners were out on the yard again, heaving for breath, dodging around, wary should the shooting restart. Three soldiers appeared above the wall to our left, and the prisoners scattered for cover. A platform had been erected and the camouflaged figures were now looking down into the yard, pointing their machine guns with only one mesh fence between us.

A corporal shouted an order. 'Número!'

Nothing happened, no one made a move.

Once again, he shouted, this time louder. 'Número!'

Prisoners stuck their heads out tentatively from behind the broken walls of the máxima. The corporal sensed the mistrust among the population.

'Come on,' he shouted. 'No one is going to get shot.'

Slowly groups of prisoners gathered and made their way toward the soldiers.

'Form lines of ten!' shouted the corporal.

Eventually, with some bumping and confusion, we formed ten abreast in rows down the yard. An officer joined the soldiers on the platform and oversaw the count. Twice it came to 147.

'*Faltan siete*!' the officer shouted for the second time.

As he started the third count, someone shouted from the back, '*Hay siete muertos, señor.*'

This seemed to satisfy the officer, and we were dismissed. But the soldiers remained, armed and ready. Prisoners wandered around in groups, talking quietly among themselves, the atmosphere very subdued. Most of the foreigners, including myself, went back to the cell not knowing what else to do. We were no sooner there when we heard shouting from the main jail. I jumped up to see lines of soldiers spaced a couple of yards apart, stretched from the centre of the pavilions all the way round through the broken gates and down the road towards the river. A continuous stream of prisoners stumbled between the soldiers, being beaten, punched and kicked as they ran. Outside in the máxima, it was strangely quiet. Word had it the prisoners from the CPO were being taken to the Casa Amarilla.

The same officer returned and ordered another count. Everyone filed together as before and número was taken. 'Now,' the officer barked, 'when the small door in the gate is opened, you will run to the yard at the rear, is that understood?'

'*Si, señor,*' the prisoners replied as one.

My chest tightened at the thought of what lay ahead, but there was no time to ponder as the small metal door flew open with a bang and prisoners made their way through. Shouting and yelping started as soldiers vented their anger on the men from the máxima. I hung back until the last few remained, hoping to delay the moment, praying it wouldn't be so bad.

But I was wrong. Stooping and stumbling through the gate, a vast sea of camouflage was the first thing that hit me, soldiers packed so close together they resembled a frenzied mob. The second thing to hit me was a gunstock crashing into my right ear. I saw it coming, but there was no way of preventing it. My adrenalin surged; I had the strangest feeling I was running as fast as I could, but I wasn't getting anywhere. Everything was happening so slowly. They lashed and beat the prisoner in front of me, then planillas rained down on me combined with punches, kicks, gunstocks, batons, even steel helmets. I stumbled twice but managed to scramble up and carry on, the fear of being beaten to death spurring me forward. I ran on. All my senses could pick up was a mixture of colour and pain.

Then suddenly I was out of the gauntlet and in the centre of the cancha, reeling like a punch-drunk boxer. I'd taken the most beats I'd ever received. Struck 20 or 30 times, every part of me hurt so much I wanted to cry. My right ear felt the size of a football. It throbbed like hell. We were ordered into a line around the perimeter of the yard, told to strip and squat with hands on heads. Franz was next to me. I had a little trouble with this position, still dizzy from the beating, and stumbled forward onto the palms of my hands.

A mean-looking soldier, his face shield up, made his way over and levelled a full-length shotgun. 'What's the matter with this one?' he said, drawing closer. 'He doesn't know how to keep still.'

Franz obviously thought he was coming to my rescue when he said, 'We're fourteen foreigners here, sir, he doesn't understand.'

The soldier made his way behind me, saying, 'Oh, he doesn't understand? Let's see if he understands this!'

The grimace on Franz's face and his look of horror somehow told me to expect the sudden darkness that came. I cannot recall what happened after that or how long I was unconscious. The next thing I knew Franz was shaking me awake. He virtually dragged me up and helped me put on my shorts. I had no idea where my plimsolls were. Using Franz as a crutch, I hobbled around the outside of the yard, dodging soldiers lashing out with planillas, and back into the máxima. We'd taken a few half-hearted beats along the way, but by that time I was just a mass of pulsating pain and they didn't have too much effect.

Once through the máxima gate, I slowed to a crawl, out of breath, throbbing from head to foot. Locals in the yard were laughing and joking, rejoicing it was all over, reliving the moments with their friends. It was just another day for them, and they were alive to laugh about it. I entered our cell through the hole in the wall. Everyone looked badly beaten, dried blood caked their filthy bodies, their clothes in tatters. I looked down at myself. I was barefoot, legs filthy, bloodied and bruised. My shorts in shreds, my shoulders and back burning off with pain, my ear throbbing. Looking at the others, I had a good idea what my face looked like.

I leaned against the wall to the side of the hole and closed my eyes, so glad I was still alive. Tears burned as they flowed down my face and onto my bare chest. There had been moments running through the soldiers when I thought I wouldn't make it, but something had been there to help me on. Emotions swelled in my chest as I stifled a huge sob. Opening my eyes, I wiped away the tears. By the look on everyone's faces, they felt the same way too.

The bruising made it difficult to move about, but it was better to stay active or our limbs would seize. 'Hey, guys,' said Alex from the window perch. 'There are trucks in the jail.' I struggled up to join him and, sure enough, four covered army trucks were parked in the CPO compound. Around them, bodies littered the ground, the concrete soaked with blood. Soldiers began dumping corpses into the trucks. We started to count: there were a lot of bodies.

'*Miren, gringos!*' someone shouted through the hole. Everyone turned to see three locals crouching down, looking in. '*Gringos! Hay un autobús a fuera!*'

What? What were they saying? A bus? What are they talking about?

Franz spoke to one of them. 'Hey, this guy says there's a bus outside waiting for us. He's been sent to tell us.'

We thought it was a trick to get us outside.

'What fucking bus?' I shouted, making my way to the hole to see. The yard was full of prisoners, but a clear path between them led directly to the open door where a vigilante waved frantically at me.

The máxima crowd erupted with pleasure. '_Gringos_! _Libertad_! _Libertad_!'

A few others joined me. I shook my head in disbelief. 'Hey,' I shouted, 'they're fucking serious. Let's go!'

We left the knick-knacks we'd collected during our stay and ran through the crowd, who cheered and put their hands out to shake or slap ours. Halfway down on the right, I spotted Psicario. '_Hasta pronto, amigo!_' I shouted as I passed him, slapping his raised hand.

'_Suerte_, Frank,' he replied, wishing me good luck. I eased my way through the steel door filled with emotion and sheer relief to be getting away in one piece.

Even though we could see the old Dodge school bus sitting on the road below, it was still hard to believe we were leaving the hellhole. Six vigilantes handcuffed us individually outside the máxima gate and instructed us to board the bus quickly, find a seat and keep our heads below the window line. If we failed or looked up, they assured us we would be beaten with the hardwood clubs they wielded. We ran in single file with heads lowered, down the steps and into the bus. Once we found a seat, we dropped our heads to our knees. It was anybody's guess what would happen next.

# 11

# AFTERMATH

The bus drove off slowly with vigilantes standing over us, tapping heads to remind every one of us to keep them down. I stayed low not wanting any more punishment. Whatever it was they didn't want us to see wasn't important. Unknown to them, we'd seen it all from the window of our cell. The journey lasted only a minute or so, and when the bus came to a halt, we were ordered to dismount and sit on a row of benches a few yards away.

Directly in front stood a two-storey house painted white with a concrete stairway running up the outside of the building to the upper floor. Behind the house, a wide river coursed its way through the rainforest, the thick jungle foliage running hazily back as far as the eye could see. Four vigilantes kept watch with a keen eye. I stared over to the far bank, watching birds take flight and skim the fast-moving river in search of food. A vibrantly coloured butterfly floated cautiously within reach and gave a splendid display of purples and reds. I became lost in a moment of tranquillity. My thoughts reached out to Sam and loved ones, and to all the things one took for granted back home.

For the first time since we'd sat down, I took in my position. The river and jungle to my left. To the right, a roadway skirted with cinder-block buildings, beyond which lay thick jungle. I turned in my seat. Behind me stood the feared Casa Amarilla. In the distance, I could see the destroyed CPO and máxima compounds, and all around hundreds of soldiers patrolled and interacted with purpose.

The Casa Amarilla resembled a castle in an odd way. The walls were 25 feet high set in an oblong with circular turret-type guard towers built into the corners giving the whole place a rounded, medieval look. One large building sat in the middle, the roof just visible above the walls. The main gates, ten feet high, faced me. There was a lot of activity in that area, soldiers and vigilantes alike. The amphibious vehicle came towards us slowly, reminding me of a predator on the hunt, an animal on the prowl.

Twenty yards away, it turned right and headed down in between buildings. I assumed the white house in front of me was the dirección. I looked amongst the prisoners and vigilantes coming and going, then rubbed my eyes in wonder: coming towards me with a vigilante was my friend Ivor from Margarita.

Nearing, his voice boomed, '*Hepa*! *Como estamos*, my frien's?' He may have been dressed in a brown shirt, shorts and plimsolls like every other prisoner but, as always, an aura of controlled presence surrounded him. 'Hey, Frank, how are you my frien'?' he asked, gripping my manacled hand. His eyes drifted over the filthy and beaten foreigners. 'You need cigarettes?' he asked. Affirmative replies prompted him to shout to a passing prisoner, who palmed Ivor's money and took off to procure a pack.

Help came when least expected. That particular day it was Ivor.

It lifted my spirits seeing him again. Ivor resided in the building known as the anexo to the right of where we sat. It housed 180 'workers' of good conduct status. The man escorting Ivor was the jefe de régimen, who was in charge of all the vigilantes. He gave a short speech about how lucky we were to be out of the máxima. Pressure from several embassies had prompted the move and because Ivor had spoken highly of our group we would be given the chance to prove ourselves.

He pointed to our right. 'You can all live in the *esquina caliente*,'
I translated this to mean 'hot corner'. I found it difficult to take

in, still shell shocked. My thoughts during the short bus ride had been that they'd made a mistake, or the embassies had intervened and we were about to be taken back to Margarita. We were the only foreigners in the whole Venezuelan penal system to have been sent to El Dorado and now we were being moved from one hell to another.

With a cool breeze blowing in from the river, we enjoyed a cigarette and waited for an orderly to bring new uniforms. The clothes arrived, handcuffs were removed and we changed quickly. Conscious of security, the vigilantes replaced the handcuffs and we marched in single file 150 yards back to a building halfway between the anexo and the Casa Amarilla. The Casa Amarilla loomed large as we neared, the walls taking on a yellow tinge. A feeling of death and misery hung in the air. The hairs on the back of my neck bristled.

A number of soldiers escorted a couple of bleeding prisoners into a doorway at the far end of the building we were heading for. In a storeroom, we collected a foam mattress each, were told to sit on a concrete bench and within a short time they provided a meal of hot soup and bread. It transpired that the *cantina* was also part of the same building. Having managed to escape the máxima with a little money, several of us bought cigarettes and a vigilante removed the handcuffs. Since my arrest, my belly had shrunk to such an extent that the soup and bread, though of meagre proportion and substance, satisfied my hunger. We relaxed some, smoking and talking in comparative peace.

Before too long, we were marched off carrying our foam mattresses in the direction of the esquina caliente. A metal door separated our cell from the rest of the building; it measured twelve yards by five. The heat was insufferable – so intense the place easily earned its nickname. Swarms of flies buzzed around inside. A few local prisoners looked up in astonishment as we piled in. Three heavily barred windows faced the prison and before I had a chance to familiarise myself with the new surroundings, someone gave a gleeful shout. In the corner of the cell partitioned off with lengths of corrugated-iron sheeting I could see a small cubicle. A hosepipe capped off with a piece of wood had caused Alex's premature rejoicing. It worked perfectly well and we fought each other playfully over who would shower first. With no one acknowledging the three residents of the esquina caliente, they looked on in bewilderment, possibly wondering what they had done wrong to merit their space and tranquillity being taken away by our presence. We washed pain and dirt from our bodies under the cool water, gently in places where the blood had dried. When I'd finished, I saw the multitude of cuts, scrapes and bruises covering my body. My right ear was still acting as conductor to an orchestra of dull throbbing pains. We'd taken a real beating that morning, but at least we were alive.

Once the water evaporated from our bodies, the heat seemed to intensify. I dragged the mattress to a space under the window with the faintest hope of catching the breeze. Within minutes, the mattress was soaked in sweat. I closed my eyes, the horrors of the past 24 hours flashing before me. After a while, all conscious thoughts vanished and I fell into a deep sleep.

Being shaken by Mike, I woke with a start. 'Hey, Frank, c'mon, we got some food!' he said, passing me a bowl, explaining a vigilante had brought it while I slept. Two prisoners served the food through the open doorway, a vigilante and several soldiers stood behind, urging us to be quicker. '*Rápido! Rápido!*' they shouted. Groggily, I made my way to my mattress and began eating the rice with my fingers. Although it was warm, it still had the knack of making me heave to swallow.

Not long after, we were taken outside for número. Our headcount came to 17. During the count, I noticed the building opposite for the first time. It was a large garage workshop with vehicles inside, bonnets raised. To the side and behind a huge mango tree lay a junkyard of old vehicles; amongst the weeds sat an old rusty American school bus. Before I had a chance to take in any more, we were herded back inside by shouting soldiers and, to our relief, we took no beats. The door was slammed and padlocked: it was our first night out of the máxima.

An hour later, Ivor came to the window and called my name.

I jumped up and we shook hands through the bars. We talked for an hour at least, he debriefing me on what had gone on since our arrival in the máxima. The riots and massacre had been provoked by Vasquez, who prompted the hard-handed treatment of prisoners with around-the-clock lock-ups, the distribution of inedible food, and constant physical mistreatment at números and mealtimes by the Guardia Nacional and vigilantes. It was only a matter of time before it had exploded. According to Ivor's sources, sixty-seven prisoners had died in the CPO, seven in the máxima and another eighty were wounded. His information seemed pretty close, more or less tallying with what we had witnessed.

I asked about the trucks and bodies. He answered with a wry smile, saying the corpses had been taken down river and fed to the piranhas. I couldn't believe what I was hearing.

'And the others?' I asked.

He told me there were over 1,500 men crammed into the Casa Amarilla, a prison built in the 1950s to hold 500 men in cramped conditions. José and Ricardo were still alive, as were Carlo Pino, Chivo Loco and the others. Only two from Margarita had died. One was a guy called 'Tio Gordo' ('Fat Uncle'), whom I knew from pavilion four. He was shot dead by the guardia. The other person I knew very well: it was Ernesto, the pastor from the evangelist church. He'd been one of four men beheaded by inmates during the violence. Ivor was well informed. He also told me four prisoners had escaped during the riots – three rich Colombians who lived in Sing Sing and Carlito, the electrician from Margarita. He'd helped them bypass the alarm system and in return they took him along on a waiting boat. Ivor also said that after a week or two, when things settled and there weren't so many soldiers around, we would be allowed outside during daytime. I believed him because the jefe de régimen was an acquaintance of Ivor's from Valencia and as such treated him favourably – like being able to stroll about in the cool night air while we sweated in the esquina caliente! We said goodnight and he was gone.

Two hundred yards away, darkness on the edge of the rainforest brought its jungle chorus, which grew louder and louder as the minutes ticked by. Behind the dense foliage, frogs croaked throatily while insects and animals called out in reply. The prison had been well positioned: it felt as though the whole site had been cut out of the jungle, making it almost impossible to escape. The night also brought hoards of mosquitoes that bit relentlessly.

No sooner had I fallen asleep when I was woken by something scurrying across my bare legs. My heart jumped. I sat up quickly and rubbed my eyes. In the darkness, I could see black shapes running and climbing everywhere: the place was alive with rats! Before I had time to blink an eye, another rat, at least a foot long and as black as coal, ran over my mattress and across the room. In the gloom, I saw other foreigners awake and sitting, watching the rat's progress; however, the three locals slept on regardless. The rats gathered in strength, climbing the eaves, darting along roof girders and then regrouped on the floor. Although there were scores of them, they didn't seem to bother anyone. No one was attacked or bitten, and eventually we all fell asleep again. By daybreak, there wasn't a rat to be seen, their place taken by thousands of flies.

Número and breakfast passed quickly and the local residents went off to work. Later that morning, the prison doctor came over and pronounced us all fit and well. He was an amicable old man and very friendly towards foreigners. We chatted for a while about England, which he'd visited with his wife some years before. Somehow the conversation turned toward my talents with paper and pencil and before I knew it I had promised to sketch a portrait of him if he furnished me with the materials and a clear photo. Two days later, he returned with a large drawing pad, pencils, a rubber and a photo of himself taken 20 years earlier. It was the first of many drawings I would do during the months to come in El Dorado.

After being locked up for a week, the jefe de régimen came and gave another little speech. Speaking clearly and concisely, he said that, in his opinion and that of other vigilantes, we had behaved well and would be allowed to sit outside each day after número. We could walk north as far as the dirección and 100 yards in the opposite direction. We could also walk to the canteen once a day but should anyone try to escape or be found where we shouldn't be, every last one would be thrown into the Casa Amarilla.

The first days out of the esquina caliente were heavenly. I spent most of my time sitting by the dirección looking out over the river. I also noticed a public telephone hidden under the stairway. Below on the bank, a concrete quay jutted five yards into the river. At its end, stone steps disappeared into the fast-flowing water. The positioning of the quay created a large pool on one side and I would see prisoners washing in the waist-high waters. In the distance, a half-mile upstream on the opposite bank, lay the gold-mining town of El Dorado, shimmering hazily in the midday heat.

Every afternoon a strong breeze gathered pace along the river and within minutes a torrential downpour would come from nowhere, the droplets sometimes as big as marbles. We'd noticed two or three small waterfalls falling from the garage roof opposite and it wasn't long before we'd acquired some old five-litre water tubs and started collecting it for our daily drinking water.

We were getting to know a few of the locals from the anexo. They were always keen to sell things to the gringos and within a week we'd procured a long length of cable, a paint-tin cooker, a cooking pot and enough food to muster one square meal a day courtesy of workers in the new kitchens behind the anexo. Food for the prison population was now being cooked in huge pots above open fires fuelled by deadwood from the jungle. We had managed to get hold of vegetables – mainly potatoes, carrots and the odd cabbage; tins of tuna and powdered milk were other supplies regularly on offer. Power lines running haphazardly outside the building provided our source of supply. Although a bit dodgy, it worked, and we could buy and cook our own food. Next, we acquired more cable and a lamp-holder with bulb: we had light. The following week, the locals moved out; they'd probably had enough of us by then!

The jefe de régimen would check us from time to time to make sure we hadn't 'run away'. One day, he asked if we would like to help unload a supplies truck. I'd seen the vehicles come by every few days, some carrying papayas, others meat, vegetables and boxed or tinned goods. Where the food went, no one knew, but it certainly wasn't dished out in the rancho each day.

Six from our party unloaded the truck into a heavily padlocked storeroom. Lifting and moving boxes and crates, bags of this and that proved to be heavy work. After we'd finished, the vigilante in charge said we could take a few things as a reward. In a cardboard box I packed oil, rice, blocks of raw sugar, powdered milk, tins of tuna and bags of maize flour. It was a good haul, and the box grew heavier with every step as I struggled back to the esquina caliente.

We were allocated more work after that, like trekking into the jungle with axes and machetes accompanied by two locals to collect deadwood for the kitchen fires. There were five other parties like ours, and we would sometimes meet along the same paths as we carried tree trunks on our shoulders back to the jail.

I hadn't seen Ivor around for a while. His friend, the jefe de régimen, would tell us no more than Ivor had been transferred back to Valencia for whatever reason. He obviously knew more but wouldn't disclose. It was a blow; I'd miss his easy-going manner and happy face.

Christmas had come and gone. We'd managed to buy some stolen chicken breasts that were destined for the vigilantes and feasted on them with potatoes and carrots. We also brewed rice liquor and got incredibly drunk on it. The guardia presence notably decreased in the new year; even the amphibious vehicle stopped its constant prowling. The *jefe* also found a new job for us: tidying up the storeroom at the back of the comando. He told us we were allowed to keep any old bed frames we found amongst the equipment as well. The job took four days to complete and amongst the jumble of things we managed to find enough parts to make six complete bunk beds; two solid spring frames atop cinder blocks made up the remaining beds needed. We were off the floor and away from the rats: a good start.

We also retrieved an old ceiling fan, which Juan Carlos and I managed to get working, strapping it tightly to a roof girder and jerry-wiring it. It wobbled at times but worked quite adequately. During our time at the comando, we spotted four brand-new lockers, keys in doors, just waiting to be stolen. One by one, we carried them down past the gate of the Casa Amarilla and across the grass to our cell, hoping no vigilantes would spot us.

Alex and I were carrying the last one late one morning as they were serving rancho at the gate of the Casa Amarilla. Hundreds of prisoners were milling around inside. Some way back in the queue for food, I saw José and Ricardo waiting in line, both looked bedraggled and the worse for wear. We saw each other simultaneously.

'*Hepa*, Frank,' came the shout. I greeted them in return and motioned to Alex to drop the locker. I asked if there was anything I could do for them. José only had time to shout money and cigarettes, pointing to one of the kitchen orderlies, before vigilantes moved him roughly along. Ricardo managed to point to the same guy. '*A el!*' he shouted, as he was served and moved along.

I gave the kitchen orderly 1,000 bolivares and a pack of cigarettes I'd bought from the canteen. 'You must give these to José and Ricardo,' I urged him.

'*Si, Si,*' he replied, '*no problema.*'

The vigilantes turned and noticed I was still there. We were moved on with threats of violence and abusive language. Alex and I took the last locker and disappeared quickly.

In mid-January, the German consul visited, bringing money and mail for everyone. I treasured the letters I received from home, reading them repeatedly until the words swam in front of my face. And the money was very helpful. I was now able to buy bits and pieces from the canteen and decent meals from the kitchen thieves. Things were looking up . . . until the jefe de régimen decided it was time we passed número around the back with men from the anexo. Those men may have been 'good conduct' prisoners but every one of them was a rogue and more vicious than any at San Antonio. There were always problems of some sort during número outside the anexo. Soldiers would beat latecomers who had delayed proceedings. Sometimes the old night vigilante would open up early and we'd have plenty of time to get there; other times he would forget us completely. There would be 14 missing and we would have to dash 100 yards and around the corner where soldiers waited, ready to lash out as we joined the end of the queue. Anexo números were never pleasant and rarely was there a time when one passed without some kind of violence.

One morning after número we were talking to the night vigilante before he went off duty. He was 75 years old and had lived in El Dorado for most of his life. I asked him if he remembered Papillon.

'Oh yes,' he replied with a smile, a faraway look in his eyes, remembering back to his youth. 'He's very famous, you know, he wrote a book,' he said at last, as if telling us something we didn't know. We weren't about to spoil his reverie and let him ramble on. The stories he told of those long-gone days were gruesome but fascinating in their own way. Papillon was a legend in these parts and, according to him, there were still records of his release in the dirección dating back to 1945. He tottered off eventually with a smile on his face, happy to have shared his memories with us.

During the day, vigilantes used small golf carts to travel about the compound. They were mainly used to carry heavy pots of food around the jail at rancho time with two kitchen orderlies sitting on the back, smiling at people as they passed, as if parading on some sort of carnival float. There were three of them and I would often see them being charged up in the garage. I knew one of the mechanics, Antonio, from Margarita. He had lived in the enfermeria there. He sported a drooping moustache that gave him the look of a Mexican bandit. He'd been taken from Margarita on the first transfer but had quickly used his talents to secure himself a job in the workshops. I mentioned the old bus to him, asking him if it was a runner.

'Why? Are you thinking of escaping in it?' he asked me, deadpan.

'No,' I laughed. I suggested he speak with the prison director and tell him we could renovate it to be used as the prison bus if he would find the needed parts. His eyes took on a distant look, then he smiled and tweaked his moustache; he was probably thinking of the brownie points.

'I'll do that,' he said, shaking my hand before we parted. I never thought any more of it.

Some days later, Harald was bushwhacked by a couple of knife-wielding locals from the anexo whilst relieving himself a short distance inside the jungle. Luckily, he was only carrying 5,000 bolivares. That very day, I asked Antonio if he could provide me with a suitable piece of metal so I could make a knife. With the seven-inch length of steel he gave me, I made myself a protector. Except for número, I carried it with me wherever I went. I'm happy I never had to use it; nevertheless, it gave me a sense of protection should I have ever had need of it.

Some of the guys managed to acquire tubs of white emulsion paint from the stores' vigilante and with broom heads we painted the dark walls inside our cell. It transformed the grimy, bare cinder-block completely. The esquina caliente began to look like home. The German consul had brought Alex a guitar, a radio and a Walkman with tapes, so now we could catch up on international news and listen to music. An outdoor grill was built with rocks and a metal grate we found amongst the auto junk, and we sometimes cooked outside under the mango tree across the road using deadwood from the jungle.

Most of the guys started bathing in the river each day, the water cooling our bodies from the burning sun. We dug a garden around the outskirts of the cell, filling it with small ferns and flowering plants taken from the edge of the jungle. The flowers attracted huge colourful butterflies and dragonflies, bringing a sense of normality to our world.

I remember February brought a plague of flying beetles. According to the locals, it was an annual event. They were gruesome-looking creatures, four inches long with an oval armoured shell, six barbed legs with clawed feet and an ivory head that made them look like prehistoric rhinoceros complete with horns. They would land from out of nowhere and cling to clothing. They were harmless; as it happened, the locals considered it a good omen if one landed on them and would walk around with their beetles fastened to their shorts, displaying them proudly. Harald decided he had to have one as a pet and kept it on a branch near his bed.

One day, Alex bought an anaconda from a local. The snake was at least six feet long. He carefully stripped off the skin, with a plan to use it to make wristbands. That night we cut the snake into chunks and fried it with garlic and potatoes. As Europeans, we ate many peculiar creatures during our stay at El Dorado, freshwater ray being one. It is a huge fish with a wingspan a yard across and a stinging barbed tail, but it is also almost boneless and tastes delicious. We tried alligator once, but nobody liked the tough, sinewy meat. All these animals were bought from locals who had caught them.

Harald once came back with a yard-long iguana and decided to play a little joke on me. I was napping on my bed when a tap on my face woke me. Opening my eyes, I was confronted with a prehistoric monster an inch from my nose. The look on my face prompted everyone to roar with laughter – when my heart stopped pounding, I joined in with them.

At the end of February, Ferdinand left us. His constant letter-writing and appeals had earned him early repatriation to Holland after serving only 11 months in Venezuela. It was something of a record. The two countries had a repatriation agreement but it usually took twenty months to administrate the paperwork. Ferdinand was very lucky to get away so early. We lined up to see him off. He climbed in the back of a small police van to make his way to Caracas from where he would fly home. Franz was the next to go in early March. Although he'd lived most of his life in Ibiza, his Dutch nationality assured him the right to be repatriated to Holland. He'd served 26 months in Venezuela.

That month, an official visited from the British embassy. She'd flown in to Ciudad Bolívar and hired a taxi for the five-hour drive. She brought money and letters for everyone and promises that repatriation talks between Great Britain and Venezuela would soon be under way. There was no agreement to date. I received one letter in an official-looking envelope, so opened it right away only to find to my dismay a county court poll tax demand for £64, plus the costs and interest that had accrued from the previous November. The debt was three years old, the letter four months. I couldn't believe it. I wanted to laugh, but I was too angry. How they had found me in the middle of the jungle baffled me completely.

She stayed for an hour during which time I gave her a letter I'd written to Sam, as she said she'd be going to Margarita the following week. She seemed quite impressed with our living conditions – if she'd seen the conditions in the máxima, she would have had a different opinion. After she'd gone, I used the public telephone for the first time. I called collect and asked Chrissy if she would sort out the poll tax mess. She was relieved to hear I was alive and well. She said people at home were concerned for my safety: the riots at El Dorado had been global news. She told me reports on the national news back home had said there were 11 dead and numerous wounded. I could have told her a different story.

A few days later, Antonio turned up with startling news. While trying to speak to the *director*, he had found out Vasquez wasn't there any more. Apparently, the local police had arrested him for playing a part in the escape during the riot. I didn't believe him at first, but he insisted that what he was telling me was true. The three Colombians had been caught and when questioned by the PTJ told them they'd given Vasquez 15 kilos of cocaine for his help. Our old friend had been locked in the police cells for some days. On finding out who he was, local thugs in there beat and raped him, and ripped out his gold teeth. All fascinating stuff, and whether it was true or not didn't matter, it sounded like good news at the time and I said as much.

'What about the bus?' I asked.

'Oh yes, the bus.' He replied. 'I spoke with the *sub-director*. We can start on it immediately.' He sounded enthusiastic and if he was as keen as I was, it would be an interesting project to pass the time.

During April, prisoners in the Casa Amarilla were close to rioting again. People had climbed onto the roof to protest and were threatening blood strikes, when prisoners gash themselves open with knives. Rumours had spread of a mass suicide bid. Conditions inside the Casa remained diabolical, with no water or toilets and no beds. It was a daunting sight, a giant, barred cage from floor to ceiling in a concrete frame. I saw it several times whilst working at the comando. As the road passed the Casa gate, it rose steeply then levelled out. At the top of the incline I could see directly into the compound. From floor to roof, hundreds of bedsheets were tied flat across to the bars, people using them as makeshift hammocks because there wasn't enough room for 1,500 men to sleep on the floor.

True to their word, late in the month and over a period of three days, 135 prisoners cut their arms and legs in an official, documented protest against being transferred from their prison of origin. A hunger strike would have had no effect, as most were starving anyway. They were busy days for the medics.

I spent a lot of time on the bus during April. It had been well stripped of parts, but with a little help we pushed it to the back of the garage and began to work on the body while we waited for replacements to arrive. I concentrated on the interior and bodywork, spraying it a medium blue, while Antonio worked on the engine and transmission. Panels ran its whole length and I masked them both sides and painted in white letters six inches high CENTRAL PENITENTIARIA ORIENTAL EL DORADO. There were perks: I was allowed to stay out after lock-up and wander about in the cool night air.

After six weeks, the moment of truth arrived. Antonio connected a freshly charged battery and turned her over. Black smoke belched from the exhaust as the engine caught and revved. Everyone in the garage cheered, and after some fine adjustments the engine idled smoothly. We were proud of our achievement; it had taken many weeks of hard work but was worth every moment – best of all, the time had disappeared.

During May, a delegation of administrators from the Ministry of Justice in Caracas arrived at the prison and stayed for two weeks, sleeping at the Guardia Nacional comando and working in the dirección each day. Their job was to establish work records and the conduct status of prisoners at El Dorado for consideration towards future benefits. It was a joke! The place was a shambles: prisoners in the Casa were on the point of rebellion, with people on rooftops protesting. I actually saw Carlo Pino up there several times during my visits to the canteen. Strapped around his thigh was a wide bandage, proof that he had taken part in a blood strike. We would greet each other with a wave.

On one visit to the canteen, a pleasant surprise awaited me: there, behind the grille of the serving hatch, stood Ciro, my old companion from San Antonio. He'd managed to grease the right palms and got away from the Casa and into a plum job running the canteen. He still had the same old cheeriness and offered me unlimited credit in his little cantina. I asked if he could get things inside the Casa, and he replied he could do that without a problem. With the little money I had, I did the best I could, sending maize flour to my friends regularly, sometimes cigarettes. I felt for the guys in there; they were treated brutally, and as bad as the esquina caliente was, it was luxury compared with the Casa Amarilla.

Much confusion arose when the time came for the foreigners to see the delegation. Files were lost, paperwork misplaced, entries were back to front – it was absolute chaos. In the end, they allowed Kike, who spoke excellent English, to sit at a computer and type all our details from scratch. It took a couple of days and, eventually, they had all the information they needed, including files for each one of us containing proof of work and good conduct, all stamped, signed and in triplicate.

When my paperwork was finished, I waited in the office upstairs for the *sub-director* to sign and stamp them. I asked him if the old records of Papillon were still around and if so, whether it would be too much trouble to find them. He was only too happy to oblige. He went off, returning a few minutes later with a dusty old ledger and leafed through the pages until he found what he was looking for. There, in faded ink, halfway down the page, was the entry: 'Charrière, Henri. *Poner en libertad* 19 – *Octubre* 1945', along with other details about him. Beneath, was another entry for someone named Picolino, with the same date, same year. Amazing! There it was, right in front of me, proof of the legend Papillon. It's a moment I will remember for ever.

Several more foreigners left El Dorado in June. Mike went first, the American embassy arranging a transfer for him. He would spend a few nights in Los Teques prison near Caracas, then move on to Santa Ana jail in the Andean foothills, close to the Colombian border, reputed to be the best in Venezuela, if there was such a thing. I was sad to see him go; we'd always got on well and we'd been through some tough scrapes together. Four Spaniards followed him shortly afterwards: Sal, Juan Carlos, Xavier and Juan. All four had asked for repatriation and were happy to go.

We were down to seven: two Brits, two Spaniards and three Germans – the esquina caliente seemed huge with half our number gone. One night in June, we heard a broadcast on Alex's radio that 26 prisoners had escaped from the jail in Barcelona. The mass breakout prompted me to jokingly suggest we escape from El Dorado by strapping several water containers together to construct a raft. The others dismissed it as a crazy notion. It was.

In July, prisoners in the Casa Amarilla were on the rampage. Scores had mounted a rooftop protest, more gashed their limbs and word was out of a mass suicide pact among the population. News bulletins concerning El Dorado were broadcast regularly on the radio and the troubles were attracting a lot of media attention. Someone must have taken notice eventually because two weeks into the month three long, green Guardia Nacional buses rolled up to the jail and took 170 prisoners back to their own jails.

At the beginning of August, the buses returned. One was destined for Margarita this time. I was desperate to get back to San Antonio, but my name wasn't on any lists in the dirección – Tammier and I were the only ones to make enquiries, as none of the others wanted to go back. We were told the seats had been allocated and the buses were full. Prisoners from the Casa Amarilla had priority.

That same day, with a little monetary persuasion in the right places, I managed to secure a transfer back to Margarita for Tammier and myself on the next bus, which would be in four weeks' time. The month dragged on slowly and then excitement filled me as the day drew closer. I would see Sam again. I'd missed her so much. I would get away from this awful place and put the horrors of the past ten months behind me.

Finally, the day came. Tammier and I said our goodbyes and made our way over to the Casa, where crowds of transferees waited outside. It was to be another unforgettable journey.

# 12

# HELTER-SKELTER

The journey back to Margarita from El Dorado was slightly less arduous than the journey there. After sitting on the small tarmac cancha opposite the Casa Amarilla in the burning hot sun for two hours, we were bound tightly at the wrists with wide tape and ordered to board one of the buses. As we made our way over to the vehicles, I saw that Ciro was part of our transfer and greeted him with a wave. In that moment of distraction, I lost contact with Tammier, who I'd hoped to share a seat with on the long journey. We were to have the luxury of two per seat this time. The order came for me to sit on the right-hand side, halfway down, by the window. The bus quickly filled in a disorderly manner, with prisoners who'd been allocated seating arguing noisily about who would sit with whom. To my dismay, the creature that sat beside me smelled so dreadful I had to turn my head.

Although they warned everyone to get their heads down the moment the bus drove through the open gates and across the bridge, I could see through the bottom of the window without risking a beat, which was gratifying, as it would help to break the monotony and mean I could avoid having any contact with my immediate neighbour. As the journey continued, I began to feel apprehensive about how we would be treated at the other end. I suppose in an odd kind of way I'd grown accustomed to the relative peace and quiet of the esquina caliente. Now, small doubts began to creep into my head. I had no idea how things were in San Antonio, but I missed Sam so much I had to be with her. Had that desperate need clouded my judgement, I wondered? Whatever the outcome, it was too late to change my mind. Early memories of El Dorado were still horribly vivid in my mind, and it was to be a long time before I dreamt sweetly again. I was on my way and glad in my heart to be leaving the rainforest behind me.

From the corner of my eye, I watched the landscape flashing by. Six or seven hours later, we crossed the Orinoco by means of a huge cantilever bridge spanning the river at Ciudad Bolívar. No sooner had we crossed than darkness descended. The colder air that accompanied night-time was welcome; though, as no prisoner had been given food or water since our departure, the drop in temperature was little consolation.

I must have fallen asleep, because a sudden jerk snapped me awake. Bright lights shone through the windows, blinding me briefly, as the bus drew to a sharp stop. Still groggy, I initially thought we'd arrived on Margarita. I raised my head to look and, seconds later, received a whack on the head from a soldier. It turned out we were at a filling station. My head throbbed as I tried in vain to get back to sleep. Through the night, the odd light would flash by the window, piercing my tired eyelids.

Daylight slowly seeped into the bus, carrying with it a deep-blue empty sky. Another hot day loomed on the horizon. The sun rose higher, heating the bus's interior to the point of discomfort. The only good outcome of this was that the sweat dampened the tape around my wrists and, with a few tugs and twists, it became loose enough to be almost comfortable. I kept this breach of conformity concealed; I didn't need a headache for the rest of the day.

In the early afternoon, we stopped at Barcelona jail to allow prisoners off the bus. We pulled up outside a 15-feet-high perimeter fence topped with razor wire. Behind the wire, men and women stood about in groups: the men proudly displaying pistols tucked in their waistbands, the women standing alongside, proudly displaying their men. A Guardia Nacional officer boarded and gave a short speech to those prisoners going into the jail. Basically, he said that the Guardia Nacional were very easy to get along with, providing two rules were followed to the letter: the first, respect the soldiers at número; the second, and most important, respect the visitors. Apart from that, he said, they could do whatever they liked. '*Plomo*,' was his last word.

The transferees were taken to the main gate, 50 yards away, where they simply meandered inside, slapping high-fives with their comrades. We, in turn, disembarked and were told to sit on the kerbside while soldiers took turns to eat and drink at the comando. I sat with Ciro, who lifted my spirits with his laughs and smiles. He was a good companion on days such as this, as nothing seemed to get him down. We sat for almost two hours in the scorching sun, still taped and without food or water.

Prisoners behind the fence began shouting at us, but my mind was miles away. I was perhaps unconsciously distancing myself from this wretched place, wanting to make haste for Margarita. I guess 20 or so prisoners boarded the bus, and we set off again, with heads bent low. After reaching the port of Cumaná, we waited another hour to board the ferry. I was thankful the dreadful journey would soon be over. I would be back with Sam and in my little room in pavilion four that night.

The crossing was smooth, and the four-hour trip passed quickly and without sickness. It had grown dark on the crossing, and I imagined it was around seven when we docked in Margarita. Within the hour, we were in San Antonio jail, sitting in rows outside the enfermeria. Salazar came along with his clipboard, shouting names and the pavilions we had been assigned to. When my name came up, I tensed for a few seconds. '*Pabellión cuatro*,' Salazar said. I breathed a sigh of relief.

We passed número and marched off to our respective pavilions. Familiar sights greeted me, as Flores escorted our party of seven through the gate and towards pavilion four. A prisoner named Perez and I were let into four, the rest he took to five, Ciro among them. I considered how he'd managed to fix that one, but then realised he was on home ground. Besides, Ciro was a talent all on his own. Walking into four, I was hit instantly by a sea of faces and the pungent smell of marijuana. It took me back to my first night.

I looked around for a familiar face, ignoring the flotsam that begged and scrounged. Carlo Pino was the first I recognised. He carried a huge knife and guarded the corridor as always. As he turned and saw me, his eyes narrowed to slits and a smile split his face. I walked up to him and took his outstretched hand.

'Hey, Frank, you made it back then?'

The begging locals left me alone immediately. It was quite a different entrance to my first, almost three years earlier, when I had arrived, not speaking a word of Spanish, and asked for my '*amigo*' Paul.

Carlo Pino took me directly to José's room, and I was shocked at what I saw. José was lying on his bed, covered in bandages from his neck down to his waist; but it didn't stop the huge smile that spread across his face as I stood, open-mouthed, staring down at him. Ricardo and Chivo Loco sat by his side. We greeted one another. Others were sitting in the corner glued to a TV show. With a wave of his hand, José gestured that I sit close to him. Ricardo moved slightly and I took my position, curious to know the story, but I held back from asking because he'd probably recounted it in detail a hundred times already. We chatted and laughed about old times. A local carried in a large pot of black beans and rice: I was so hungry I devoured two bowls within minutes. José and Ricardo told me how they'd survived seven and a half months in the Casa Amarilla, with its suicide pact and blood strikes – Carlo carried a foot-long scar on his thigh, evidence of his involvement.

Slowly, José recounted his story. On his return from El Dorado, he was immediately thrown in the máxima, accused of having instigated the protests in the Casa Amarilla. The rest were put in the enfermeria for the first week. Pavilions four and five had lain empty since an attack from the other side two months after our transfer to El Dorado.

Prisoners from pavilions two and three had banded together and attacked an unprepared four and five, killing some, wounding others and stealing everything they could carry. Following the ensuing raqueta, Salazar placed the remaining prisoners of four and five in the enfermeria, where they stayed until the first busload returned from El Dorado. They'd been back in four only a matter of weeks.

Unfortunately, José had several enemies in the máxima. Without weapons to defend himself, he was pounced on by a group carrying knives. He was stabbed 17 times and left for dead. It happened at rancho time. José had been carried inside the dirección by two vigilantes and left to bleed. An orderly cleaned him up before the ambulance arrived. He had spent three weeks recovering under guard in Porlamar hospital. Seventeen stab wounds, and a month later the guy was lying there as large as life! José was one tough *hombre*.

We were still at war with the other side, but the máxima had now become the main target. It was as if El Dorado had never happened.

My old room had been taken over by four of José's lieutenants, and I wasn't about to argue with the arrangement. I said my goodnights and walked down the corridor to find a slot where I could rest my head for the night. Many old faces greeted me and before too long I was talking to Ramon, another who'd made it back in one piece. We'd been chatting for a couple of minutes when Cardoso appeared from the room opposite. I left Ramon and greeted him, the big, friendly giant. I told him of my predicament and, without a thought, he invited me to stay in his room until I sorted out something permanent. From nowhere, a mattress appeared. Feeling safe for the first time in ages, my growling stomach satisfied, I collapsed into a deep sleep.

Cardoso shook me the following morning in time for número. I was ready for the gauntlet this time around, the soldiers yelling and swinging their planillas as we ran onto the cancha and got in line. '*Cuarenta!*' I shouted as my turn came.

Looking around, I saw many familiar faces. Twenty feet down the line, I saw the Danes, Peter and Mads. We acknowledged each other at a distance, but when we broke ranks to head back inside, we ran together. They were living in a boogaloo in los vagos, a separate part of pavilion four, next to the evangelist church. We agreed to meet up at breakfast time, when vigilantes opened up for the day.

Inside the pavilion, I walked the corridor for a while, still wearing the brown prison uniform issued in El Dorado. Juan Carlos, a Colombian member of José's gang gave me a pair of his jeans and a T-shirt. At first, I looked him up and down, weighing up whether I could fit into his clothes. He was tall and skinny. I'd overlooked the fact I'd lost four stone since my incarceration. They fitted perfectly. I hardly knew the guy, nor he me, and the gift touched me. He and I became firm friends as time went on.

I met up with Peter and Mads after breakfast. Sitting in their boogaloo, I listened to tales of the attack and the subsequent move to the enfermeria, and the tough months they had endured during my time away. Although I'd heard José's take on events, it was still a frightening thought that I'd escaped the horrors of El Dorado only to be pitched into another war zone. The conversation turned, and it gave me a chance to borrow paper and a pen and write a short letter to Sam, which I dispatched with a runner.

Late in the morning, I was called to the dirección. The consul had arrived. One thing had changed slightly: no longer was there a vigilante on the gate; instead, it was held shut with wire and manned by two prisoners. They instructed me to jump the wall, using footholds knocked out of the cinder blocks. Excited by the thought of seeing Sam for the first time in many months, I made my way across and entered the building at such a pace I completely forgot about Mr Mellor and walked straight past him. When I first laid eyes on Sam, I was overcome with shock. I held her at arm's length, taking her in. She looked gaunt, her face thin and ashen, her eyes dull and lifeless. It took me a few seconds to register why she looked that way.

'Oh, God, Sam, what have you done to yourself?' I said, choking back the tears. We held each other tightly and cried openly.

'They said you weren't coming back!' she sobbed. 'I've got myself in such a mess.'

We vowed that this would be a fresh start. Mr Mellor cleared his throat for the umpteenth time and gained our attention. He had been very patient during our reunion but swiftly got down to the business in hand. He'd brought money and letters for everyone, he said, and had rearranged *entre vistas* for Sam and me. In less than ten minutes, he took his leave. I held Sam until the last possible moment, then scrambled back over the wall, found a quiet spot and read my letters over and over again. There had been odd shots fired between the pavilions that morning, and Mr Mellor had made a quick exit when a flurry of shots were exchanged between rooftop *garitas*.

I asked José about the gate. He told me it was a delaying tactic for when the *guardia* came in. Ironically, as we spoke, vigilantes' shotguns boomed in the background and the siren went off. The tactic may have given everyone more time to conceal their weapons and miss the gauntlet, but we all paid for it in the end. By the time a soldier had scaled the wall and untangled the wire, the angry remainder piled in with venom, kicking and beating us as we lay prone on the ground. No one escaped unscathed.

After a while, we were ordered to stand in rows and run, hands on heads, round the back of pavilion five, across no–man's–land, then behind pavilions one, two and three to a large *cancha* situated in open ground. Soldiers were spaced along the way, shooting plastic at our feet and lashing out with *planillas*. I took a few stinging pellets across my ankles, but I didn't stop. It was quite a run. Before I reached the *cancha*, I had slowed to a walk, my chest heaving from the effort. I wasn't on my own; other prisoners had slowed down around me. A screaming soldier ran up and fired his shotgun point-blank at a guy no more than a yard from me. The blast, though plastic, shredded the man's shorts and left a bleeding hole in his upper thigh four inches in diameter. The sight and closeness of it gave me the extra jolt of energy to dash the remaining 50 yards to the *cancha*.

This was a new twist to the *raquetas*. Soldiers kept up the pressure, ordering everyone into rows by pavilion number and ordering them to strip and sit with hands on heads. It was a blistering hot day, the midday sun firing the concrete, which literally burned the skin where it made contact. The excruciating pain on my buttocks and heels became unbearable, and increased as the minutes rolled slowly by. For more than two hours, we were forced to sit in the fiery heat, burning concrete causing everyone to fidget uncontrollably, while the soldiers strutted between the lines, beating prisoners at random. Why the fuck did I come back to suffer this all over again?

I gritted my teeth, my face and chest drenched with sweat, the pain so indescribably intense it was impossible to shut it out. Eventually we made our way back, on the run, through the dirección and across to the pavilions. It was just as well I didn't have any possessions that day because our pavilion had been completely ransacked.

The aloe plant was busy that night, yet, despite its healing properties, along with everyone else, I woke the following morning with huge blisters on my backside and feet. I was barely able to move without screwing my face in agony. Walking was a real struggle, each laborious step torture in itself. Running out for número proved an almost impossible task: the majority of prisoners hobbled there and back racked with pain. I spent the rest of the day lying on my stomach.

Visiting hours on Saturdays always promised a somewhat peaceful day, but I noticed another change of routine – the rooftop garitas were manned with armed prisoners during those hours. Although no shots were exchanged, we had to be constantly alert in case the fragile truce on such days fell apart. A vigilante also stood at our gate, controlling visitors, the wire having been untangled before they entered the jail.

Through the gate, I noticed girls selling their wares outside the enfermeria. I could see Sam from where I stood, but the vigilante wouldn't let me pass. It transpired that I would need to go through the whole routine again with the new *director* before I could sit with her at weekends. I was gutted.

After the first week, I moved in with Peter and Mads. Los vagos was separated from the rest of the pavilion by a cinder-block wall. It measured thirty feet by fifteen, with two rooms taking up the far end. The rest was filled with boogaloos, made with wire and bedsheets. A hole in the floor, with a six-foot-high wall around it, functioned as the communal toilet. A length of plastic piping with a crude valve on the end constituted a shower of sorts in the same area. Peter and Mads shared a boogaloo in the right-hand corner, a space ten feet by six with a bunk bed, table, paint-tin cooker and television. Mads offered me the top bunk, with Peter beneath. Mads rolled out a thin mattress and bedded down on the floor each night.

September passed quickly, the day in, day out sudden explosive sound of gunfire never ceasing. Raquetas became an almost weekly occurrence, opening old wounds, adding to the bruising; the blisters barely healed.

Something quite new came along in October: the Ministry of Justice declared that attendance at educational classes would count towards benefits. Of course, it didn't appeal to many; but it sparked my interest. Volunteer teachers came in from the street each day and held classes in the salón. I joined a model-boat building class. It got me out and away during the day and gave me something else to think about, instead of the constant madness around me. Rufini, the corrupt kitchen vigilante, had been placed in charge of the benefit book, and each day he would come around and put a tick against my name. It proved a good little moneymaker for him, because a lot of the better-off prisoners, who didn't want to work, simply gave him money each week and received a tick.

On the grapevine, I heard that Juan, the electrician who'd taken over from Carlito, was about to be released onto the street on a working benefit. The two-wire 110-volt system wasn't difficult to understand, so I asked Rufini if I could take the job. I told him a bullshit story about being an electro-mechanical engineer back home, and it got me the job. And what a number it was, being out and about from morning número until eight or nine at night.

Salazar wanted me to live in the enfermeria, but I refused, preferring to stay with the guys I knew. With my new-found title, I could go anywhere in the jail without a problem; even into the anexo, where I would head whenever the siren went off. I escaped many raquetas this way, although there were odd times when I was out of position and inescapably found myself caught up in them.

My job was to repair the jail's electrical system, which was extremely dangerous, with overloading and cables burning out on a regular basis. There was no protection at all – no earth circuit existed, melted breakers had been bypassed and cables wired in directly. It was quite a task, but the challenge was exciting. The first project was to sort out the lights in the *director's* office. After a few days, and much salvaging of old electrical items, I sorted the problem. He was amazed to have all four fluorescent lights working at once, and all via a single switch! It may sound ludicrous, but that's the way it was. There wasn't a switch, socket or light that worked properly in the whole jail. I realised Juan had barely kept the place ticking over; he hadn't actually fixed anything.

I saw a lot of Sam with my job, as part of it was tending six Singer-type sewing machines in the anexo. Sam and five other girls machined children's clothing for a woman on the street, who owned several clothes shops in Margarita. They received a pittance for their long hours, but there was always plenty of work. Sam would sometimes ask the other girls to call me out to repair some invented problem with their machines and, on those occasions, I would wander over and talk to Sam for hours, while pretending to fix the machine.

The month of December in 1999 brought catastrophe to Venezuela. Initial reports estimated that up to 50,000 people on the mainland died when heavy rain triggered severe flooding and landslides. Congress declared a state of emergency. Hugo Chávez, the new president, dealt with the crisis incredibly well under the circumstances. We watched events unfold on television news bulletins each night. San Antonio had been under three feet of water for two days, undoing a lot of my hard work, but fortunately most of the damage wasn't permanent.

It was during that month that I became interested in the country's politics. Chávez had brought about radical change: a new constitution came into force at the end of December. It basically meant a new democracy, human rights, and an end to torture and inhuman treatment. Unfortunately, the penal code wasn't altered at that point, so beatings and raquetas continued as before.

I started to complain to the embassy about our treatment, sending letter after letter to Caracas, and I encouraged other foreigners to do the same. It was the start of my mission to put an end to the brutality and torture.

In January, six new foreigners arrived: three men and three women. Two of the men were Brits. One was 'Poco Pelo' (nicknamed as such by the locals because of his thinning hair), a quiet sort, who minded nobody's business but his own. He bought a small boogaloo in los vagos. The other was Danny, a likable young tearaway 'cockney rebel' who was either completely crazy or just didn't give a flying fuck. I could never work that one out. Nevertheless, he was a good sort, with a heart of gold and a bad cocaine habit.

Of the other new arrivals, Joey was a Canadian Filipino. A nice guy, but totally hooked on crack. 'Spiritual' would sum up Joey in one word: he felt so connected with nature, he could charm dragonflies to land on his finger; butterflies, too. I witnessed it many times. He had a serious asthmatic condition and, on occasions, would be rushed to the dirección, where an electronic nebuliser, donated by the Canadian consulate, was kept. His crack-smoking habit caused many attacks, but it didn't stop him – the drug had a good hold on him. Angelique came from South Africa, Monica from Germany, and Suzanne from Austria. All three spoke excellent English and were good-looking girls. They caused quite a stir among the male population, competing with Sam for wolf whistles and catcalls.

The months passed quickly. I became a workaholic, installing new circuits throughout the jail. The job may have had its rewards, but the downside came in the middle of the night, when, on numerous occasions, I would be woken to repair burned-out floodlights on the guard towers outside the prison walls. Soldiers accompanied me throughout the repair, and they were never a problem, yet somehow it was hard to communicate with them, as they'd caused me so much pain and suffering.

The new *director* was quite liberal in his thinking. As a devoted Chávez supporter, he welcomed the dramatic changes being made to the country. In February, he allowed entre vistas in the anexo gardens at weekends. It made a big difference to be able to sit with Sam without supervision.

It was during those early visits that I noticed another change in Sam. She'd made many male friends during my absence, guys I didn't know or particularly like. I would often come across her laughing and joking with slimy characters, and she would pull a face at being interrupted. I seriously began to wonder if my surprise return had cramped her style. I knew she'd been approached many times and bombarded with love letters while I was in El Dorado. My concern for and overprotection towards her appeared as jealousy in her eyes and caused many arguments.

To add to my anguish, Mads blurted out one night that I should keep an eye on my woman, as she'd spent a lot of time with other guys while I'd been away; he'd even seen her kissing them more than once. I didn't want to believe it – as if it wasn't bad enough just getting through each crazy day, now I had this eating away at me. I confronted her one day, and her deep frown and emphatic denial confirmed what Mads had said. I knew her well enough to see the lie behind her eyes.

This created a huge rift and started the decline of our relationship. We weren't the same any more and, although the last thing I wanted was to lose her, I had a heartbreaking feeling that it would be only a matter of time before we went our separate ways.

From that moment on, I ploughed all my energies into my work. The máxima was a shambles, having only two thin cables running through the wall from the evangelist church next door. I needed to run heavier cables from a distribution box 30 yards away. On my first day working in the máxima, I bumped into Psicario. He had made it back from El Dorado. He told me that, after we had gone, he was detailed to a working party that was made to clear rubble away. They lived in the ruins of the máxima for months afterwards.

It was difficult to talk openly with Psicario, as, on these particular jobs, a vigilante accompanied me. Although Psicario was my friend, the máxima was the enemy and my loyalties, if I had any, were with José and Ricardo. If I appeared over-friendly, word would soon get back. These were difficult times, and I tried to sit on the fence as much as possible. I knew many of the jail's population, and it would have been wrong of me to take sides. It was never my war anyway; but the others wouldn't understand that way of thinking, it was alien to them.

One day, whilst fixing a fuse board on the wall outside the salón, a familiar voice greeted me. '*Hepa*, Frank!' I turned to look. It was Santo Loco, the guy I'd battered in pavilion four. He was standing behind the gates of the enfermeria, grinning at me with his rotten teeth. 'Hey, *amigo*, give me a cigarette,' he said.

'What?' I answered incredulously. 'It wasn't so long ago you wanted to kill me, now you want to be my friend! Are you crazy?'

'Ahh, that's in the past now. You beat me well that day – give me a cigarette, eh?'

What could I do? I saw Santo Loco regularly after that, and every time I saw him it cost me a cigarette. He'd been put in the enfermeria for his own safety; he'd obviously upset a few people in the pavilions, because there was a price on his head.

In March, a 65-year-old Scottish woman called Irene came into the jail. She suffered with ill health, to such an extent, in fact, her two daughters flew from Scotland to Margarita to fight for her freedom. A tabloid newspaper sponsored one of their visits, with a reporter in tow to embellish the story. Sam and I chatted with him for a minute or two and told him nothing of any value but, a month later, when I phoned home, I received a severe rollicking from Chrissy. The press had knocked on her door, demanding her story – of how I'd left her and run off to South America with a blonde bimbo! She was told it was the love triangle story they were looking for, it was what the readers wanted. Chrissy told them to 'go away', or words to that effect, refusing the £10,000 offered. I was livid! The reporter hadn't done his homework. I'd been divorced for two years before I even met Sam.

That same month, Jiminez appeared back on the scene. He hadn't been at San Antonio on my return. He had been promoted and his rise in status encouraged him to strike with a vengeance. After the first raqueta under his charge, he had his soldiers remove our gate completely, leaving our side of the prison wide open. Armed prisoners sat each day in the gardens, ready and waiting for any possible attack. One day, José was inspired to remove the barred section from the apex wall of the workshops. A gang of prisoners dragged it down to our open gateway and propped it up, fastening it in place with wire stripped from the link fencing. It weighed a ton and proved a crude but effective deterrent: it became much easier to jump the wall than try to move it. Two prisoners dragged open and closed the makeshift gate when vigilantes needed to pass for rancho, the rest of the time it remained wired shut until lock-up each day. Jiminez was beside himself with rage and raquetas became fiercer than ever.

The new millennium brought with it serious investigations by Amnesty International and other organisations into human rights abuses in prisons in Venezuela. Torture and physical abuse inside jails were on the increase despite new laws and changes to the constitution. I wrote to Prisoners Abroad several times, giving details of the situation and explaining that embassies weren't doing enough to curb maltreatment. They, in turn, used their influence through the Foreign Office to put pressure on the British embassy in Caracas. It was a long, slow process, but the wheels had been set in motion.

The new constitution didn't stop Jiminez and his henchmen ignoring the law, wreaking havoc at every possible opportunity, beating prisoners mercilessly and destroying what little property the inmates possessed. To get away with this, the soldiers used a loophole in the penal code that gave them licence to enter the jail, claiming they took such actions to quell rioting and rebellion. Jiminez's interpretation of the penal code obviously didn't sit well with the foreigners, who continued to complain to their respective embassies.

Six months after taking the electrician's job, I'd almost completed my task. The *director* had taken me out of the jail several times to install a new system in his house beyond the grounds. On those occasions, his lovely wife would feed me like a king. One day, I staggered back to the jail carrying two overflowing bags of fresh vegetables. The *director* had plied me with cans of beer as I worked and, not having drunk alcohol for so long, it didn't take many before I was three sheets to the wind. Soldiers on the gate saw the state I was in, but the *director* guided me past them and to my pavilion. Later that week, I suggested to him that the prison needed a security lighting system and he financed it without a problem. Within a couple of weeks, a dozen large halogen lights dotted the jail, working from two switches in the dirección. I could do no wrong in the *director*'s eyes and my working benefits were mounting each day.

Danny moved into the enfermeria in May. His 'habit' had caused some problems with his creditors on our side and it was the only option available, other than hospitalisation. Salazar had been sacked the month before and, even though I'd made it easy to light up the four corners of the jail, Marin, the new jefe de régimen, insisted I stay out to switch the lights on, which left me with a lot of spare time in the evenings. Sometimes I would sit and talk to Sam through the gate of the anexo building, other times I would climb onto the dirección roof under the pretext of repairing something and sit there smoking a cigarette or two, watching the stunning sunsets.

Many times Danny would hide behind one of the hedges after número, wait until the soldiers had gone, then crawl commando-style over to the kitchens, where he would wait for me to come through. Marin caught him with me many times, but Danny would just laugh, and it was always infectious, because Marin would laugh too and shake his head. Danny was too much for him, and he always went unpunished, just for his cheek! Joey, meantime, moved into the kitchens to give him easier access to the dirección should he suffer an asthma attack. The three of us spent many evenings sitting under the stars. Marin eventually gave up on Danny and moved him into the kitchen building too.

A Colombian named Cristantio ran a small coffee stand from a lean-to that stood outside our gate. It also doubled as his accommodation, as he slept in the back. One evening, we were discussing El Dorado – he had been in the main jail when the soldiers had come in shooting. The conversation then turned to religion. Cristantio had become spiritual in a big way since his return and, when I asked why, he showed me his Bible. It had a nine-millimetre hole almost all the way through it! Apparently, out of sheer fright, he'd dropped to the ground holding the book against the back of his head as a soldier levelled his gun to shoot him. The bullet entered the Bible with such force it knocked Cristantio out cold, but the book saved his life in the process. An incredible story, but I believed every word. I saw the Bible with my own eyes.

I began to spend more time in los vagos, reading, drawing and listening to the local radio rock station. Now and then, I would be called out to repair sewing machines or the odd electrical problem, and still stayed out each evening after número, enjoying the cool night air with Danny and Joey. The war between the sides continued without a break, and I was caught up in many raquetas. After one particular episode, I lost my head, refusing point-blank to repair anything for the guardia ever again. I was adamant, whatever the cost. Why the fuck should I do anything for them when they continually beat me for no reason other than that I lived in pavilion four? Once I'd cooled down, I worried that I would lose my job. On the contrary, the *director* understood my feelings and told me to carry on as normal, but just inside the jail. Cristantio took over any work for the guardia, which suited me, as he was also working to enhance his benefits.

In June, two more Brits arrived. 'Ben' and 'Neil' had been caught with a huge amount of cocaine on board their boat. They moved into los vagos but kept themselves very much to themselves most of the time. Our section of the pavilion was quickly filling up with foreigners, and I knew the increase could be used to our advantage. There were now more people to put pen to paper and campaign against the brutality.

The following month, Venezuela re-elected Hugo Chávez as president. I watched his speeches on television. He claimed there was stiff opposition to his efforts to create, in his own words, 'a revolution without arms'. Earlier in the year, he had ordered 70,000 members of the military to participate in a countrywide public works programme, conducting a census, providing medical care to the needy, renovating schools and hospitals, even removing garbage. He was determined to get the country back on its feet and away from the long-standing economic crisis it had suffered.

There was evidence that 'interested parties', linked to corrupt elements in past administrations, were seeking to sabotage his efforts to stabilise Venezuela's national economy, inciting nationwide riots and strikes. The US president's name cropped up regularly as 'the main leader of imperialism worldwide'. It appeared Chávez didn't respect the American administration at all: he never spoke a kind word about it, nor the USA.

In August, sad news filtered through to San Antonio. Rival gang members had ambushed Ivor at Tocuyito prison in Valencia. He was shot in the head with his own gun and died instantly. Ivor had been much loved and respected by everyone, friend and foe alike, and many sombre faces walked the jail for days afterwards. José asked me to draw a portrait of Ivor from a small photo he'd been given by one of the girls in the anexo. Try as I might, I just couldn't get the eyes right; even in the small photo, Ivor's eyes were alive and mischievous. I had the strangest feeling he was standing over me as I drew. It made the hairs on my neck and arms tingle. In the end, the likeness was good, and José was pleased, but for me there was something not quite right. I would miss Ivor.

Time moved on. Shots were exchanged daily between pavilions, the routine never ceased. Raquetas continued in their brutal manner, despite the fact that embassies were talking directly with the Ministry of Justice in Caracas, complaining bitterly about the treatment of their nationals. Every three months, an embassy official came to the prison, bringing Prisoners Abroad money and letters from home, and keeping everyone informed on the progress of our complaints. Occasionally, I would bump into the Dutch consul on the grounds outside the dirección. Jab was a regular visitor and voiced his concern to me about conditions at San Antonio. He was a complete gentleman and would play a leading role in changes to come.

Christmas Day arrived with the sounds of excitement, as men groomed and smartened up with what little clothing they possessed. The jail would open for visiting, loved ones and family members arriving soon. The carnival atmosphere was already evident in the pavilions, as men waited for the hour. Sam and I had been incarcerated for four years, and I hoped this special day would heal the rift that had grown between us.

The prison opened its gates. I made my way over to Sam and we talked a while, both trying to reconcile our differences, but, as we spoke, I realised the bond was broken: things weren't the same any more.

At 2.30 p.m., I returned to my side, to watch kids running about playfully, women walking arm-in-arm with their menfolk. It was almost time for the visitors to leave, when – bang! bang! – two shots rang out from the direction of pavilions one, two and three. Half a minute later, the siren went off, and approximately 50 soldiers ran into the prison, shotguns booming, Fals chattering.

Absolute chaos followed: children running in every direction, screaming and howling, their mothers chasing after them, shrieking in horror. On our cancha, a horde of prisoners ignored the shooting and began shouting abuse at the soldiers, threatening them with violence. Some were even trying to physically disarm the soldiers, wrestling weapons from them. The air was electric. An incredibly chaotic few minutes followed before the shooting died down. No one on our side had provoked the shooting, and we were furious. The guardia had behaved like animals to cause such distress to women and children.

Prisoners on the yard stood firm; more joined from pavilion five. They continued to shout abuse at the soldiers, as visitors were quickly gathered and escorted out of the gate. The situation created by the guardia was spiralling out of control, the air buzzing to a fever pitch: where, and how, it would end would be anyone's guess.

A corporal had the presence of mind to move among his men and, without delay, we were locked up and told there would be no rancho or número later that day. In the evening, agitated prisoners stalked the pavilions, forming groups, making plans. I spent the whole time watching events, noting actions, wondering if this was, once again, the calm before the storm.

# 13

# BREAKDOWN

The next morning, I woke to an eerie silence. There was a noticeable tension among the prisoners, everyone waiting for the inevitable.

'*Agua verde!*' shouted a lookout.

My thoughts were interrupted. My heart rate jumped up a notch; adrenalin shot through my body like an electric current as prisoners pushed their way towards the unlocked door. It burst open to disorder and confusion as we funnelled out. Boom! Thwack! Boom! I ran like crazy, making it to the cancha with only one beat across my shoulders. Boom! Tat-tat-tat! There were scores of soldiers, the noise was deafening. Down I went, somewhere in the middle of the yard, taking a kick in the ribs, which knocked the wind out of me. I lay wheezing, as soldiers gave it their all for a few minutes. Then it fell silent.

We lay still, waiting until the order came, and when it did, we quickly got to our feet and formed rows with hands on heads. What followed will remain with me for ever. The first beat I received as we ran to the other side came from an aluminium baseball bat delivered by a brute of a soldier, a sergeant, in fact – I remember seeing the insignia on his sleeve when he swung his arm back. The blow hit me square at the base of my spine, and I dropped to the ground, momentarily paralysed, as other prisoners jumped over me, continuing their run to no-man's-land. The sergeant bent down and screamed at me to get up and run, raising the bat to strike me again.

Some unexplainable force always came to my rescue during moments like these. I managed to scramble up, escaping the bat, and stumble on for a few yards until I got my momentum. I looked back at the sergeant. 'You'll get yours one day, you bastard!' I called out, though he probably didn't hear or understand me.

Turning my head, I found myself running head-on towards a soldier 15 feet in front of me, who was preparing to fire his shotgun. Veering to the left into a patch of rough grass, I avoided the collision but, as I passed him, I heard the boom! I was a good 20 feet from him when pellets hit me, stinging like a hundred needles plunging into my back, right arm and right leg. Luckily, I was far enough away to make the shot non-piercing, but it hurt like hell all the same.

Only halfway across no-man's-land, I saw in front of me a line of crazed soldiers spaced ten yards apart. By the time I reached the cancha, I was gasping for breath. In rows, we stripped, and that's when I noticed the mess in my shorts. The blow from the bat had caused me to soil my pants. I felt angry and humiliated. Thoughts of a slow, agonising death for the sergeant filled my mind, and I vowed I would repay him one day for his brutality.

Jiminez strode out, as we sat naked on the cancha, and decided to play a cruel joke. For his amusement, he ordered each pavilion in turn to sing the national anthem. Soldiers walked up and down the lines, beating prisoners who weren't singing. There were many macho types who refused to sing, preferring the beats. Even though I'd been there for years, I didn't have a clue. I knew the tune, but not the words, so instead I sang my own version, inventing it as I went along, the lyrics filled with hatred and death towards Jiminez and his thugs.

Suddenly, I received a whack on the head from behind. A young officer bent down and looked me in the eye. 'I understand English,' he said, and walked on. Two hours later, we ran back to our cells and were locked up for the rest of the day.

That evening, news filtered through about what had happened the day before. An argument had broken out between two wives, visiting their respective men. The guys got involved and one shot the other, killing him instantly. After that experience, Christmas time would never be the same.

It took a few days to recover from the raqueta but, during the week, I began to lose my senses. I weighed just ten stone. I was unable to stomach the rancho food and, although I scrounged bits and pieces of decent food wherever I could, I was constantly hungry. A madness came over me. I'd had enough.

Not bothered if I lived or died any more, I decided to go on hunger strike to protest against the conditions. On the first day of January 2001, my birthday, as the call came for número I lay on my bed until a soldier entered the boogaloo and summoned me outside. I declined, and refused to work also. The first couple of days were very uncomfortable and I was desperately hungry but, as the days went by, the hunger pangs disappeared and were replaced by a strangely calm warmth within me. On the fifth day, as I got weaker, I began to hallucinate. The few real friends I had were concerned for my well-being, but I told them not to interfere.

By the end of the week, I had become delirious. I was shaking with a fever. On the morning of the eleventh day, while slipping in and out of consciousness, I vaguely remember someone shouting to bring the medic. I recall being lifted from my bed and wheeled on a trolley into bright sunshine, through the main gate and into an ambulance. The bumping and bouncing as it drove off threw me around so much I eventually passed out.

I came round on a trolley in the hospital, with a tube in my arm and a saline drip hanging in the air above me. I lay there all day, gathering strength as bags were replaced, and by the early evening I was fit enough to sit with the doctor in his office. I told him of the atrocious conditions in the jail and the disgusting food I couldn't keep down. He concluded I had a stomach ulcer and wrote a letter to the *director* of San Antonio, urging him to allow me a special diet. I knew there was no ulcer but wasn't about to argue. The doctor gave the letter to Chuito, my escort vigilante.

My friends welcomed me back into los vagos that evening with a helping of sardines and boiled rice. I was ravenous and ate it greedily, falling into a deep sleep within minutes of finishing. The next day I spoke with the *director*, who ordered Rufini, the kitchen vigilante, to issue me with a bag of raw vegetables twice a week. Rufini was not happy at having to give away food he normally sold to line his pockets. I returned to work the following day, feeling weak but filled with a sense of achievement as I collected my vegetables from a very reluctant Rufini.

I saw Sam that day. She said she'd been worried for me but showed her concern with anger, telling me what a fool I was and that if my friends hadn't made such a fuss in the dirección, I would surely have been left to die where I lay. I hated to admit it, but she was right – nobody gave a damn.

Some days later, whilst working on a fuse board in the dirección, an orderly, a cocky young piece of shit, made rude comments about Sam, gesticulating with his hand close to his mouth as he did so. I saw red, and chased him through the anexo gate. He was too quick, and I couldn't catch up to him, so I returned to my work. Ten minutes later, once he'd forgotten all about it, I saw him standing by the dirección gate, talking to Pablo, the prison plumber, a guy I only knew slightly. I walked up behind the orderly and placed the sharp end of my screwdriver against his throat, not quite piercing the skin.

'If you ever say anything about Samantha again,' I said into his ear, 'I'll stick this screwdriver in your eye, you cocksucker!'

'*Si, si*,' he replied, eyes wide with fright. '*Está bien!*'

That wasn't an apology by my way of thinking but, just then, Flores, the vigilante, walked past and stopped to take in the scene. '*Está bien?*' I said, getting angrier, then, without a thought, head-butted the orderly. Something snapped as my head connected with the bridge of his nose. Pablo stood back, open-mouthed. Flores smiled, shook his head and walked on. I returned to my work only half satisfied.

I started to get to know Pablo a little more after that. We began exercising together in the mornings after breakfast, and soon became close friends.

Months passed, the raquetas continued and the war between the two sides went on without a break. In April, an influx of foreign prisoners boosted our numbers: three Nigerians, two Dutch, a Brit and a Mexican. Zaffa was a huge, muscly black guy, who commanded immediate respect from locals. He was a proficient kick-boxer and totally fearless. Sonny, a well-spoken Nigerian, wasted no time in setting up a business selling cigarettes. In general, the Nigerians were an unpredictable bunch, schemers and scammers mostly, but Laddie became my favourite, a true lady's man, and when he flashed his toothy white smile, the anexo girls loved him.

Phillip and Stephan were the two from the Netherlands. Stephan's girlfriend, Ellen, was in the anexo. The Brit was a young guy called Lee. Tough in his own way, he hardly ever complained about the raquetas and beatings. We just called the Mexican 'Mexico' because no one could get any sense out of him, let alone his name. Completely mad, he would laugh wildly at vigilantes and soldiers alike, whenever they beat him. He would always sing out his number loudly at número, which never failed to get a laugh from other prisoners, much to the annoyance of a scowling Jiminez.

Under supervision, the girls from the anexo were allowed over to our side a couple of times a week. With José greasing the right palms, Alexi Castro, José's lieutenant in pavilion five, would have them doing aerobics on the cancha to music booming from a portable stereo system. Juan Caldera, a Panamanian from my pavilion, also held karate classes for them once a week. It proved good interaction and lifted morale all around.

One Thursday afternoon that month, while the girls relaxed on our side of the prison, gunshots rang out from the other side. A minute later, before they could fully understand what was happening, the air was filled with the wail of the siren, closely followed by the sound of shotguns. The *director*, who was watching, virtually had to run the girls back through a horde of screaming soldiers firing guns and waving planillas. They found many weapons that day, the guys being more concerned about getting their girls to safety. It was yet another example of how things in San Antonio could turn around in seconds.

The following month, heavy rainfall flooded the prison grounds once again and, with trepidation, I waded throughout the prison in knee-high water to switch off the main breakers with a wooden stick. The water flowed with such force through the dirección and into the anexo gardens, it was difficult to walk without holding on to something.

Pablo was struggling to clear the drains, so I helped once the water level dropped. Walking outside to survey any damage caused by the flooding, I saw Sam walk towards the gate. I thought I'd introduce Pablo to Sam, and when I did something resembling a coy smile passed between them. I should have seen it then, but I didn't: loving eyes never can see, or so they say.

'We already know each other,' said Sam.

Some months previously, the *director* had initiated the outfitting of a dentist's room in the prison. In truth, it was an old electro-pneumatically operated chair bolted to the concrete floor in a bare cinder-block room in the enfermeria with a door tacked on the outside. The visiting 'dentist', for want of a better word, came to the jail a few days after the flooding receded and requested I repair minor electrical damage in his 'surgery'. As I was fixing a foot switch at the chair's base, he offered to give me any treatment I required when I'd finished.

I smiled and said no, thank you. Inside, I cringed, remembering the one and only time I'd gone to him with a toothache a few months into my sentence. He was a pig farmer on the outside – his reason to visit the jail was to collect swill – and his gloveless hands had reeked of manure as he probed inside my mouth. After three injections in the gum, which had no effect whatsoever, he twisted and yanked the tooth out with a pair of ancient, peeling, chromium-plated pliers, as his assistant held me down on a chair with his knee on my chest.

It didn't take long, but the pain during those few seconds was indescribable. He gave me the tooth afterwards. There was nothing wrong with it – the hole being no bigger than a pinhead and he

222

could have filled it in seconds. It was to be my first and last visit to the prison *dentista*. I finished my work, smiled, and left as quickly as I could, still shuddering with the memory.

In June of that year, a group of people from Prisoners Abroad visited San Antonio as part of a tour of Venezuelan jails where Brits were incarcerated. All the vigilantes were on their best behaviour, full of smiles and benevolence. The party was aghast at the conditions inside the jail, the armed prisoners on the rooftops and the vast array of weapons proudly shown to them in pavilion five by Alexi Castro. They went away with a very clear idea of what life was like in San Antonio, promising to change things using their connections at Amnesty International and other human rights groups.

Things were on the move at last – but they were not changing fast enough. Tragedy hit our group a few weeks later when Joey suffered a severe asthma attack. He'd made his way to the dirección to use his nebuliser only to discover the vigilantes had been lending it out to all and sundry, and of course it was broken. Joey begged Marin, the jefe de régimen, to call an ambulance. Apparently, Marin had laughed at Joey, telling him to stop acting the fool and go back to the kitchens where he slept. Joey died on the floor with no medical help whatsoever. It was a tragic loss for his friends. The Canadian consulate was up in arms over the incident, demanding an investigation into why it had happened, a little too late in our opinion. As usual, the truth was covered up and, after a couple of weeks, nothing more was ever said about it.

We held Mass in remembrance of Joey in the salón. At least 20 of us, men and women, attended the service. A visiting pastor named Roberto, a regular to the jail, presided over the Mass. I made Roberto's acquaintance that day. He was a kindly man and gave everyone a chance to voice their thoughts about our friend. Joey's death affected me deeply for weeks. Each night Danny and I would talk about him, remembering his crazy habits. It was as though we could feel him in the air around us. I was convinced more had to be done to stop the barbaric treatment, and I didn't have too long to wait.

One afternoon, shots came from the other side. It had nothing to do with us, but the soldiers came blazing in as usual. In previous months, many soldiers had taken to wearing plain green T-shirts without nametags. It proved one thing to me: they knew they were breaking the law and were dressed that way to escape recognition. One soldier came directly at us on the run, so revved up he couldn't get the rounds off quick enough. I instantly recognised the commanding officer in the background: it was the sergeant who'd beaten me with the baseball bat on Boxing Day. Many were peppered with plastic that day, including me. The backs of my hands were covered with red weals where I'd tried to protect my face from the pellets.

Some nights later, I became deeply engrossed in a speech by Chávez broadcast on the television. He mentioned a provision in the new constitution that stated human rights violations committed by the military would now be dealt with by civilian courts, ensuring offenders would be tried and punished accordingly. This was the opening I had been looking for. I wrote a letter to the embassy that night, virtually demanding to take Guardia Nacional soldiers at San Antonio through the courts for human rights abuses. Although it was unheard of for a prisoner to do this, I was adamant. I sent the letter with the pastor Roberto some days later and waited for a response.

The following Sunday night, the mood inside the pavilion was one of high spirits. A lot of alcohol had been consumed over the weekend, and the better-off prisoners were more than a little drunk. Peter and Mads had moved into Cardoso's room some weeks before – it was better equipped than los vagos. I now had the boogaloo to myself. My only furniture was a single bed and Paul's old bedside table, which Sam had rescued when I was sent to El Dorado. I was lying on my bed, smoking a cigarette, listening to music on my radio, when a loud thumping noise from the other side of my wall had me up and on the edge of my bed. The banging continued for a few minutes, then a part of the wall in the far corner of my boogaloo caved in and bits of cinder block fell to the floor. Other people stuck their heads in to see what was happening. Crash! Crash! For a few moments, I had a terrible flashback to the máxima in El Dorado.

Fragments of wall continued to fall to the floor until a hole a couple of feet round became visible. Although angered by the unexpected intrusion, I remained silent in case the demolition team turned out to be gang leaders. A bleary-eyed face appeared through the hole: it was José. He looked up and smiled. '*Hepa*, Frank!' was all he said before his head disappeared and the banging continued. Before long, there was a hole in my wall, three feet high by two feet across, and the floor in my boogaloo was covered in rubble.

José stepped through gingerly, then stumbled on the mess he'd created. As he sat on my bed, the smell of whisky hit me; the man was completely drunk. Carlo Pino came through, followed by Chivo Loco: both were as intoxicated as José. I began to get nervous; after all, it wasn't every day three drunken murderers crashed through the wall.

'*Que paso?*' I asked José, trying my best to appear cool. He placed a finger to his lips, and motioned Carlo Pino to close the curtain to my boogaloo and shut the population out. I didn't quite know what to do or say, so I made a feeble joke. 'If you wanted to see me that badly, why didn't you wait till the morning and use the door?' All three fell about laughing.

They stopped when José leaned close to me. 'Someone's going to die in here tonight,' he whispered in my ear. The smell of whisky on his breath was overpowering.

'Not me?' I said in mock horror, my heart pounding. These guys were very unpredictable at the best of times and, with so much whisky inside them, anything was possible.

'No, no,' he laughed, 'you're my friend!'

Sudden relief rushed over me. 'Who's going to die then?' I whispered back, now part of the conspiracy.

'A *sapo*,' he said. Sapo was prison slang for a snitch.

With that, José got unsteadily to his feet and opened the curtain to my boogaloo. He had everyone's attention instantly, shouting to a Colombian guy who sold drugs for him, calling him to the centre of the room.

Carlo Pino and Chivo Loco grabbed the guy and forced him to his knees. The Colombian, visibly shaking, pleaded for mercy as José accused the guy of ripping him off over money owed for drugs given on credit some weeks earlier. José lifted his shirt and brought out a foot-long knife. Carlo and Chivo stood back as José brought the hilt crashing down on the Colombian's head, splitting the skin. Blood poured from the wound and ran down his face. 'You're going to give me my money tomorrow, aren't you?' slurred José, bringing the knife hilt down again, not even giving the guy a chance to answer. The Colombian's face was streaked with blood that dripped down onto his shirt, soaking it crimson.

I sat mesmerised by what was going on. But surely this wasn't the sapo? José dismissed the Colombian with a wave of his knife and the words, 'Tomorrow, or you die!'

The Colombian crawled off into the far corner to nurse his wounds. Most of the prisoners in los vagos were relatively new and had no idea what José and his two companions were really capable of. My friend stood in the middle of the room, swaying drunkenly, and gave a lecture regarding respect and how they knew nothing about real suffering. I sat rigid, my mouth wide open.

He caught my eye. 'See that guy over there,' he said, pointing at me. 'He's a real soldier. Went to El Dorado with us. If anybody fucks with him, ever, I'll cut them into pieces personally!' He almost shouted the last part. Fuck, I thought, what's going to happen now? With a nod from José, Carlo lifted his shirt, pulled a .38 automatic from his waistband and passed it over to his leader.

In a dangerous mood and very drunk, José staggered over to where Mancho lay propped on one elbow. He dragged the surprised informer off the bed by his shirt and ordered him to kneel down in front of him. We all sat transfixed and silent, nobody daring to move or utter a sound. José held the muzzle of the .38 automatic close to the man's forehead. Mancho started to sob, then plead. 'Please don't kill me!' Those were to be the last words that passed his lips.

'Cocksucking *sapo*! You know what happens to people with long tongues,' replied José coldly. While the gun at his head drew Mancho's attention, Carlo Pino, a cold-blooded killer of repute, moved in behind the kneeling man and, with practised motion, slipped the loop of a home-made garrotte over Mancho's head and pulled it taut around his throat, instantly tightening the wire while at the same time placing his knees between the shoulder blades. It was as though Mancho accepted the fact he was about to die. Like a lamb to the slaughter, he didn't even put up a struggle. At one point, both men toppled backwards, Mancho landing across Carlo Pino's legs, but Carlo kept his grip tight for almost two minutes during which time, with his eyes bulging, Mancho's legs and feet twitched uncontrollably. His sphincter muscle loosened and his bowels emptied, a dark wet patch appearing around his crotch as his bladder discharged.

Although I was a couple of yards from the scene, the smell hit me immediately. I fought to suppress the vomit rising in my throat. After more than four and a half years in Latino hellholes, I'd almost become immune to the unending cycle of violence and murder. What had happened to me? It didn't seem that long ago I was wining and dining clients in fancy restaurants; now, I was witnessing yet another act of cold-blooded murder with little compassion.

José watched Mancho's life force drain from his body with a huge smile, then knelt down, removed a suture kit from his pocket, broke the seal and proceeded to sew up the snitch's mouth – it was an established ritual for that kind of execution.

'He won't be talking to anyone else,' he laughed. His whisky-glazed eyes looked around the room. 'Are you all watching?' he shouted. 'This is what happens to people who talk!'

Still nobody uttered a sound. Eighteen prisoners had been forced to watch the horrific execution and not one dared say a word for fear of a repeat performance. While all this was going on, Chivo Loco was busy ripping up a sheet he'd snatched from the nearest bed. The owner was another English guy, and he wasn't about to argue. José and Chivo quickly fashioned a makeshift noose and hung Mancho's now lifeless body from one of the concrete window slats. There it would stay until the following morning when it would be discovered that, once more, there was one short at six o'clock headcount. From past experience, I knew that every single one of us would pay for that act of retribution. José, Carlo and Chivo made their way back to the other side, leaving their audience shaken and speechless, a hanging corpse and the hole in the wall grim reminders of the evening's events.

In the morning, running out for número, we had no option but to pass the gruesome sight of Mancho's hanging body. We lined up and nobody said a word. The count was taken. 'Falta uno!' the officer called.

A couple of soldiers went into the pavilion to search for the missing prisoner. They came back a minute later and said something to the officer in charge.

'Everybody down, hands on heads!' he shouted.

Prisoners left the line and fell to the ground and, within seconds, soldiers were in amongst us, beating and kicking and lashing out at everyone. We lay for an hour in silence, nobody moving a muscle; finally, we were herded back into the pavilions and locked up for the remainder of the day. I spent the time cleaning up the rubble and rearranging my boogaloo, making it smaller. There was now a cavity between my boogaloo and the next, which led to the hole and directly into the corridor of pavilion four.

The next day, every prisoner in los vagos was summoned to the dirección and questioned by the *director*. I told him I was asleep all evening and didn't see a thing. I could see in his eyes he didn't believe a word, but he dismissed me with a shrug of his shoulders. Nobody in los vagos spoke about it openly in case they were overheard and word filtered back.

The following day, everything was back to normal. It was as though the incident had never happened. During my morning exercise with Pablo, he asked me what had gone down. I refused to talk about it and carried on walking, so he didn't push it; however, he was very keen to know about my relationship with Sam. I considered him a friend, so discussed my feelings openly.

When I next saw Sam, she told me she'd had news that an uncle in her family had died. She was very upset about it but, try as I might, I just couldn't muster the sympathy to console her. The daily madness around me made it impossible to empathise with her, and we ended having a blazing argument. The following day, I was so angry I failed to turn up at the anexo for our entre vista, and the next time I saw her she refused to talk to me. I spent the next two weeks trying to reconcile our differences, all to no avail; she wasn't interested. It was the beginning of the end for Sam and me.

During August, news filtered back that Sam and Pablo had been seen holding hands and kissing in the anexo gardens. I didn't want to believe it, so I confronted her. She denied it completely, but I knew her well enough. The deep frown and the shake of her head told me she was lying. It wasn't long before I saw them walking arm-in-arm. It was a cruel game she had played to hurt me, and it worked well. I now had a broken heart to contend with. I slowly began to lose my mind. I still loved Sam; every time I saw her and Pablo together, it was like a knife twisting in my gut.

I talked it over with Pablo – he wasn't interested in my feelings at all. He was smitten by her. So much for friendship. It was then that it finally dawned on me: the sneaky bastard had befriended me to get closer to Sam. I'd confided in him about our struggling relationship and that was how he had repaid my trust. What a complete fool I'd been.

I spoke to Sam, telling her that if she was going to carry on seeing Pablo she should keep her affairs to the anexo and not on our side, where the locals had started to ridicule me about it. Fights with other prisoners were getting to be all too frequent as I tried to retain the credibility it had taken me so long to earn. I flipped in the end. No longer in control of my temper, I gave her one last chance to stay away. The next day, the girls would be coming over for games, and I warned her if she showed up and carried on her nonsense, I wouldn't be responsible for my actions. I was wasting my breath; I knew her well enough to know she'd be there.

That evening, a rage possessed me and, throughout the night, I filled a plastic bottle with urine. I hoped and prayed Sam would stay in the anexo, but when the girls came over, there she was, dolled up and bold as brass, sitting with Pablo under a tree by the workshops. I walked up to them, the plastic bottle tucked inside my shirt. As I came closer, I shouted, 'I fucking told you not to come over here!'

'Fuck off,' she replied. 'I'll do what I like.'

With that, I pulled out the bottle and tipped its contents over her head. Pablo didn't say a word, he just sat there watching. I walked off and sat outside my pavilion, seething with uncontrollable anger. Sam came past a minute later. I shouted abuse at her until she walked through the gate and out of sight.

Ten minutes later, she reappeared, hair washed and dressed in fresh clothing. A shouting match followed in the middle of the cancha, and people gathered to watch. A minute later, Chuito, who was overseeing the games, took the girls back to their side. I wasn't very popular among the prison population at that moment, so Pablo took the initiative and shouted abuse at me. I didn't want to fight him over it. I knew I could beat him – that wasn't the problem: I just knew I would kill him.

I hated Sam so much for what she had done that whenever our paths crossed, I would shout obscenities at her and things would end in an intense argument. I really was going insane with it all. It's strange when I look back: after the beatings and humiliation I'd suffered over the years, all it took was a woman to break me!

Early in September, I was called to the dirección. The public prosecutor, the *fiscal*, was there to take a statement with regard to human rights abuses by the National Guard soldiers. I couldn't believe it was actually happening. Tammier, who was living in the enfermeria at the time, came with me for moral support and to help with translation, as he spoke better Spanish. We were taken outside to the comando, where the fiscal and his assistant waited in the comandante's office. We were made somewhat comfortable by the fiscal, and I made a statement, picking out several faces from photographs pinned to the office wall. I saw pictures of the sergeant and his henchmen who had beaten us that day. Surrounded by the very soldiers I was instigating proceedings against, I felt very intimidated. We were thankful when it was over. I never found out what happened to the rest, but I didn't see the sergeant again for six months.

Things changed dramatically for a while. We took número in an orderly fashion and, if any trouble arose, the guardia went to the side where it had actually happened. The times they went to pavilions one, two and three, they carried on with their usual beating frenzy. On our side however, because of the foreigners' presence and our consular backing, no one was physically punished during raquetas. It wasn't long, though, before the locals in four and five, with their crazy way of thinking, ruined our hard work. Killings and shootings continued and the inevitable raquetas followed. But not content that we weren't getting beaten up any more, while sitting on the cancha they started to provoke the soldiers, goading them with shouts and obscenities. Under orders not to beat anyone up on our side, the soldiers were visibly angry and frustrated. They wouldn't take it for long without some sort of violent retribution. Something dreadful was bound to happen.

Late in September, I applied for a transfer to Santa Ana, the prison where they had relocated Mike. I needed to get away from San Antonio; I couldn't stand it any longer. My job took me to the anexo on a regular basis. Inevitably, I always saw Sam and we would argue. There were times when I was so wound up I wished she would drop dead at my feet. I no longer had control over my mind where she was concerned.

One week into October, a prisoner was killed on our side. The siren went off and soldiers came in with their usual gusto, shotguns booming. No gauntlet and no lashes followed but, as we lay on the yard, an order rang out. '*Los extranjeros por aca!*'

As we foreigners got to our feet, we were told by an officer to sit at the edge of the cancha, facing pavilion four. Not thinking, we did as we were told. A moment later, the soldiers set about everyone left on the yard, beating them in a wild frenzy.

This wasn't supposed to happen. We'd been duped. Although foreigners escaped the beating, our fellow prisoners hadn't, and I knew immediately it was Jiminez's ploy to cause friction amongst us. Listening to the yelps and shrieks behind me, I worked out a plan and, later that day, spoke with José, who confirmed my suspicions when he told me other prisoners were complaining about our 'special treatment'.

Emphasising that it would only work if they stayed quiet and didn't antagonise the soldiers, I told him what I had thought up. It took a while for it to sink in, but he agreed the basic idea was good. He gathered the foreigners outside pavilion four the next day and spoke to them as one, saying the law applied to everyone, not just the foreigners, and that the next raqueta would be different: when the soldiers called the foreigners out, everyone would stay still. From recent events, one thing had become very clear: pressure was mounting on the Ministry of Justice from all directions. For a while, at least, things had changed, and we were about to change them even more.

A few days later, a prisoner on the enfermeria rooftop shot Juan Carlos, the Colombian who had given me the clothes on my return from El Dorado. Juan was standing alongside the dirección gate when two bullets hit him in the chest; another scored a groove on the right-hand side of his head. He managed to pull his gun and return the fire, and, as he fell, another prisoner grabbed the gun and ran back to our gate, passing it to one of José's men, who quickly hid it. The siren went off and we scattered, running back to our cancha, bracing ourselves for the soldiers. That day we would see how united we really were.

The soldiers burst in with shotguns booming, but no one took a beat. As we lay there, the order rang out once more. '*Los extranjeros por aca!*' I looked up to see men fidgeting, as if to rise.

'No fucker move!' I yelled out loudly.

'*Nadier mueven!*' others shouted in Spanish.

Everyone lay still: the plan was working. It gave me such a good feeling inside, I choked up with emotion. The soldiers hadn't a clue who was a foreigner and who wasn't, so they restrained from beating anyone. We went through the routine, sitting in rows stripped naked with hands on heads. I saw José sitting two rows in front of me; he looked around, caught my eye and winked.

At that moment, Jiminez spoke to one of his men briefly, and then shouted, '*Los Británicos! Cónsulada!*' It was a trick, the consul wasn't due for another three weeks.

'Stay where you are!' I said loudly enough for everyone to hear. Nobody moved. Jiminez scowled at me, eyes afire with hatred, the scar down the side of his face turning deep red as he stormed off.

Eventually, we were herded back inside the pavilion and locked up. My boogaloo had been slashed open, things scattered around the room; a painting and several drawings I'd been working on lay on the floor, imprinted with boot marks. All my photos had been ripped off the wall. They had been through the place like a tornado and, as I tidied up and counted, I discovered that two precious photos of my daughter were missing. This had been Jiminez's doing. I sat on the edge of my bed, head in hands, completely devastated.

At five o'clock, they opened up for rancho. I wasn't in the mood to face anybody, but two soldiers insisted there would be a headcount following the meal. As I stepped out of the door, a soldier swung his planilla low, catching me with the thin edge across my shins, breaking the skin and sending shooting pains up my legs. 'Tell that to your consul!' he said, pushing me roughly toward the rancho queue.

Three weeks into October, I was summoned to the dirección with a couple of other Brits. In a large office sat the *director* with Jiminez and Jab, the Dutch consul. Joining three Dutch prisoners, we stood against the wall. Jiminez's eyes narrowed when mine made contact with his. He knew I'd instigated this meeting. Jab then delivered a scathing attack on Jiminez's blatant disregard for the law and his maltreatment of prisoners during raquetas. Jiminez leaned back in his chair with an arrogant look and denied everything.

'Liar!' I exploded. 'I've seen you myself and so has everybody here. You even wear a glove, so you can beat prisoners harder.'

'You,' he retorted with a sneer, 'you're a troublemaker . . . always complaining.'

'Yes, and I'll continue to complain until you stop treating us like animals,' I said, shaking with anger. I hated the man. He was dangerous, but I wouldn't be intimidated any more. Jab ended the meeting by informing the *director* and Jiminez that it wasn't going to stop there, he would talk to the Ministry of Justice personally.

Some nights later, I crawled through the hole in the wall to talk with José. When I got there, he and Ramon were deep in conversation. Ramon looked up and down the corridor to see that no one was within earshot and closed the door behind me. A moment later, he produced a hand grenade. I looked on with little concern. I'd ceased to be amazed by the weaponry these guys could get hold of; all it took was money. It was one of three, each costing them 60,000 bolivares. José had placed a man in the church three weeks earlier, and the plan was that this recruit would break a hole in the wall small enough to crawl through, run across and throw the grenade into the máxima, hopefully killing everyone in there. Oh, fucking hell no, I thought.

'When's all this going to happen?' I asked, dreading the answer.

'Tomorrow night,' José replied with a smile.

# 14

# BREAKTHROUGH

Waking early the next morning, my first thoughts were of José's plans. Psicario was confined in the máxima and I had no way of warning him. All I could do was detach myself. The day passed quickly enough, though I was ever mindful of the raqueta that would inevitably follow. Inwardly, I hoped the attack would be called off at the last minute, but I knew those guys well enough: they meant business.

Night-time came. I worked outside until around nine. No exchange of gunfire had taken place all day and a surreal atmosphere enveloped the pavilions. Returning to my boogaloo, I found it hard to settle; people in los vagos, oblivious to what was about to happen, carried on as normal. Around midnight, two shots rang out, followed by an almighty explosion, which echoed like thunder around the jail. BOOM! The blast startled me to such an extent I literally flew off the mattress and became entangled in the mass of bodies that dashed this way and that. Fuck! Then the wail of the siren, and soldiers piled in.

'*AGUA VERDE! AGUA VERDE!*' prisoners shouted. The steel door flew open with a bang. We ran like the wind to the sound of shotguns and the spitting of fire in the darkness: yet another hair-raising experience, another excuse for the soldiers to return to their customary ferociousness. We reached the cancha, itself illuminated by a floodlight on the roof of pavilion four, giving the soldiers a macabre look as they stormed around, flogging prisoners in their fury. My protectors were certainly with me that night, as I escaped the whole episode unscathed. It was probably 1.30 a.m. by the time we re-entered the pavilions, and 2.30 a.m. by the time everyone had tidied up and settled again.

I went through to see José, who appeared very disappointed. His man had lost his nerve as lookouts in the máxima had opened fire on him. He had pulled the pin on the run and thrown the grenade at the máxima gate from a few yards away, then dashed back to the hole in the church wall. The grenade had bounced off the bars and exploded harmlessly outside. Thank fuck for that, I thought, while at the same time trying to appear as disappointed as José. He looked up, his face set with determination. 'No matter,' he said. 'We've got two more grenades, and sticks of dynamite.'

Dynamite! This was getting out of hand. José had procured six sticks of dynamite from a nearby quarry, and that wasn't all. Ramon had two litres of petrol, contained in old whisky bottles, buried behind the cancha. Why was he telling me this? Was he testing my allegiance? My mind spun around in turmoil – what with this crazy war and breaking up with Sam, I could foresee another massacre like the one in El Dorado.

Some days later, the embassy official turned up at the prison. She wanted to talk to the Brits, one at a time, in a small office inside the dirección while the rest waited outside. It was inevitable that I would be in Sam's company for a while. I wished things could be back to how they were because, as mad as I was, I still cared. It was then that she hurt me so deeply it sent me over the edge. She just came out with it.

'I think I'm pregnant, Frank.'

I stared at her, stunned, unable to speak. I wasn't sure if she was saying it to hurt me, or just stating a fact. My head was reeling with the news. I could hardly gather my thoughts.

'Come on, Sam, where the fuck did it all go wrong?' I managed to say eventually.

'It's you, Frank, you've changed so much – and so have I.'

'How? What do you mean?'

'A lot of times, I felt you weren't there for me. You moved away, Frank.'

'But Sam, it wasn't my choice.'

Sam was about to say something else, but my name was called.

The woman from the embassy greeted me with a watery smile. 'How are things with you, Frank?' she asked.

'Things are bad here, and about to get worse,' I blurted out and, without thinking, said, 'You've got to get us out of here, or we're all going to die!' I went on to tell her about the grenades, dynamite and petrol bombs, and the hundreds of other weapons being readied for war. 'There's going to be another massacre, right here in San Antonio. I know it.' I was raving by the time I'd finished.

She sat through my speech expressionless. Surely she could not be that heartless, I thought. A few seconds passed. 'I think you're exaggerating, Frank,' she said to me at last. I lost my temper, accusing her of being totally uninterested in our welfare. I admit I became offensive. She dismissed me, saying I was distraught and over-imaginative. I left the office completely disenchanted with her. Surely she could not have been that naive. She had been in Venezuela long enough to know how the prisons worked. I left the office determined it wouldn't end there: I'd get around her indifference somehow. I wasn't sure how at the time but knew a degree of cunning would be required.

Sam's news really knocked the wind out of me. I lost my mind completely; all I recall about the next few weeks is that I took to walking around the prison grounds naked like an absolute lunatic, filled with anger, goading people to fight with me. Everywhere I went, a dark, heavy cloud shadowed me. What few friends I had avoided me during that time, as intense hatred filled me at every waking moment, my head ticking like a bomb, ready to explode at any second. I cried like a baby whenever I was on my own. I had reached the lowest point of my life, my sanity hung by a thread.

I cannot clearly recall what happened during those days, but perhaps there was a fragment of good spirit that remained with me.

Something stopped me from acting on my emotions. I will never know why, but thank goodness it did, because slowly the madness wore off and rationality returned. Though still terribly distressed, I began to get a grip of my senses and concentrated on the mission at hand: eradicating the brutality.

Danny began working for Cristantio at his coffee stall and slept on the floor inside. Cristantio was a trustee of sorts and wasn't locked up at night. In late November, we met there to make a handful of posters, which we intended to stick on the walls wherever we could during the next visiting day. The posters explained that the constitution of Venezuela had made corporal punishment illegal and should their loved ones be beaten for no reason, the prisoners' families were to report the abuses to the papers and to the courts. It was their duty.

Marin was furious, rushing around ripping them down, tearing them to shreds, but we were right behind him with more. In the afternoon, Danny actually managed to stick a poster on the noticeboard outside the dirección gates while Marin was at his desk. Every visitor went home that afternoon having read our messages, and our act of bravado gave me the lift I needed to set me on the road to recovery. Danny turned out to be an unfaltering ally and a trusted friend, and slowly I let go of any infatuation I had with Sam and returned to work. Fuck her! Let her get on with it because no good would come of it in the end, I thought.

Juan Carlos, the Colombian who was shot outside the enfermeria, had returned from hospital swathed in bandages across his chest and around his head. Though lucky to have escaped with his life, he shrugged and laughed about his experience. Everyone was happy to see him and, although Marin had put him in the enfermeria, he came over to see us daily.

Changes had been made during the weeks of my temporary insanity. A new *director* had taken over and moved Freddie, the Colombian drug baron, to another part of the enfermeria, his 'double room' becoming one cell, separated from the rest of the building with a metal barred gate outside. Eight problematic prisoners lived in there, away from the rest of the population. One of them was Jon Hiro, whom I'd met when I first arrived at San Antonio and who was by now a long-standing friend. He'd served eight years of a thirty-year sentence for several counts of murder. He'd been responsible for a number of killings in the jail and over the years had been moved from pavilion to pavilion. He possessed a strange outlook, in as much as he knew he would die in there one day, resigning himself to an inevitable violent death. It was an openness that astounded me. One day, Jon asked me outright if I would like him to shoot Pablo. He said all it would cost was 50,000 bolivares! Forty quid to get my revenge! How cheap life was in San Antonio. I seriously considered it for some time but eventually dismissed it. I needed to forget Pablo, not feed my hatred against him. Jon Hiro seemed disappointed, but it didn't affect our friendship.

The salón had also been converted to house 15 extremely dangerous prisoners with nowhere else to go. The jail now had many different groups of prisoners, all at war with each other; the animosity was getting out of hand.

In late November, I began a new relationship with a girl named Carmen, who was serving five years for manslaughter. Her boyfriend on the street had beaten her regularly, and in the end she shot him dead. Carmen was a foxy, five foot two, dark-haired 40 year old with a gypsy look and went by the nickname '*la Gata*' (the Cat). My job meant I could still come and go whenever I wished, so our meetings were frequent. She worked alongside Sam in the machine shop and, as Sam had done in the past, Carmen would call on me to 'repair' her sewing machine. Sam wasn't overjoyed with my presence on those occasions, and we would glare hatefully at each other.

A week into December, I learnt that Sam's pregnancy scare had been a false alarm, but I still hated her for what she'd done.

That same week, Danny became unpopular with all the guys on our side. In a drugged stupor, he had sneaked out of Cristantio's coffee stall in the dead of night and jumped the wall by the dirección in a crazy bid to escape. He landed almost in the laps of soldiers sitting under the canopy on the other side. They battered him senseless, then handcuffed him to a barred gate in the dirección. Danny had somehow managed to open the cuffs and escaped again. He was eventually caught, roaming the grounds, completely off his head on crack. At three o'clock that morning, with everyone fast asleep, the siren went off. Soldiers came in, shotguns booming. We ran in a crouch to the concrete pad just inside the main gate. There we sat for almost an hour, passing número six times before the soldiers were satisfied. Danny was one crazy motherfucker, and I couldn't help but laugh at his escapades, but nobody else saw the funny side. Marin locked him in the enfermería for the duration and kept a keen eye on him at número to make sure he didn't pull the same stunt again.

Danny, however, managed to get out the following weekend by joining a Bible class held by Roberto, the visiting pastor, in the anexo gardens. Danny and Angelique, the South African, had feelings for each other and this was the only way they could be together. I was in the garden spending time with Carmen that day and while chatting to Roberto, the subject of email cropped up in conversation. A flash of inspiration took me to ask him if he could send an email for me.

'Of course,' he said. 'No problem at all.'

I excused myself and rushed back to my boogaloo, where I composed a quick letter to Prisoners Abroad, explaining what I'd told the official from the embassy a month before and declaring that an all-out war was imminent and we would all perish in the inevitable massacre. I literally begged them to put as much pressure on the British embassy in Caracas as they possibly could as soon as possible. I wasn't kind to the British official in my letter, emphasising what I saw as her blatant disregard for our safety and well-being. I was back in the anexo within the hour, and gave Roberto the letter and the Prisoners Abroad email address in London. I thanked him sincerely for his help and he assured me he'd send it that night. I returned to my boogaloo pleased with my unforeseen good fortune and satisfied that it had been a very constructive day.

The following week, Mads went free. He and Peter had received five-year sentences and their time was up. Mads had obviously spent his time and money lining Rufini's pockets to get his working benefits and good conduct status, whereas Peter had not, preferring to squander his money on drugs and gambling. Peter moved back in with me, angry at Mads over his early release.

Meanwhile the war continued, as did the raquetas, the soldiers now wary of whom they were beating out on the yard. They still came in wearing plain green T-shirts, however, to avoid detection. Christmas and the New Year passed easily. I sneaked Carmen into my boogaloo on several occasions, where, despite the lack of privacy, we made love many times. She was quite a noisy lover and the other guys in los vagos ribbed me constantly over it, but at least no one was tormenting me about Sam any more, which suited me fine. Peter wasn't too happy about being ejected each time but that was tough shit, in my opinion; I was enjoying the contact and love of a woman for the first time in ages and I wasn't about to let anyone spoil it.

One week into 2002, Juan Carlos, the Colombian, was shot again, but this time fatally, inside the enfermeria. Someone had come up behind him and blown his face away. Soldiers had arrived and fired tear gas through the gate and into the corridor. Danny witnessed the whole thing and became a victim of the ensuing raqueta. The guardia confined their punishments to the enfermeria and didn't come over to our side at all. I watched from outside the kitchens, where I'd been repairing a walk-in refrigerator. Every inmate in the enfermeria received three lashes as they lined up outside, hands up against the wall. I could feel the pain myself, cringing at the sound of swishing blades and the yelps that followed.

Having a newly elected democratic government and constitution meant nothing to the Venezuelan guys. They were so set in their ways, they accepted punishment as a part of their everyday lives. I still couldn't grasp how their minds worked, even after so many years. For them to wantonly invite and accept this damnable treatment still had me scratching my head in bewilderment.

A few days after Juan Carlos's death, Ricardo was released on confinamiento after serving five years and two months. His father, Francisco, whom I'd met on occasion, had upped his roots in Puerto

La Cruz and bought into a restaurant franchise at a fancy hotel in Porlamar. He'd worked hard behind the scenes, greasing palms and obtaining the right paperwork. Ricardo had a family home and a job to go out to. José, on the other hand, had been arrested with a false cédula, which had only become apparent when he applied for his benefits. He needed to pay a lot more to officials to get around this discrepancy. There was no problem about that, he told me, he had money and it was only a matter of time.

That same month, the evangelist church on our side was extended into the unused building at the rear. Originally built as a dining room, it accommodated concrete tables and benches running the whole length of the building. Demolishing the back wall of the church to make a doorway, tables and seating were removed and placed around the area for prisoners and their families to sit at on visiting days. Four ten-foot lengths of seating placed in a square outside pavilion four became a regular hangout for the foreigners. We nicknamed it 'Fantasy Island'.

The evangelists grew in numbers as boogaloos sprang up inside the extended church, their occupants overjoyed they had so much space. I, however, was one of the few who knew the real reason behind this new idea, as José had confided in me yet again. Sixty feet of window slats faced the máxima and pavilions opposite. Ten members of José's gang, led by a guy named Raymondo, were ideally positioned to keep an eye on the comings and goings of the enemy.

I knew Raymondo well – we'd almost come to blows one day when he'd threatened me with a huge knife for lack of 'respect'. I didn't care for his arrogant, macho attitude and had told him so in no uncertain terms. Ramon had stepped between us and broken up the argument, but Raymondo still held a grudging respect for me because I had stood up to him that day. He and his men were part of a long-term plan to attack the máxima in force, using grenades, dynamite and petrol bombs. José said this time they wouldn't fail; he would wipe out every last one.

While work in the church progressed, one event caused the most terrifying raqueta to date in San Antonio. People in the máxima had broken one of the window slats to get a better shot at our garita. The bullets must have gone over the top, narrowly missing the guard tower in the far corner, because a soldier in that tower and the one close to the main gate began shooting down onto our cancha. Prisoners scattered as nine-millimetre bullets ripped into the pavilion walls, sending fragments of cinder block flying everywhere. The siren went off and soldiers came in. Guard tower soldiers fired indiscriminately in all directions, soldiers running towards the gate thought they were under fire from prisoners and opened up with their Fals.

I'd been lying on my bed reading a book when it kicked off, and ran at a crouch with the others to the cancha, bullets zipping past our heads and smashing into the pavilion wall above us. Thoughts of a massacre filled my head, as my heart pounded with sheer terror. I made it to the far right-hand corner of the yard just as the soldiers came in wearing gasmasks, firing tear gas. One white-hot canister hit a prisoner in the chest, burning the skin on his torso, his throat and face. He dropped to the ground, writhing in agony. It was Ruben, the very same guy who'd bungled the first attack on the máxima. Many prisoners gathered in the corner of the yard, huddled together, seeking safety in numbers. Bullets continued to whistle overhead, and it was a miracle no one was killed.

As the gas thinned, Jiminez took control, raising his pistol and shooting one prisoner in the leg as the guy ran from pavilion five. He then ordered everyone to form rows in the centre of the courtyard and strutted between the ranks like a cock of the walk, in his element to have caused so much terror. Still shaking, I stood at the front of one line and glared at him with such contempt he must have felt the energy, because he turned quickly and fixed his evil gaze directly at me. We stared at each other for an age, neither backing down, our eyes narrowed to slits, pure hatred passing between us. Everything else ceased to exist for those moments. He finally swaggered over to me, our eyes still locked on each other.

'I'm going to speak to the embassy about this,' I said to him quietly as he stopped, inches away from me.

'You can speak to whoever you want,' he replied with a sneer.

I would have gladly put a bullet between his eyes at that moment. He turned and walked away.

The next day, I happened to be at Cristantio's, drinking coffee, when I noticed the bars on the makeshift gate had several semicircles literally chewed out of the metal where bullets had struck and ricocheted, and the 50 or so bullet holes in the pavilion walls would surely interest the embassy official the next time she came. Let her tell me I was imagining things, I thought!

Another act of madness took me that day. I ran out to evening número armed with pen and paper, stopping in my tracks when I reached the cancha. I slowly walked past a row of soldiers and began to write down their names. Some placed their hands over their nametags when they noticed what I was doing. I'd written several names down when the sergeant in charge came over and snatched the piece of paper from my hand, tore it into shreds and dropped the pieces to the ground.

'Get in line,' he shouted at me. While I made an obvious show of looking at his nametag, he prodded me with the barrel of his machine gun, screaming, 'Get in line!' I stayed put. He prodded me again, but harder, and I stumbled back. The yard erupted with shouting from the prisoners. As I stood my ground, the sergeant released the safety on his machine gun and prodded me yet again. Prisoners raised their fists, shouting defiance. The clacking sound of breech mechanisms could be clearly heard above the din as soldiers readied their guns. I knew I was pushing my luck: I could quite easily have been shot for provoking them in this way. Shaking with a mixture of fear and anger, I finally turned and made my way back to a space in the line. Cheers rang out from inmates around the yard. It felt good to have so much support, but I have to admit it was an insane thing to have done. I went inside with the rest of the prisoners after número. Marin could switch the fucking lights on himself!

In February, the new *director*, who seemed more liberal than his predecessor, allowed the girls from the anexo to walk freely around the jail on visiting days. It was quite a sight to see Sam hovering in the wings, waiting to see Pablo, only to discover his wife and two children in attendance. I saw them arguing many times. Meanwhile, I was still seeing Carmen.

Two days after Valentine's Day, the jail was full of visitors. I was passing the time of day outside Cristantio's coffee stall when Sam and Sarina came by. Sam stopped to talk to me, though I don't know why she bothered because, as time had gone by, I didn't know where I stood with her and we always argued – one day she would be all sweetness and light, the next like a woman possessed; she had probably always been like that, but I hadn't noticed because I'd loved her so much. Maybe she was right in one way . . . she had changed. Regardless, I acknowledged her and, after a few minutes of small talk, she blurted out again that she was pregnant. My stomach churned, but I didn't show it: I wasn't going to give her the pleasure of upsetting me. 'Oh yes?' I said nonchalantly. 'And is Pablo happy about that?'

'Don't talk to me about *him*!' she spat. 'He's a brute! I finished with him last week.'

It was news to me. She looked at me expectantly, waiting for me to say something. Well, well, well, I thought to myself, keeping my face straight but smiling inwardly. 'Yeah,' she continued, 'I couldn't believe it when I found out. I threw the test kit at the wall, I was so mad.'

Just then, along came Carmen. '*Hola, mi amor*,' she said with a huge smile. I returned her greeting with a hug and a kiss, and we walked off together, her arm linked through mine, leaving Sam and Sarina standing there.

Three days later, I was summoned to the dirección. Sam and I were to appear in court the following morning for our benefit assessment. When the time came, we were locked in the back of a jeep, similar to the one we were brought to the jail in, along with four male prisoners and one female. Sam appeared to flirt openly with the guys along the way, hoping to rile me, but I didn't play the game and chose to ignore her instead. This time we were driven to the large Criminal Court building in La Asunción, the island's capital, and were placed in separate holding cells.

When our time came, we were handcuffed together and taken up 12 flights of stairs to the top floor. As we climbed the concrete steps, I looked down at the cuffs, then up in the air, saying, 'You've got a cruel sense of humour, God, that's all I can say!' Sam glared at me.

Inside a large office, we sat together in front of a secretary, who told Sam she had earned a remission of two years and four months for her work and good conduct. The secretary turned to me and told me I had earned one year, eleven months and four days.

'What,' I said, 'that can't be right? I've worked every day and have good conduct too. Why is it different?' The secretary went on to tell me I had a gap of ten months, between November 1998 and September 1999, where there were no records of me working, and I had a bad conduct mark for the same period. It came to me: El Dorado. Fuck! All the effort we'd made to get the paperwork done for the delegation from Caracas and it wasn't even in my file! I didn't have time to argue my case, as we were quickly dismissed, cuffed together again and taken back downstairs to the cells. On the way down, I noticed Sam was smiling. I was seething, and determined to find the underlying cause of it when I got back to San Antonio. Sam continued to flirt on the way back and I continued to ignore her.

The next day, I went to see a prison social worker. She went off to get my file from the records office and, after a moment's inspection, told me that all records for the period I'd spent at El Dorado had been lost in the Caracas flooding during December 1999. I was fucked, and there was nothing I could do about it. I wasn't allowed to go out on confinamiento, as I had no family on the island, no job to go to and lacked the necessary paperwork to live in the community. Double fucked! I left, not wanting her to see my disappointment.

Some days later, the woman from the embassy flew in from Caracas. She greeted me angrily, producing a copy of the email Roberto had sent to Prisoners Abroad on my behalf. They had obviously been on to her superiors.

'Well, what did you expect?' I said. 'Your attitude's painfully apparent, you don't care whether we live or die here.' I told her I wanted to show her something before she left.

'What?' she snapped.

'Wait and see,' I replied, as I rose from my chair, picked up my letters and money, and walked out.

I waited for her by the dirección building and, half an hour later, I showed her the gate and pointed to the pavilion wall opposite, peppered with bullet holes, then described the raqueta in detail. 'I don't make things up and I don't exaggerate. Those are real bullet holes.' She kept a poker face, but I knew I had finally got to her. I watched her walk away, sure she'd left with a slightly different attitude.

The system set José free at the end of February. It had cost him a substantial amount of money. A young guy by the name of Elidio took over our side. José had placed him in charge a few days before his release. Elidio came from a large family of illegal arms dealers on the island and owned a brand-new, 18-shot automatic Glock pistol to prove it. His mother and José had become lovers over the previous months and José was going to live with her on his release. Elidio loved to shoot the gun. Climbing up to the garita each morning, he would empty the magazine at the other side in one burst. No one in the jail had anything to match the Glock, which earned Elidio much respect from prisoners on our side. Everyone except Raymondo, who was openly envious of the relative newcomer: a man in his early 20s, who refused to take orders and kept him and his gang out of the circle.

In March, the government decreed a census be carried out throughout the prison system. We lined up, gave personal details, sat for mug shots, gave fingerprints and were weighed by a visiting doctor. Unsurprisingly, I had lost a lot of weight. I now weighed 63 kilos (9 st. 9 lb). Rufini had stopped my supply of vegetables months before, claiming each time that there wasn't enough to go round. I gave up bothering him in the end, realising that the only way to get anywhere would be to go on another hunger strike, but I'd been down that road before and the outcome had not been a success. I had money, but there was nothing to buy except bits and pieces from the canteen behind the enfermeria, rice and flour being the only supplies available. I had no real contacts any more, and I could not ask visitors unknown to me to buy food, as most were untrustworthy:

they would pocket the money and make some excuse that they had lost it or it had been stolen. I knew this because I had tried and lost money, along with many other foreigners, in the process. More to the point, I could not afford to lose what little I had.

During the third week of March, Elidio was ambushed and murdered by Raymondo and his gang in the very room he'd taken over from José. Elidio took 12 bullets in the head and chest; the walls of his room were sprayed with blood and brains. Inevitably, a raqueta followed. That night, Raymondo and his men took control of our side of the jail. During the days that followed, his men knocked a hole through the wall in los vagos to the church next door, and another between the church and pavilion five. No one was allowed to use these 'doorways' except Raymondo and his followers. They would pass from one part to the other constantly, all carrying an arsenal of weapons, and Raymondo the coveted Glock.

Raymondo posted a 24-hour watch up on the rooftop garita during daylight hours and at windows in the new church extension through the night. A rota ensured every prisoner took a two-hour shift on garita duty. I discovered my name wasn't on any list and when I queried Raymondo about it, he simply said I didn't have to do it and not to ask any more questions. Maybe his respect for me had grown, I didn't know, but I wasn't going to push it; I was quite happy with his decision.

At the end of the month, Peter went home to Denmark. He'd served three months more than his partner Mads. The Danish consul picked him up at the gates and took him to Caracas, from where he flew directly to Copenhagen the next day. Peter had served three years and seven months, almost three-quarters of his five-year sentence.

The same week, Mr Mellor arrived unexpectedly with exceptionally good news. He held a meeting in the dirección with both men and women present. The Ministry of Justice had agreed to transfer the British prisoners to Santa Ana, near the Colombian border. He produced paperwork for people to sign if they wished to go.

'I've got a pen right here,' I said immediately. 'Show me where to sign and get me away from all this bullshit.' I looked across at Sam as

I uttered the last words; she was staring at me defiantly. I signed the paper without hesitation. Danny snatched the pen from my hand and signed. Tammier came next, then Lee, Ben, Neil and Poco. Sam and Sarina declined, saying they were content to stay where they were. I bet they were, and I was happy to hear it: being near Sam when she had the baby would have crushed me. Even now, at four months pregnant, the sight of her rounded belly saddened me.

At last, something had been done, and I put it down to Prisoners Abroad. Mr Mellor said it would be several weeks before the administration would be sorted, then we'd be on our way. Those who'd signed up thanked Mr Mellor profusely, and everyone beamed happily at the end of the meeting, including Mr Mellor, possibly glad to get us off his back. It wasn't long before news spread of our impending move. Danny was ecstatic, as Angelique had been transferred to Santa Ana the previous month, thanks to her embassy's involvement.

Before we knew it, we were halfway through April. I became more and more impatient to get away from San Antonio. Constant comings and goings during the night by Raymondo and his men made it almost impossible to sleep. The space in front of the hole between my boogaloo and the next had become a crack den during the day; the unending striking of matches to light pipes glowed through the thin material of my boogaloo wall and clouds of crack smoke filtered into my space. To top it all, I'd contracted scabies. I had a good idea it had come from a blanket that Peter left behind. I'd lent it to Lee, who slept in Cardoso's room, and he, in turn, I found out, had lent it to one of the locals who always seemed to be scratching himself. It wasn't long before the whole of my body was covered in scabs that itched uncontrollably. My ankles, already badly damaged over the years, were a mass of weeping sores. The filthy conditions made matters worse, and there was no medicine at the surgery – it had been stolen by the orderlies and sold. I had also stopped seeing Carmen, as I didn't want her to get infected too, and I would be going away soon anyway. She understood and we parted amicably.

Tension on our side became intolerable as news came through

that José had put a contract on Elidio's assassins: a million bolivares for the death of each person who had been involved. Elidio's mother had been devastated by her son's death, and the couple were looking for revenge. Money was no object. It kept Raymondo and his gang constantly on edge, to the point of paranoia, in fact – many prisoners would risk their lives for that kind of money.

One night in early May, despite Raymondo's vigilance and round-the-clock garitas, someone from the other side managed to lob a grenade through the window slats at the rear of pavilion five. I was sitting with some Brits, talking about the transfer, when it happened. The explosion was so loud it shook the ground and startled everyone.

'Fucking hell,' I shouted in sudden panic, 'that's a grenade! We're under attack!'

Shots rang out in the background. Raymondo's men were dashing about like headless chickens, in and out of holes, as the siren went off.

Another fearful raqueta followed. Sparks flashed from the soldiers guns in the darkness and we were beaten badly. The whole episode was like a quick visit to hell. Two hours passed before they herded everyone back inside. The grenade had exploded in Ciro's room. He wasn't in there at the time; however, his room-mate wasn't so lucky. He'd been asleep in his hammock four feet off the ground and the blast took a good part of his right leg and hip away. It left a crater in the floor three feet in diameter; blood was spattered everywhere.

They took Raul to the hospital on the point of death. News came back that he was in Porlamar hospital and had received two hours of intensive surgery. He was alive but only barely. A few days later, he was taken off the critical list. A week after that, Ramon surprised me with two tubes of cream he'd acquired; he said it was to treat my infections. I didn't know what to say to him, I was taken aback by his act of kindness.

The following Wednesday morning after breakfast, the British guys were called to the dirección and told we'd be leaving for Santa Ana later that day. My bag was packed within the hour and I sat counting the minutes. Inevitably, the day passed so slowly it was as if time was standing still. What we didn't know was that since Mr Mellor's visit seven weeks before, six other foreign prisoners had also applied to be transferred to Santa Ana. Money had changed hands somewhere along the line and they'd jumped on the bandwagon. They were a Colombian named Leon, three Nigerians – Zaffa, Laddie and Sonny – Phillip, the Dutch guy, and a French girl from the anexo called Veronique.

After evening número, a vigilante opened the pavilion door and told us to go to the dirección. I spotted Pablo looking through a window slat in Cardoso's room as we made our way past. I couldn't resist saying one last thing before I left that evil place behind me for ever. I had to wish him luck with Sam; he was going to need it. Laughing loudly with a joy in my heart, I shouted, '*Adiós, Romeo, suerte con la loca!*' He spat at me through the window, but missed. I laughed even louder and walked on.

We spent an hour waiting in the dirección, then were handcuffed and shoved inside two police vans waiting outside the gate. There were 13 of us altogether. Unlucky for some, they say, but I considered it the luckiest day of my life.

# 15

## TOO GOOD TO BE TRUE

The journey to Santa Ana was completely different from any other transfer. Although handcuffed inside the vehicles, no prisoner was maltreated. This wasn't a punishment transfer, but a voluntary one. By the time we reached the ferry port and boarded, I was brimming with euphoria, as though all the tension of the past five and a half years had dissolved; a feeling I cannot describe adequately with words alone.

A half-mile out to sea we were uncuffed and allowed to stand by the deck rails; what an experience to breathe in fresh sea air. After a while, we were taken upstairs to a spit-and-sawdust-type lounge, where we sat and ate snack food served at the bar. Guards were positioned by the door, and we were left alone. Through the stern window, we watched the twinkling lights of Margarita slowly fade into the distance. I felt overwhelmed at the thought of leaving San Antonio behind for ever.

I had said goodbye to Carmen and some of the other girls I knew earlier in the day; Sam and I hadn't spoken, we just stared at each other from a distance. Filled with a feeling of betrayal, my love for her had turned into an equally strong hatred.

'Good fucking riddance,' I said aloud as I turned my back to the window. A few guys agreed wholeheartedly, but they didn't know what I really meant.

The crossing was relatively smooth, and I suffered no seasickness. This particular ferry was heading towards Puerto La Cruz and again we were allowed to stand at the rails as the mainland became visible; just before landing, however, we were handcuffed and put back in the vehicles. Puerto La Cruz is a beautiful city. I'd seen it briefly on the way back from El Dorado, albeit only from the side of my eye; now, we watched the city lights through the grilles as we sped on into the night. No one was tired. We sat in the darkness, still not believing what was happening. There were eight in our vehicle and five in the other, which was smaller.

Tammier, who always fancied himself as a bit of a rap singer, began to sing, making the words up as he went along:

> Everybody listen to what I'm sayin',
> We don't have to do no more prayin',
> Listen carefully to my rap,
> Cos you know what I'm saying ain't no crap,
> Y'all agree there ain't nothin' sweeter
> than leavin' the jail in Margarita . . .

We fell about laughing. Despite my body being covered in sores and the flesh on my backside still raw from the last raqueta, I was overjoyed to the point of bursting. We had heard good reports about Santa Ana, some of them almost unbelievable. There were no raquetas, vigilantes weren't allowed to carry firearms inside the jail, and there were restaurants, shops and educational classes of every kind. I couldn't see it myself – it all seemed too good to be true. After much debate, we agreed, however, it would be – it had to be – better than the awful place we'd left behind.

Late into the night, I fell into a semi-sleep, head hanging, being jerked awake here and there whenever we hit a rough patch on the road. When daylight came, we were well on our way, with more than a third of the distance covered. During the morning, we passed a huge lake on our left before reaching the outskirts of Valencia. Memories of Ivor filled my mind: how he'd saved my hide on that first night, how he'd screamed at me for choking Pescado, the way he'd led the attack on the pavilions, how he'd been there to meet us out of the máxima in El Dorado. Except for Tammier, nobody else in our vehicle had known Ivor, so I kept my thoughts to myself, smiling inwardly at the memory of him. He had been a tough no-nonsense villain through and through, but the man's heart had been made of gold.

In the afternoon, we stopped for fuel in the small town of Guanare. Ten minutes out of town, we pulled up outside a roadside café, where, to our amazement, we were taken inside and given a meal and water to drink. We used the toilets and were back on the road within the hour. With full bellies and our thirst quenched, the general feeling was of jubilation. I had a positive feeling about Santa Ana; the filth and stench of San Antonio had already become nothing more than a bad memory.

By nightfall, we were climbing the Andean foothills. The air inside the vehicle grew thinner and colder as we rose higher and higher into the mountains. We felt the dramatic climate change, with everyone shivering, and rubbing their arms and legs vigorously. We arrived outside the gates of Santa Ana jail just before midnight. It had been a 30-hour trip: nothing like the horrendous journey to El Dorado, but memorable in its own way. We passed through two gateways manned by Guardia Nacional soldiers – there was no shouting and no abuse; in fact, they were almost pleasant as we passed número. The dirección area was huge and silent, with corridors running off either side and a gate at the far end, 30 yards away. Once through the gate, the cold air bit through me.

The prison was nothing like I had imagined. It felt so tranquil. Set 3,000 feet up in the mountains, the place was so big it was impossible to take it all in as a vigilante led us down a floodlit path and into a building with the sign '*observación*' hanging above its barred entranceway. I was shivering uncontrollably by this time: the only clothing I had with me were the lightweights I'd worn in Margarita, where the temperature had always been in the mid-80s.

In the observación, we were left to our own devices. I claimed a space, and tried my best to settle down on the concrete floor after putting on several layers of clothing. But it was no use. I was chilled to the bone, making it impossible to sleep. The other guys fared no better. Eventually, fatigue and the excitement of it all got the better of me and I dozed fitfully, waking every now and then, teeth chattering with the cold.

Morning came. The sun climbed over the horizon and the air grew warmer. A vigilante took us straight to the dirección, where our first port of call was the doctor's surgery in the hospital wing. There they served a breakfast of hot porridge and a bread roll. I had warmed up by the time I stepped on the doctor's scales. He tutted when he saw the scabs that covered my body and gave me two bottles of pink lotion to eradicate them. He tutted once more when he assessed my frame, now just skin and bone, and saw the needle climb to just 63 kilos. I then gave a blood sample, after which he excused me to do my own thing. It would be my first chance to take a good look at the prison in daylight.

From the dirección gate, a set of steps went down to a walkway under a canopy of corrugated asbestos, which led to the main buildings 200 yards away. The prison, carved out of a mountainside, stood on three levels. The dirección gate opened on to the middle tier. To my left was a basketball court and raised stage, at the far end of which two sets of concrete steps rose twenty feet to the top level. There sat a huge building, the size of an aeroplane hangar. Behind that, mountains towered into a clear blue sky. There were three main prison buildings that were three storeys high and built of red brick and concrete. Each was situated on a separate level. To my right, several paths led down to a lower level where mature gardens and trees flourished in the high altitude. One hundred yards further back and down another set of steps was a full-size football field and marked-out baseball pitch. The prison, carpeted in lush green grass, brought back memories of England – I'd almost forgotten what it looked like, as San Antonio had been a dry, dusty place except for no-man's-land, where odd patches of vegetation and wild flowers grew. With its stunning panoramic views, Santa Ana could only be described as the Garden of Eden in comparison.

I was brought back to earth when a familiar voice greeted me. 'Hey, Frank, how ya doin', man?' I heard you were comin'.' I turned to see Mike the American walking towards me. My mood lifted even higher. We greeted each other warmly, with lots of laughing and shaking of hands. 'Well, wadda ya think of Santa Ana, then? It's a real cool place, ain't it?'

'You can fucking say that again!' I replied, 'I froze my bollocks off last night.' I knew it wasn't what he meant, and we laughed.

Mike showed me around the place, taking me first to the top level. The hangar-size building was split into two segments, the front half being the kitchens and rancho area. Huge workshops full of machinery occupied the back half. Hundreds of handmade tables, chairs and beds, and wooden carvings filled the floor space. It was 8.30 in the morning and already the place was a hive of activity, machines humming and prisoners toing and froing, carrying materials. On our way round, Mike told me the whole jail was run by Colombian paramilitaries and that everything we saw was down to them. The more I saw, the more amazed I became.

He told me there was a fantastic library in the dirección and a score of educational classes to choose from, if I wanted something to occupy my time. The biggest surprise of all was the availability of a music room, complete with electric guitars, a bass, drums and amplifiers. Mike casually suggested that some day we should put a band together. With my mind reeling from what I'd seen, the remark went over my head. There was so much to take in.

Walking back to the observación building, situated across from building three on the lowest level, we passed five outside restaurants and twenty or more stalls where prisoners sold fresh bread rolls, cakes, coffee, cigarettes, fruit and vegetables, fish, meat and almost anything one could wish for – a complete contrast to what I had been used to. There was only one problem: I had no money. I'd left Margarita without a bean.

By this time, my money at home had dried up to nothing, and I was relying solely on the money from Prisoners Abroad every three months, plus the little bits here and there Chrissy could afford to send. One thing in my favour – though unfortunate for Venezuelans – was that the bolivar had dropped in value and continued to do so at an alarming rate. The allocated three-monthly £90 from Prisoners Abroad was now worth 120,000 bolivares, which would go a long way to help me get by. There was plenty of money floating around in Santa Ana and I was sure I would manage to earn some with my drawing talents.

As I neared the observación, yet another familiar voice greeted me. It was Condor, a Colombian I'd befriended in San Antonio. 'Hey, I'll catch up with ya later,' said Mike, as he turned and walked the other way. Condor had been transferred to Santa Ana along with two of his compatriots, Juan and Xavier, two months previously. All three had close connections to the head prisoners who ran the jail. And run it they did, ruling with total ruthlessness should anyone be stupid enough to break the peace. There were deaths here and there, Condor explained, but that was inevitable. With 3,000 male prisoners living in close quarters, there was bound to be some trouble but, by and large, the place ran smoothly. No one was at war, no one tried to rob anyone else, and absolutely no one carried weapons except the don and his men. If anyone broke the peace, without question they would die for their mistake, both swiftly and without mercy. Having heard of our arrival through the grapevine, Condor had already been at work, finding a good place for us to bed down. By rights, we should have stayed in the observación for a week, but his connections inside the jail got us out of there immediately. Under his instruction, we gathered our belongings and followed him to building two, where we entered a ground-floor dormitory the size of a pavilion.

On entering, the first thing to hit me was the cleanliness of the place. There were rows of shower cubicles to the left and right, a toilet area, washing and shaving facilities. We then walked through a double doorway into the dormitory, which was broken up by four-foot-high walls into cubicles three yards square that accommodated three bunk beds and six double lockers. It appeared rough and ready, but the whole place was spotless. We were allotted a place to bed down. There were no mattresses on the beds we were given, which would present a 'comfort' problem, but I was determined nothing would spoil my mood.

They called the dormitories *letras*, and we would have to pay 20,000 bolivares as an entrance fee. There was no rush for the money, however; we could pay as and when it was possible. There was also a fee of 1,000 bolivares a week to keep the place clean – a small price to pay for such comparative luxury. The letras were run in military fashion. A *cabo* (corporal) was in charge of discipline and order, and any problems that arose were to be reported to him.

When the cabo had finished his welcoming speech, I dumped my bag and made my way to the washing area, where I'd spotted an enormous mirror that ran the whole length of the room. I hadn't seen a complete mirror in years, having had to make do with tiny scraps to shave with. There had been times when I'd managed to acquire a fragment then thoughtlessly left it lying around. Usually it disappeared within seconds. I'd eventually learned to shave without one. I removed my shirt and took a long, hard look at myself, and I wasn't too pleased with what I saw reflecting back. I had lost so much weight I appeared all skin and bone, while sunken eyes and cheeks made me look ghostly. I reeled back at the sight of the scabs covering my torso; still, there was a sparkle in my eyes and a smile on my mouth. I had come this far, I had survived, surely things could only get better.

At lunchtime, I made my way to the rancho, which was set inside the large building. Four, fifty-yard-long concrete tables ran half its length and the queue of prisoners stretched right around and outside the door. The food wasn't à la carte, but it was a definite improvement on the slop dished out at San Antonio. I managed to keep it down, which was something in itself. Once I was settled in, I would buy and cook my own food.

After I'd eaten, I bumped into Mike and we spent the afternoon laughing and joking, remembering the scrapes we'd been through in Margarita and El Dorado, especially the massacre and the crazy day in the máxima when we crawled through the rubble with bullets zipping all around.

'They beat the fuck out of us, didn't they?' laughed Mike.

'Yeah, but we're still here to laugh about it,' I replied.

After Mike's transfer in June 1999, he was meant to spend a couple of nights in Los Teques jail in Caracas before being moved on to Santa Ana. It had turned into seven months. He had been here now for almost two and a half years and had become somewhat complacent. I, on the other hand, was filled with wonder, like a child in a sweet shop, amazed at the staggering contrasts. Mike gave me a mattress and blanket to ward off the chilly night air and a bowl of food he'd cooked that morning.

At five o'clock, vigilantes blew whistles to sound lock-up. Half an hour later, número was taken outside the letra in an orderly fashion, no gauntlet to run, no beats; it *was* too good to be true. I spent the evening lying on my bed, listening to the noise of the letra, a smile on my face, still unable to take it all in. At ten o'clock, the noise died into silence. Apparently one of the rules: no noise after ten at night. It was a blessing in itself after many sleepless nights in Margarita. I thanked my angels for protecting me and fell into a deep, untroubled sleep.

The next day was a visiting day and over a thousand visitors turned up to see their husbands, brothers, fathers, sons and friends. The whole place took on a carnival atmosphere, every part of the jail teeming with people and stalls, and restaurants so busy it resembled a small town. Hundreds of beautiful girls strolled about, some of them eligible, but I kept my distance: I wasn't about to get caught up with anyone else. The painful episode with Sam still burned inside me and I was determined that no one would ever get the chance to hurt me again. Sunday was the same, with most of the visitors being Colombian and arriving from either San Cristóbal or from the frontier town of Cúcuta. I spent the day wandering around, or sitting on the football pitch, where I could be alone with my thoughts.

On Monday, the local consul honorario from San Cristóbal visited with his assistant. His name was Roger and his assistant's was Zulay. Roger said Zulay would visit us monthly with letters and money from home. He explained he was usually out of town but should we need to see him urgently, he would do his best to come. Zulay was a petite Venezuelan woman who spoke very little English, but with my fair command of Spanish we understood each other perfectly.

The next day, while taking in the sun outside the letra, I saw the don for the first time. When he came towards me, it became obvious who he was, as a group of seven men fanned out behind him, glancing in all directions protectively. He turned the corner and headed for the dirección, his entourage following closely. So that was the man himself, I thought. He wasn't much to look at, but the power he wielded in the jail was immeasurable. I felt a deep respect for him: if he could control 3,000 Latino prisoners, he had my vote of confidence. The week passed by, and at last I stopped shivering, getting used to the change in altitude and climate.

On the way to the dirección to check out the library, I had spotted a crowd of girls playing table tennis on the raised area in front of the basketball court. Hordes of locals were gathered round, staring at them, and giggling, so I wandered over to have a look. Among the girls, I saw Angelique, the South African from the anexo in San Antonio. She hadn't seen me, so I crept up behind her and whispered hello into her ear. She jumped up with a start before she turned around and greeted me warmly with a huge smile and a hug. The locals eyed me menacingly, as if to say, 'Who's this new gringo to suddenly appear and hug our precious gringa?'

'Danny's here,' I said.

'Yes, I know,' she replied, 'but he doesn't really interest me any more.' I wasn't surprised with all the attention she was getting from the guys around her. Angelique was a very pretty woman. I hadn't spent much time with Danny – he'd been busy feeding his habit.

Angelique told me she participated in a guitar class and that I should call in to see her sometime. We chatted for a few minutes before I went in search of the library. I took out a couple of readable books from the 150 or so titles available in English, which had been donated over the years by other foreign prisoners. There were over 60 foreigners in Santa Ana from every country imaginable, and I got to know most of them during the months that followed.

In July, a new official from the consulate in Caracas came to visit.

She brought letters and Prisoners Abroad money. At last, I paid my entrance fee to the letra and seven weeks' cleaning money, which pleased the cabo. That same month we heard, through Leon, the Colombian on our transfer, that Raymondo had been shot and killed in San Antonio during an internal conflict in pavilion five. Someone had earned himself a million bolivares of José's contract money. Leon was in regular contact with a friend by phone and we were kept well informed as to what was going on in San Antonio.

During the latter half of July, a violent clash occurred between two groups of prisoners in Santa Ana. A gang of Venezuelan prisoners had managed to smuggle arms into the jail and attacked a rival gang in building one. How they thought to escape without punishment was anybody's guess – everybody knew the rules, but inevitably some prisoners chose to ignore them. Within ten minutes, the don ordered their execution. The gang's leader was chopped to pieces and four of his unlucky followers shot dead. All five lay in a bloody heap outside building one as a warning to others. The paramilitary faction were not to be toyed with. They were very serious and dealt out punishment quickly and without hesitation.

A raqueta followed the killings, but it was nothing like the raquetas I'd been used to. We sat on a basketball court behind each building as they searched each letra. No shooting or beating took place, but when we were locked up afterwards we discovered the soldiers had ransacked the letras and personal belongings had been destroyed in the process. Up in arms, prisoners complained bitterly to the prison bosses, who in turn held a meeting with the Guardia Nacional comandante in the dirección later that day. Nobody knew exactly what was said during that meeting, but it never happened again in all my time in Santa Ana. And to prove they had made their position clear to the comandante, two weeks later three newly inducted prisoners, who'd robbed a house in San Cristóbal, raping and killing the mother and daughter, were hacked to pieces in building three and carried through the jail on flat-board stretchers. That sort of crime was not tolerated, especially if an appeal by the victims' family was made to the bosses. The don's men summoned every available prisoner outside to witness this gruesome spectacle. A couple of thousand spectators cheered wildly, as orderlies carried the blood-soaked stretchers towards the dirección. I was quite happy with the result but couldn't see anything to cheer about. Without doubt, Latino prisoners were a bloodthirsty breed. No raqueta followed that incident, proof indeed that even the local Guardia Nacional were in awe of the Colombian paramilitary group that ran the jail.

In August, I was asked to paint banners for the upcoming sports week in September. I'd already become known as '*Artista*' after painting a sign outside the bakery some weeks before. A local guy from building three came to negotiate on behalf of the prison bosses. Four days into working on the banners, the don himself came along to inspect my work. He appeared suitably impressed and said I would be rewarded for my trouble.

However, the local who was supposed to pass on the money ripped me off and I never saw a single bolivar for my work. I searched him out daily and hassled him, but each time he came up with an excuse. It wasn't hard to figure out why I hadn't been reimbursed: the guy was a hopeless crack head and had spent the money on rocks. After a week of getting nowhere, I gave up.

A few days later, the don and his entourage walked by, and he stopped to thank me for the banners. I nervously explained I hadn't been paid, as he'd promised. The don's face took on a contemplative look. He spoke to one of his men before turning back to me. 'I'll deal with it,' was all he said before walking on.

I had no idea what he meant at the time, but a week later I realised I hadn't seen the local around for a few days. I asked Condor, who told me the guy who'd ripped me off had been taken to the máxima, where he'd been stabbed to death on the first day. I was shocked for a while; prison bosses obviously took things like stealing and defrauding very seriously. They also had power to decide who went to the máxima, sometimes a death sentence in itself. In our letra, the cabo in charge dished out in-house punishment. If anyone was caught stealing, he would receive a good pistol whipping and possibly be stabbed in the arm or leg, then expelled from the letra to whichever place would have him. If he was foolish enough to be caught a second time, which many were, he would end up in the máxima and never be seen alive again.

In late August, Mike and I got together with two Colombian guys called Carlos and Felix and formed a band. Carlos, one of two prison electricians, knew the beat to tunes he called *músico europeano* and played the drums with flair. Felix, who presided over the guitar classes in the dirección, played bass and he could run off the bass line to 'Hotel California' as if he had written it himself. Mike played lead guitar and I played rhythm. We practised four afternoons a week in one of the larger classrooms until we could play a dozen songs reasonably well.

We became quite proficient and played to an audience of around a thousand – prisoners, visitors and girls from the anexo – one Saturday in the middle of September. It was, in fact, the very same religious day on which we'd had that first party on the cancha in San Antonio all those years back. We weren't brilliant by any means, but everyone applauded our efforts, especially the female *directora*, who requested we play for her and a delegation of highly placed officials from the Ministry of Justice a few weeks later. Not only was I enjoying myself, I was earning brownie points in a jail where the benefit system actually worked.

In October, Leon informed me Carlo Pino had been murdered at San Antonio. All hell had broken loose after Raymondo's death and many had been taken to the enfermeria to split the warring gangs, Carlo Pino included. It was ironic that he died by his favourite means of killing other people: a gang had jumped Carlo and their leader had strangled him with a garrotte.

One week after receiving the news, the consulate official from Caracas came on her three-monthly visit, bringing letters and Prisoners Abroad money. She told me Sam had given birth to a baby girl. It creased me inside; I had tried my best to forget Sam, but she'd crept into my thoughts daily since leaving Margarita. Now, even the consul was reminding me of her. Would I ever get her out of my life completely?

Christmas came around quickly. Many Latino prisoners brewed

home-made rice liquor, but in Santa Ana the majority went one step further and distilled it into pure firewater known as *michi*. It rattled the brain to drink more than a cupful and the whole population, including visitors, became completely drunk on it during Christmas visiting days. It took vigilantes an extra hour to clear out the visitors at the end of each day. The drunkenness carried on into the new year until the bosses put a stop to it. If allowed, the Latinos would party day and night for weeks on end, but guys would start to fight amongst themselves and nobody would turn out for work. The don decided enough was enough and placed a ban on michi for the foreseeable future. Everyone obeyed without argument, which pleased me, because once liquor took a hold all sense of reasoning went out of the window. The prisoners could turn aggressive in a heartbeat.

The routine had returned to normal by mid-January. I continued to draw portraits for people and was never short of customers; it helped to pay my way in the letra, buy a little food and cigarettes. I phoned home once a month, always call collect − I knew it cost Chrissy a small fortune, and she wasn't well off by any means, but she insisted I call. In early February, she had news that lifted my spirits. She'd been clearing out old paperwork at home and discovered a retirement plan that I'd started in 1987, when I still owned the company. My bank had kept paying the direct debit, even in my absence, until my overdraft had run out. A kind gentleman from Allied Dunbar informed Chrissy I wasn't entitled to the full amount, as the payments had been stopped by the bank in 1997, but a tidy sum was still forthcoming. Unfortunately he couldn't give her the cheque without my permission.

I told her it would not present a problem. I would write a letter giving her power of attorney and request the consul witness it. What a turn up for the books. I'd completely forgotten about the policy. Luck was on my side again. I wrote the letter that night and waited eagerly for the consul to show. Zulay turned up the following week, witnessed my letter and endorsed it with the consular stamp. I was in business. With my new-found windfall soon to be on its way, I gave thought to how much it would cost to buy my freedom. I was past my confinamiento release date, and it would mean I would have to apply for and buy all the necessary documents, grease the right palms, find and pay a family who would vouch for me, arrange for somewhere to live and pay rent – all the things I needed to do to become eligible for release on parole into the community. Costwise, it would be cheaper to stay in jail until my official release date, when I could leave the country directly from prison. I'd also heard it was safer in Santa Ana than it was on the streets of San Cristóbal, especially for a foreigner. Terms of parole meanwhile dictated that I would have to stay in Venezuela for a further 12 months. After much deliberation, I decided to stay put, live comfortably and let things run their natural course.

I opened a credit account with José, the cantina proprietor in building two. The Colombian had no problem waiting for his money and I ate well. I still went to the rancho for breakfast, but the rest of the time I cooked meat and fish with a variety of vegetables. Within weeks, I gained weight, and began exercising every morning.

One day in May the head of education, a woman also called Zulay, approached me in the music room and asked if I would be interested in taking a class to teach English. I thought it over briefly: it would go towards my benefit, so why not? I agreed there and then. Zulay was visibly pleased and told me she would arrange the days and let me know. Two weeks later, I held my first class in front of twenty-six pupils, sixteen girls from the anexo and ten men. I was very nervous, and explained I wasn't a teacher but a prisoner just like they were, that my Spanish was far from perfect and they would have to bear with me. Several piped up they could understand me perfectly, which boosted my confidence.

Zulay had pointed out the basic format I would teach: numbers, days, months and colours; parts of the body; basic phrases and simple verbs. Once into my stride, I thoroughly enjoyed the two-hour session and looked forward to the next class in two days' time. Zulay appeared ten minutes before the end and stood at the back. Afterwards, she implied she was very happy with the way it had gone and would be talking with the social worker with regard to my benefits.

In July, I received £200 from Chrissy through the consulate. By this time, the value of the bolivar had dropped even more. The country had lapsed into a deep recession and my £200 was worth just over 300,000 bolivares. I'd run up quite a bill at the cantina – 180,000 bolivares in total – and José was over the moon when I cleared my account. Most people paid him in dribs and drabs, as was their way, but it wasn't mine. Nevertheless, José offered me unlimited credit should I want it. I declined.

I now had the cash to eat well and not go without. I carried only a small amount of money with me at any one time – no matter what the rules said, it would have been asking for trouble to pull out a wad of notes – and the rest I carefully hid away. And it was lucky I did. Only a week later, I went to the toilet in the middle of the night. When I returned, a little voice in the back of my head told me to check my jeans pocket. I had only 10,000 bolivares in there, but it was gone. I'd been away for less than a minute, so it had to have been someone in my cubicle. I was so mad I couldn't sleep for the rest of the night. My suspicions lay with a guy on the bottom bunk, a Colombian named Condi whom I'd seen smoking a lot of crack here and there. It was only a couple of days before some of my paints disappeared and the large pot I used for cooking.

I spoke to the cabo in the morning and told him who I thought was the culprit. He wasn't the slightest bit interested because it wasn't too much money. I was also accusing one of his paisanos. I made the mistake of losing my temper, saying that if it had been one of his countrymen who'd been robbed he would have taken a different attitude. Word spread and I wasn't made very welcome for the next few days; so much so, I decided to change letra.

A guy named Jimmy Garcia, who attended the English classes, owned a cubicle in 2D on the first floor. Jimmy was an amicable character and we got on well. Letras 2D and 2E were set out differently. Each person bought his own space and partitioned it off with plywood and a lockable door. I paid the entrance fee, gave 5,000 bolivares to the vigilante in charge of the número lists and Jimmy welcomed me into his space the next day. By way of gratitude, I cooked a decent meal that night and gave him an extra English lesson. I'd landed on my feet, being much happier there than in the open-plan dormitory style of 2A.

That same week, Poco Pelo, the English guy, went out on the street on a confinamiento benefit. He'd been busy behind the scenes, paying off the right people, and had a little place to go to in San Cristóbal. I wished him well, not thinking I would see him again, and he was gone.

I began phoning Chrissy from a set-up in the sports coordinator's office owned by a Colombian guy named Willie from 2A. It was his 'little' business and cost me around 10,000 bolivares every time I called, but it wasn't as expensive as Chrissy paying for collect calls at £25 a go. In late August, Chrissy answered the phone in a foul mood. She had seen Sam a few days earlier. Sam had been released and was back in my home town in England with her baby girl and was six months pregnant. It was a garbled conversation and I couldn't make head nor tail of it. She told me she was going to change her number and that I wouldn't be privilege to it. With that, she hung up. I didn't even get the chance to defend myself. I phoned again . . . engaged.

I left the dirección totally deflated. Sam was still causing me heartache after all this time. What the hell had she been saying to make Chrissy so angry, I wondered? Whatever it was, she'd fucked me up again!

# 16

## THE FINAL TWIST

I had shared the occasional confidence with Sam over the years, of course, and unaware of exactly what had been said between Chrissy and Sam back home, I wrote to Chrissy that same evening, apologising for something I was unsure about. She was my lifeline and I needed to put things right. Sam had probably elaborated on the little she knew and made a whacky story from it. Chrissy had believed her.

Six weeks later, the embassy passed on Chrissy's new number. It had taken her that long to realise the truth. I phoned as soon as I could, and we talked it over and by the time I replaced the receiver we were friends again. I paid Willie his 10,000 bolivares and made my way back to the room I shared with Jimmy, pleased that Chrissy and I had cleared up the misunderstanding.

I had almost run out of cash by now and went cap in hand to José to ask for credit. He was delighted to have me owing him money again, a quirk of many Colombian businessmen in the jail. Even though they were ripped off occasionally, for some unfathomable reason money owed meant more to them than cash in their own pocket.

Over the next few months, a lot of things happened. I befriended a few foreigners from the letra across the landing. 2E was reputedly the best letra in the building and spaces were rare. Among them were

Eko and Olaf, two guys who shared a room. Eko was an educated, articulate guy from Indonesia; Olaf, a big friendly Russian due for release on a work benefit thanks to efforts by his girlfriend's mother, Myrian, a Colombian from Cúcuta. Myrian was a genuine, helpful 60 year old with a vast amount of knowledge regarding the Venezuelan prison system. She was chasing release papers for another couple of guys, and I would meet her several times during the visiting days that followed. It was obvious to anyone who knew her that she loved to do this and, as I got to know her better, an idea hatched in my mind.

Phillip, the Dutch guy on our transfer, also lived in 2E and ran a small cantina there. I would often spend time chatting with him, drink a coffee or two and listen to reggae music unleashed from his boom box. Phillip was cool, smoked lots of pot and was friendly with everyone – until someone owed him money, that was. Then Phillip was *un*cool and barraged his debtors with a stream of abuse until they paid. During a visit to 2E, I talked with Eko about the possibility of moving in with him when Olaf came up for release. Eko warmed to the idea and readily agreed.

Distressing news came my way concerning Danny during that month. His habit had got him into considerable debt with the prison bosses. It had been easy for him to get credit from a dozen different dealers in each building and he'd worked it to the hilt. Of course, all the money went back to the bosses and, in effect, he was in debt to the don. To my knowledge, he owed more than two million bolivares. Danny was taken to a room in building three, where he was beaten and threatened with a slow, painful death. His nonchalant attitude had them guessing (I had decided he really was mad after all). They actually hung him by his neck until he blacked out to get a reaction from him, and still nothing. I'm sure they let him live only because of the inevitable repercussions from the British embassy should he die in suspicious circumstances.

The don placed Danny in the rehabilitation wing in building three. No drugs were available in there and, whenever he left the building for any reason, a minder accompanied him. It was a great set-up for those who seriously wanted help, courtesy of the bosses. And Danny needed help, that was for sure.

Somewhat trivial compared with Danny's problem, but of concern to me, were my ankles. Even after 18 months of comparative sanitation in Santa Ana, they were still giving me trouble. I'd tried creams, lotions, potions, injections, even plant cures concocted by a local, but they were still covered in open sores that wept continually. The condition had baffled the doctor. All I could do was bathe them every night, wrap them in bandages and put up with the discomfort.

It wasn't long before Olaf went to the street on his work benefit and I moved in with Eko. I thanked Jimmy for his hospitality and companionship then, after paying the entrance fee and the customary bribe to the roll call vigilante, moved into 2E. Being Indonesian, Eko was quite a cook and we shared the occasional feast together. With three paint-tin cookers firing at once, he would dish out some incredible meals.

During my stay in 2E, I discovered most foreigners were receiving money from home via Western Union and paying trusted visitors to collect it on their behalf. It was quicker than waiting for the consul each month and well worth paying a little for the service. I asked Eko about it. Oh yes, he told me, he and Olaf had used the service on many occasions. We would talk to Myrian on the next visiting day.

The following week, armed with Myrian's full name and details, I rang Chrissy and asked her to wire me £500 via Western Union. One week later, I received close to one million bolivares, which I hid very well indeed. With that amount of money, I believed I could surely get the wheels in motion to secure my release. My English classes were earning benefits and I had the necessary cash: it was time to make my move. The outstanding work benefits from San Antonio totalling five months were in question and I wondered how I would go about claiming the two months' remission I would receive from it. That, and the seven months I'd already earned at Santa Ana, would take me to a release date in March 2004.

I began to spend time around the education department, getting to know the social workers better, taking them candy and cakes on occasion, or helping here and there with the odd *colaboracion* – prison slang for financial help – when the photocopier mysteriously ran out of ink in the typist's office, or any of the many other acts of God that needed financial assistance in order to crank the wheel one more notch. It took several weeks of persistence and talking to the right people before things were on the move. The amount of paperwork involved to release someone was mountainous and I was just on the lower slopes.

I was left with the problem of the remission due from Margarita. A social worker in Santa Ana told me if they were to deal with it through normal channels, it would be months before San Antonio responded. I felt two months less in this godforsaken prison system was worth talking to Myrian about the next time I saw her. When visiting day came around, I asked if she would like a short vacation on Margarita, during which time she could call in at San Antonio and arrange for my benefits to be passed over to the local judge in San Cristóbal. Myrian was delighted I'd asked her and, with her help, I wrote a letter giving her power to act on my behalf. I gave her half a million bolivares for fare and hotel accommodation, plus a little to eat out with. She had loose ends to tie up and would leave in two weeks in search of my missing paperwork.

Meanwhile, I made a new friend, someone I grew to respect and like immensely in the short time I knew him. 'Miguel' was Dutch and from Aruba, an island off the coast of Venezuela. I'd met him briefly here and there over the previous months after I'd taken to exercising in the morning on the yard behind building two. With the city of San Cristóbal visible in the distance, he would stand motionless looking out over the valley, watching the sunrise, smoking a cigar. Sometimes his lips would move as though praying. I never disturbed him at those times. Over time, we started greeting each other and soon became friends. Miguel was an interesting person and had done so many things in his 64 years: from the time he ran away to sea from Aruba at the age of 16, through countless adventures to the last 40 years he'd spent in Venezuela. He spoke excellent English, perfect Spanish and conducted himself like a real gentleman. One day, I asked why he stood praying to the sunrise while smoking a cigar.

'Frank,' he said with a smile, 'when I'm praying to God, I look at the sun, because without the sun there would be no life.'

'And the cigar?' I asked.

'Ah, well,' he replied with an even bigger smile, and a chuckle, 'spirit likes a good cigar.'

It came out in conversation one day that Miguel was well versed in the ancient Caribbean art of reading cigar ashes. It all sounded a bit spooky; nevertheless, I was intrigued. There was definitely more to the man than met the eye.

Round about that time, I met Jennifer, a gorgeous five foot two, blonde-haired Colombiana – with a Scandinavian bloodline, judging from her looks. She lived across the border in Cúcuta and came with her mother and child each weekend to visit her father, a new prisoner in 2B. We literally bumped into each other outside José's cantina. Our eyes met and we smiled, her expression turning coy as she lowered her eyes shyly. I was smitten. Trouble was, even though she was 28 and a widow with a small child, her mother followed her almost everywhere she went. We managed to spend a little time alone in my room, but it wasn't long before her mother would knock on my door.

After so long without the company of a desirable woman it was all too easy to fall for Jennifer. Memories of Sam had now faded away to nothing. I drew Jennifer's portrait to such detailed perfection it looked better than the photograph and she was enthralled. I was getting serious about her, and it frightened me to distraction – the work I had put into my release was bearing fruit and I couldn't possibly afford to jeopardise my efforts by falling in love with a local girl, as beautiful as she was. It would cause all sorts of complications and, besides, I didn't want the pain that would follow when the time came for me to go home. So I played it cool with Jennifer: as difficult as it was, I had to resist the emotions bubbling up inside me.

In early November, Myrian came with news from Margarita. She'd spent two whole days virtually standing outside the prison gate before being allowed to speak to the *director*. She was then passed on to the social worker and the new *coordinador de trabajo*. They assured Myrian they would send all the relevant paperwork to the social worker in Santa Ana after it had been stamped and signed by the local judge. They could do no more than that.

Myrian had also spent a whole day waiting at the large courthouse in La Asunción to speak to the judge's secretary with reference to processing paperwork quickly when it came. Again, greased palms and the promise of action. I was positive her hard work would produce results, and I thanked her wholeheartedly. She was a remarkable woman, only too glad to help, and looked for no reward. Maybe she was one of those people who I believed guardian angels guide into your life to help you along from time to time. All I can say is she appeared just when I needed help.

Miguel was another of those people who would soon prove the same. I'd discussed my ankles with him one day while taking off the bandages and revealing the weeping fleshy mess underneath. After taking several puffs of his ever-present cigar, he said, 'Do you want me to help you cure that?' There was no doubt in his voice, and it struck me I could trust this man.

'Yes, I do,' I replied simply.

'Then all you have to do is buy me twelve cigars,' he said.

I thought the cigars were for payment, but when I gave them to him he said he would keep them for the healing. I wondered what he was going to do with them – but I'd tried so many things without success, I was more than willing to give anything a shot.

The following day, I met Miguel at his favourite spot and we watched the sun climb in silence, its early morning blush delighting the eye with pastel shades of delicate colours on mountain flanks.

'Well,' he said after a while, the cigar clenched between his teeth, 'are you ready?'

'Ready as I'll ever be,' I replied with a nervous smile.

Inside my room, Miguel explained that he'd smoked three of my cigars the previous night while praying to the revered Indian chief he once knew in spirit. Open-mouthed, with my feet propped on the chair, I watched on as he lit a cigar with three matches twisted together, mumbled a string of words to his inner being and chewed the end awhile. With eyes pinched tight, he eased the cigar from his mouth and spat the mixture of saliva and tobacco directly onto my ankles. While doing this, he broke other cigars, using the leaves to make a poultice. He puffed away, cigar after cigar, more saliva, more leaves, the room filling with smoke as he puffed furiously, exhaling clouds of smoke around my ankles while chanting strange words. Miguel began to shake here and there but only momentarily as he continued this ritual for the hour it took to completely cover the sores with tobacco leaves.

Throughout that hour, my body had tingled from head to toe, the hairs on my arms and neck had stood on end. I was totally fascinated. A sign of spirit presence, he assured me. I quickly replaced the bandages to secure the poultice and made the exhausted Miguel a coffee. I walked around the rest of the day with a warmth inside; I hadn't felt so peaceful in years. I don't know to this day if it was what Miguel had done or my own rediscovered belief in spirit but, a week later, under instruction, I removed the bandages and slowly unpeeled the tobacco leaves. Beneath, for the first time in almost two years, were patches of fresh pink skin where the open sores had been.

I was astonished but, unlike me, Miguel shrugged his shoulders, telling me to leave the poultice on for a few more days. Two days later, the sores had edged in crusty scabs and another layer of skin had grown over, giving them a darker shade. They were healing. I thought of all the money I had spent on medicines to cure the condition, and all it took was a packet of cheap cigars and the friendship of a true spiritual warrior. Within weeks, the scabs had dropped off and fresh skin covered my ankles.

After a meeting between the Venezuelan and US governments, Mike, along with three other Americans, was accepted back into the United States on condition of parole. He was delighted. I knew in all probability I'd never see him again and wished him luck; then he was gone. Whenever Mike sprang to mind after that, I always had that picture of us crawling through the rubble in the máxima at El

Dorado. A truly unforgettable moment. Mike had gone, and I hoped I would also be going home soon. I needed to speed the wheels and phoned Chrissy to send more money.

In December, Danny surprised everybody in the jail when a vigilante escorted him to the dirección for transfer to another prison. It transpired that the consul had arranged it secretly. Danny had been working on the move during his consular visits every month unknown to anyone. Those were the only times his 'minder' had to wait outside. He'd bluffed the bosses for months about money he was about to receive and just disappeared, owing the paramilitary gang over two million bolivares. What was the man thinking? I knew all along he was in some kind of shit but to rip those guys off was asking for trouble. During Zulay's Christmas visit, she told me Danny had been shot in the leg by a Colombian gang member in a prison 200 kilometres away. It wasn't a mortal wound but was certainly a reminder that the arm of the Colombian paramilitaries stretched far and wide. Danny was lucky to be alive.

Christmas time was another drunken fiesta for the inmates of Santa Ana and their visitors. People came from the streets to party. Gallons of michi had been distilled in each letra during December – the place was awash, the smell of it hanging in the air. Eko and I had decided to make our own hooch early in December too. A twenty-five-litre tub had been fermenting for three weeks, its contents including two kilos of rice, eight kilos of sugar, four kilos of strawberries ordered through the cantina, and half a block of yeast procured from the prison bakery. It tasted sweet, like strawberry wine, but had the kick of a mule. Eko and I spent most of Christmas in a drunken haze and slipped into the new year in a comatose state.

The new year brought brighter prospects, as I would be in court in February for benefits and a new release date. If all went well and the people in Margarita had done their bit, I would be free to go home sometime in March. My ankles were healing nicely, the only thing visible a slight colour change. The English classes were going well, and we had moved on from basic to more complicated tuition. Word got back to Zulay, who, pleased with my labours, arranged another visit to the social worker. During that visit, she informed me paperwork had arrived from Margarita. It was what I'd been waiting for!

However, reading through the newly dated documents, my smile faded: it looked like the dates had been changed concerning the time worked. I still had my one year, eleven months and four days from before, but the last day of benefit had been changed to 22 May, the day we left for Santa Ana. It meant I wasn't going to receive the two months' remission from Margarita. My heart sank. I left the social worker's office a little dejected.

Soon after, I met a guy called George, a local man from San Cristóbal who visited Santa Ana on occasion to seek out English-speaking prisoners. Tammier introduced me to him one Saturday. George, a big, friendly, peaceful guy studied English at the university in San Cristóbal. In passable English, he said to me, 'I want learn to speak your language. Not American English – the Queen's English.' He always carried a textbook that included pictures of London and the Thames. An avid listener to the BBC World Service, he respected the way presenters spoke. George came across as being a little odd but was interesting in his own way. We became firm friends and would spend at least an hour each visiting day speaking the Queen's English. In February when my benefits hearing came around, I was surprised to learn he had been to the local courts to give me a character reference.

I was now surrounded by people helping me, and most of them for no more reward than the satisfaction of doing so. My faith in humanity had stopped crumbling. I put the episode of the lost remission from Margarita to the back of my mind and began to look forward to my release in May, only three months away. The time passed quickly. I was liaising with the consulate and keeping them informed, and speaking to Myrian and George to keep the mountain of paperwork flowing in San Cristóbal. I spent hours in endless queues carrying bags of candy, waiting to see the social worker to ask for news. She grew a little tired of me and said she would make a point of finding out to stop me bothering her. My persistence had worked: my release date would soon be written in stone.

I spent most of my spare time either with Miguel, listening to his tales, or lying on my bed reading. Occasionally, I would walk around the football field and sit by the perimeter fence, far away from everybody; the ideal place to contemplate. At weekends, I spent most of my time with Jennifer, inevitably getting closer, and I even toyed with the idea of asking her to come home with me. But a strong urge told me that when I was released, I needed to be free of any commitment.

In April, the social worker met with the judge's secretary. My day of release would be 24 May 2004, providing I could produce proof that I'd never committed a crime in Venezuela prior to my arrest. I'd never been in Venezuela before, so how could I have committed a crime other than the one I had been arrested for? It was a new twist nobody had warned me about and one that needed sorting quickly. The paperwork turned out to be a simple document called an *antecedente* and it would need to be stamped in Caracas. The Ministry of Justice stated that they had no record of me committing a crime on Venezuelan soil. It was that simple, but it cost me 20,000 bolivares and several bags of cakes to get a result within two weeks.

By the beginning of May, the prospect of going home filled me with excitement. After all the beatings, hunger, humiliation and filthy conditions, El Dorado, the madness of San Antonio and the drastic difference of Santa Ana, at last I was three weeks away from leaving my chosen hell behind for ever. I say chosen because I did choose it. I chose to go against my intuition and had paid the price. So had Sam, unfortunately, and that I can never deny.

Chrissy, my saviour, had booked a flight for 12.10 a.m. on Monday, 26 May. My release date on Saturday, 24 May at 8 a.m. would leave me with two days to fill. I didn't have too much money left – the bulk had gone to pay for the flight – and I would have to be careful with what little remained. I asked Zulay to book an overnight coach to Caracas and gave her 30,000 bolivares to purchase the ticket. It all sounded so simple.

A vigilante came for me early on the morning of my release. I was packed and ready to run the gauntlet one last time, only this time to the slap of hands and not planillas. I would never hear that siren wail again, except for something similar on Armistice Day in my home town. The next time I hear it, I thought, I'll stand with the rest and pray. I left the sea of smiling faces and walked out of the letra carrying my holdall. I was taken straight to the dirección, quickly processed and virtually ejected through the main gate. It happened so fast, I found myself standing in the street somewhat confused. I was positive the Guardia Nacional had forgotten to give me vital paperwork, something called a *boleta de excárcelación*. I had pestered the guards on the gate about it, but they waved me away angrily. 'Go, *gringo*, you are free. Go!'

Outside the prison gate, I turned away and breathed in the cool free air, my bag in my hand, passport and flight reservations in my pocket. The time was 7.45 a.m. A bright-blue sky topped the mountains around me. I walked slowly to the nearest corner, where I smoked a cigarette and waited for Zulay to pick me up as promised. I wasn't quite home yet and kept my excitement under control as best I could. I had the next two days to spend in Venezuela and I had a nagging concern the missing boleta would cause problems.

At nine o'clock, there was still no sign of Zulay. By ten, I had a feeling she wasn't going to show. I decided to follow my instincts, catch a bus to San Cristóbal and go in search of her myself. I had no idea where to start other than her office, which was closed on Saturdays. And I didn't have her mobile number. Of the 75,000 bolivares in my pocket, 50,000 of it was to be retained to pay airport tax at Caracas, Zulay had told me. I needed to find her. She had my bus ticket.

During the journey into San Cristóbal, I had a flash of inspiration. I would call George, the English student, and ask for his help. It was his town, after all. I had his number and, as soon as I disembarked, I bought a phone card and called him. Fate was kind to me that day. Not only was he in, but I'd jumped off the bus by chance no more than 300 yards from where he lived. George came out to meet me. We ate a small meal inside his house and I explained my dilemma. By one in the afternoon, we were on a bus, zigzagging across the city in search of Zulay. There was no one at the consulate, except a very unhelpful security officer staffing the gate. I left George's number and a short message should Zulay call.

With no idea where else to look for her, I would have to borrow the money from somewhere and buy a fresh ticket. But where? I couldn't ask George, he was always broke. Another flash of inspiration – Poco Pelo. But how would I find him? I asked George if, by chance, he knew Poco and, if so, where he lived. He replied in the negative but said he knew a man who probably did. With that, we climbed back on a bus and cut across the city to George's friend's house, where we were soon guided down narrow streets to the cosy little place where Poco lived. His face was a picture when he opened the door. After the initial shock had worn off, I gave Poco a hasty rundown of the situation and virtually begged him to lend me 30,000 bolivares to pay my fare to Caracas. Poco obliged without a second thought and said he'd come along to see me off. It was 4.30 p.m.: my coach would leave at six o'clock. We caught another bus into the city centre and arrived in the coach terminal at five o'clock.

The place was humming with activity. While I was looking around for the ticket office from out of nowhere a familiar voice cut through the din. I turned and looked down to see the petite Zulay standing in front of me, coach ticket in hand, smiling broadly. I was relieved to see her. She said her car had let her down that morning, but the gateman had given her my message. Things were falling into place. Zulay informed me that she'd made an error and the airport tax at Caracas was now 80,000 bolivares. Luck was with me again. With the 65,000 I had left and the 30,000 from Poco, I had enough, including the taxi fare to the airport. We sat and ate a quick meal, which Zulay kindly paid for, and we waved goodbye. Before too long, I was seated on the upper deck of the long-distance coach, heading for Caracas, scheduled to arrive in the city at eight the following morning; it was a 14-hour trip.

At ten o'clock that evening, the coach stopped at a Guardia Nacional security post, where soldiers boarded and demanded to see paperwork from passengers. All I had was my passport stamped with an entry visa dated November 1996 and my flight reservation. It wasn't enough to satisfy them, so I was taken off the coach and handcuffed to a metal table while my bag was removed from the luggage compartment and thoroughly searched. I fucking knew it! I was missing proof of my release, the boleta de excárcelación. After some quick talking on my part, and a plea of clemency, a Guardia Nacional officer phoned Santa Ana to check my story. He came back scowling and allowed me to board the coach but not without giving me a severe reprimand first. I should have been given the document by law.

The same thing happened four more times during the night, and each time it became more stressful. I was taken off the coach, handcuffed to the nearest metal railing and my luggage ransacked. After the fifth time, the other passengers had grown weary of me, mumbling and tutting to each other as I boarded. I had caused five twenty-minute hold-ups and the coach arrived an hour and a half behind schedule in Caracas. I hadn't managed to sleep at all during the night, my nerves had been at breaking point with the hassles along the way. Totally exhausted and heavy-eyed, I looked for a taxi to take me to Simón Bolívar airport in nearby La Guaira. The fare was 12,000 bolivares, which left me with 82,000 plus change.

On reaching the airport, however, an official at the information desk told me the ticket counter for my flight would not open until 11 p.m. There was nowhere to sit in the airport concourse, so I hung around for an hour until several security police told me I couldn't wait in the airport building; I would have to leave and come back later that evening. I spent the rest of the day wandering the outskirts of La Guaira, ever wary of muggers and thieves. I sat at a busy bus stop for hours, watching people come and go, arm clasped around my holdall, avoiding eye contact with strangers who passed by.

By nine o'clock that evening, I was reduced to a bag of nerves and decided to wait around the airport for the remaining two hours, no matter what they told me. Security was intense at Simón Bolívar and I was questioned several times while I waited. At last, the ticket counters opened and I made my way over. After collecting my ticket,

I discovered it included airport taxes! All the running around and the stress of the previous day had been unnecessary.

I reached customs at 11.30 p.m. and handed over my passport. When the customs official found my entry visa and nothing else, he shook his head, pulled me over to one side and sat me down while he dealt with other passengers. My head was spinning. What now?

Eventually, he came over. 'You have a problem,' he said to me without preamble. 'You are missing an exit visa. Something you should have acquired from your embassy.' I sat stunned, unable to think clearly. All this way only to fall at the last hurdle. It couldn't be. The customs official saw my distress. I confided in him, and asked if there was anything he could do to help. I had 20 minutes before my plane took off. The guy looked around and, with no one in earshot, asked quietly, 'Do you have any money?'

'No, I don't . . . wait! Yes, I do,' I replied. 'I have 80,000 bolivares and you're welcome to it. Just let me get on my plane!'

'Is that all you have?' he asked, visibly disappointed.

'It's everything I have in the world,' I replied, almost begging. 'Please take it and let me catch my plane.'

He seemed unmoved for a moment, then stood up and walked over to his companion. They glanced over at me as they whispered. Finally, the customs officer ambled over. Motioning me to the booth, he said, 'OK, give me your passport again.' I passed over the money and he stamped my passport. YES!! He wished me good luck as I ran through the turnstile towards Gate 14 with ten minutes to spare before take-off.

I was out of breath with exhilaration as I walked down the tunnel onto the plane, found my seat and buckled up, still not quite believing that after seven and a half years I was actually on my way home.

I'm not a religious person, but I do believe that angels and spirit exist. I believe there also exists an awesome power that is everywhere at once, a loving, non-judgemental power that keeps the universe ticking over like clockwork. The spirit of nature itself. Some people choose to call it God, I prefer nowadays not to give it a label. Nevertheless, whatever name one gives it, in the end that presence was there in my countless moments of need. I have to admit I fell by the wayside many times, but I'd made it; well battered emotionally, on the mend physically and a little more enlightened spiritually. One thing I do know for sure: if I hadn't had the experience, the pain and suffering, then I wouldn't ever have felt the pure joy of every single moment, as I do NOW.

# GLOSSARY

*a firmar* – sign (a command)

*anexo* – annexe

*asi* – like this/that

*barrio* – rough area, slum

*basta* – enough

*caballeros* – gentlemen

*cancha* – yard, courtyard

*la cola* – the queue

*comando* – command post

*confinamiento* – parole compulsory residence

*corre* – run

*cuchillo* – knife

*declaración* – statement

*de nada* – it's nothing

*dirección* – main offices

*director* – prison governor

*enfermeria* – sick bay

*entre vista* – internal visit

*está bien* – that's OK

*extranjero* – foreigner

*garita* – prisoners' lookout post

*hasta pronto* – see you soon

*hay hambre* – we're hungry

*jefe de régimen* – chief

*libertad* – freedom

*loco(a)* – crazy

*los vagos* – 'the vagabonds', an area of the prison

*máxima* – maximum security

*mira* – hey

*mosca* – a fly

*nombre* –name

*número* – number; in prison slang, headcount

*paisano* – countryman

*planilla* – slang for long, steel bayonets

*plomo!* – let's do it! (prison slang)

*por allí* – over there

*por ahí* – that way

*que paso?* – what's up?

*que queries?* – what do you want?

*rancho* – slang meaning prison meals

*raqueta* – prison slang for *requisa*: a search, inspection

*regalo* – gift

*salón* – pavilion within prison used for various purposes

*sapo* – a toad, prison slang for snitch

*sub-director* – deputy governor

*suerte* – good luck

*vigilante* – a civilian guard

Frank Kane was born in Cheshire in 1953, and attended grammar school and college. After many years working in the electrical industry, he started his own electrical wholesale business, which collapsed after 12 years of very successful trading. Since his release from prison, Frank is now settled and working as a lorry driver.

John Tilsley is also the author of *Be A Good Boy Johnny* and *Nevada Blue*. He lives in Cheshire.